THE END OF ETHICS
IN A TECHNOLOGICAL SOCIETY

The End of Ethics in a Technological Society

LAWRENCE E. SCHMIDT
with
SCOTT MARRATTO

McGill-Queen's University Press
Montreal & Kingston • London • Ithaca

© McGill-Queen's University Press 2008
ISBN 978-0-7735-3335-6 (cloth)
ISBN 978-0-7735-3336-3 (paper)

Legal deposit first quarter 2008
Bibliothèque nationale du Québec

Printed in Canada on acid-free paper that is 100% ancient forest free
(100% post-consumer recycled), processed chlorine free.

This book has been published with the help of a grant from the
Canadian Federation for the Humanities and Social Sciences, through
the Aid to Scholarly Publications Programme, using funds provided
by the Social Sciences and Humanities Research Council of Canada.

McGill-Queen's University Press acknowledges the support of the
Canada Council for the Arts for our publishing program. We also
acknowledge the financial support of the Government of Canada
through the Book Publishing Industry Development Program (BPIDP)
for our publishing activities.

Library and Archives Canada Cataloguing in Publication

Schmidt, Lawrence, 1942–
    The end of ethics in a technological society / Lawrence E. Schmidt
    with Scott Marratto.

    Includes bibliographical references and index.
    ISBN 978-0-7735-3335-6 (bound). – ISBN 978-0-7735-3336-3 (pbk.)

    1. Technology – Moral and ethical aspects. 2. Ethics, Modern –
    21st century. I. Marratto, Scott L. (Scott Louis), 1968– II. Title.

BJ59.S34 2008   170   C2007-905050-6

This book was typeset by Interscript in 10.5/13 Baskerville.

For Brigitte Maria, *sine qua non,*
with love

Contents

Acknowledgments   ix

Preface: Technology and the Problem of Nihilism   xi

Introduction: Technology:
A Canadian Preoccupation at the End of Canada   3

1   Technology, Religion, and Progress:
The Beginning and the End of Optimism   11

2   Technology, Poverty, and Malnutrition:
The End of Distributive Justice   22

3   Sustainable Sufficiency is Not Enough:
The End of Environmental Ethics   39

4   Excursus on Nuclear Power:
The End of Sustainable Sufficiency   57

5   Modern Weapons:
The End of the Just War Theory   79

6   Reproductive Technologies:
The End of Sexual Ethics   113

7   Excursus on Genetic Testing, Selective Abortion,
and the New Eugenics   138

8   Technology and the End of Politics   149

9   Technology and the End of Ethics   164

viii

Notes   181

Bibliography   219

Index   235

Acknowledgments

This book grows out of thirty years of teaching in the Department and Centre for the Study of Religion at the University of Toronto. My academic career provided me with the opportunity to exchange ideas with many fine students whom I attempted to instruct in religious ethics. I am grateful to them all for helping me clarify my thoughts on ethics and technology using an analysis inspired by the writings of George Grant.

Perhaps the most remarkable student who enrolled in my courses was Scott Marratto. I learned so much from him that, when my energy and enthusiasm were flagging, I asked him to act as my research assistant and help me complete a manuscript that had been too long in coming to birth. In the process, Scott became the co-author of this book. He was almost wholly responsible for the just war analysis of modern weapons in the latter part of chapter 5. He contributed chapter 7, which provides essential insights into the new eugenics movement and its implications for the disabled. He made substantial contributions to, and rewrote sections of, chapters 3, 8, and 9. He did much to improve the coherence, argumentation, and style of the entire manuscript. Without Scott Marratto's collaboration, *The End of Ethics in a Technological Society* would, I fear, have remained on my hard drive.

Brian McGowan, Judy Vivacqua, and Elana Summers made important research contributions to chapters 5 and 6. Many colleagues and friends read the manuscript in whole or in part and made insightful critical comments along the way. Terry Barker, Iain Benson, Scott Kline, Brian McGowan, Carl Mitcham, John O'Neill, Frank Piddisi, Catherine Schmidt, Samantha Thompson, Michael Vertin, and John R. Williams were very helpful, even when they differed with the ethical judgments expressed. The two anonymous readers to whom McGill-Queen's University Press assigned the manuscript offered many suggestions and corrections that immensely improved the quality of the final product. Jonathan Crago, Joan McGilvray, and Lesley Barry were of great assistance in shepherding the manuscript through the publication process. I thank them all. None of the above individuals, of course, is to be held responsible for any of the book's deficiencies.

I am particularly grateful to my family. My wife, Brigitte, put up with my obsessions, hobbyhorses, and inattention to our common domestic concerns with constant grace and good humour. Without her support, expressed in ways too many to number, my preoccupations might have collapsed into unfocused spleen or mindless rants. On the other hand, without the day-to-day indifference of my four children (Andréa, Michael, Catherine, and Simone), an indifference that mirrored that of our family cat, Cosette, I might have lived with the illusion that my ideas were immediately relevant. Regardless, I am still convinced that Scott's and my analysis is valuable even as I draw back from its implications for the future of my children, who will be required to live in a more and more realized technological society.

Lawrence E. Schmidt
Toronto, June 2007

Technology and
the Problem of Nihilism

In the past thirty years, many books on technology have appeared. Some are full of optimism and preach salvation through advanced techniques of energy transformation, defence capability, agricultural production, genetic engineering, artificial intelligence, or digital information systems.[1] Enthusiastic technophiles always acknowledge the (temporary) negative side effects of specific techniques but are certain that these can be eliminated or limited. Their confidence is rooted in their progressive outlook. Candu can do.[2] Technology presents us with many risks, but by facing them steadfastly, we can advance into a new age of peace and prosperity. The unfulfilled dreams of the modern project will be realized in a bright future in our new millennium.

A second type of book is critical of specific technologies, denouncing the television or the computer, space travel or antibiotics, the liquification of natural gas or the expansion of nuclear power.[3] But generally the critique of a particular technique is left unrelated to the whole modern technological drive; it is simply argued that the risks presented by some techniques are not worth taking. The task is to determine which techniques are too risky and then to abandon them. As difficult as this may be, it should not lead us to reject technology. We can't go home again, and anyway, who wants to drive a horse and buggy?

A third type of book proposes a humanist critique of the predominant role that technology has been given in our society. Technological advances, although sometimes desirable in themselves, are destructive of the culture that enables people to live together. According to this view, we must become "freedom fighters," dedicated to resisting the intrusion of technology into every aspect of our lives because "the uncontrolled growth of technology destroys the vital sources of our humanity. It creates a culture without a moral foundation."[4] We must begin to reform technology and bring it under social and governmental control.

Finally, there are alarmist predictions of doomsday or apocalypse. The end will arrive, whether with a bang (as in a nuclear holocaust) or a whimper (through slow, irreversible environmental degradation), the result not of divine intervention but of the malfunctioning of the (humanly constructed) technological system itself. The most notorious of these anti-technological tracts is the Unabomber's manifesto,[5] which was published following his threat to send more letter bombs to carefully targeted industrial leaders in 1996. The fact that the biography of Ted Kaczinski has been examined in minute detail while the manifesto has been generally ignored, if not trivialized, is a sure sign that his analysis of technology has enough truth in it to pose a threat to those who control the major sources of propaganda in liberal capitalist societies. Most have responded to the manifesto by dismissing it as the work of a crackpot. But this is too easy, if only because it articulates an apocalyptic mindset and a sense of impending doom that more and more people seem to share. Technological growth does seem to be out of control, and even a former vice-president of the United States has long accepted the view that the planet is imperiled.[6]

This book does not attempt to make definitive predictions or offer any purely practical recommendations. Rather, it seeks to relate our social crises to the transformation of ethics that has taken place in Western societies as technology has become the "house in which we all live."[7] Increasingly, those who implement the most important technological innovations, those who run the private and public corporations that fuel the dynamo, will, when pressed, acknowledge that they don't know whether a particular technique will have good or bad effects in the long run; they will also admit that they don't know what criteria one might use to determine the goodness or badness of a technical innovation. Nonetheless, they will assert, we must adopt the new device. We cannot stand in the way of progress. However, is it not clear that if we do not or cannot know whether a particular technical project (the cloning of human beings, for example) is good, and yet we argue that we must proceed with it, we are saying – if only implicitly – that it does not matter what we do?

This spells the end of ethics. By this we mean, first, that the ethical theory that has animated the modern technological system has brought us to this end. But, second, we mean that we cannot go on doing ethics in this way. The modern ethical game is over. God may or may not be dead, but ethics is. We are at a dead end. NIHILISM is written on the wall.

We accept Stanley Rosen's definition of nihilism, which is largely derived from Nietzsche: "If everything is permitted, then it makes no difference what we do, and so nothing is worth anything. We can, of course, attribute value by an act of arbitrary resolution, but such an act proceeds *ex nihilo* or defines its significance by a spontaneous assertion which can be negated with equal justification. More specifically, there is in such a case no justification for choosing either the value originally posited or its negation, and the speech of justification is indistinguishable from silence."[8] Like Vladimir and Estragon in Beckett's *Waiting for Godot*, we can and do go on speaking out of habit. But more and more, "the speech of justification" for technology – which has traditionally been called ethics and which has attempted to relate what we do as human beings to some conception of goodness or justice – has become indistinguishable from silence.

The nihilism of the Unabomber's actions is obvious to most. There was no limit to what Ted Kaczinski was willing to do – including murdering innocent human beings – to get his ideas published. What is less obvious is the nihilism of the system the Unabomber opposed. In his manifesto, the Unabomber contends that new techniques like genetic engineering will be implemented without ethical guidelines.

No code that reduced genetic engineering to a minor role could stand up for long, because the temptation presented by the immense power of biotechnology would be irresistible, especially since to the majority of people many of its applications will seem obviously and unequivocally good (eliminating physical and mental diseases, giving people the abilities they need to get along in today's world). Inevitably genetic engineering will be used extensively but only in ways consistent with the needs of the industrial technological system.[9]

The Unabomber sees that human behaviour (and human nature) rather than nature itself will be brought under technological control. Nothing in our study of reproductive technologies leads us to draw a different conclusion.

The technocrats argue that we must be resolute. There is no turn-ing back. We must not chicken out in our quest for technological mastery. We must proceed into the abyss. We must accept more root-lessness before we can become rooted again. More technology will be needed to cure the damage that technology has already wrought. The nihilists propose an ethic adapted to the demands of technology rather than a technology adapted to human nature. And the Nietzscheans (sometimes cheerfully, sometimes grimly) predict two centuries of nihilism and propose a supermanly love of the earth in-spired by the myth of eternal return as its transcendence.

By turning on an electric light one conspires in the production of nuclear waste hazardous to the health of many future generations. What has an existentialist, historicist, utilitarian, or Nietszschean ethics to say in such a context? Little, we hope to show. And yet we cannot turn off the lights and live in the dark. Our current plight would be tolerable if important ethical concerns were raised – even if no definitive answers were forthcoming. Socrates taught that the acknowledgment of ignorance is the beginning of wisdom. More recently, Hans Jonas explained that in a technological society we can know that our power is growing faster than our knowledge, not to speak of our wisdom or ethical sensitivity.[10] A sensible response would be to develop an ethics based on ignorance. However, where technology has become autonomous and dynamic,[11] the ethical questions that could impel us to acknowledge our ignorance can never seriously be raised. They are viewed as irrelevant if they would slow down the technological project.

The purpose of this book is to demonstrate that nihilism is at the heart of the technological project. While this is not in itself an origi-nal thesis,[12] no one has attempted to illustrate it through an exami-nation of specific issues that have emerged in the past thirty-five years. In each of the issues discussed, the failure to set clear and abso-lute limits to what human beings may ethically do to themselves, to other human beings or to the environment (nature) has meant the end of ethics. In suggesting that liberal ethics are at an end, we are not engaging in nostalgia for a distant past that was better than the present that is dominated by moral relativism or nihilism. Nor are we advocating a return to former values, which might be factored into the technological system. But we are advocating principles of techno-logical limitation that may serve to reclaim and protect human dig-nity after the language of liberal rights has been eviscerated by the dynamo. The basis for these principles of limitation is an ethic founded not on human rights, which, as Simone Weil taught, are derivative and contingent, but on human obligations that are timeless.[13] Such an ethic respects the needs of both the body and the soul and attends to our ignorance with respect to the possible risks and harms that accompany the technological (and other) experiments we undertake. Within this ethical framework our unknowing is not something that can be progressively eliminated as we move into a brighter future. It is, rather, an essential aspect of our being that we must acknowledge and respect. It points to a mysterious dimension of reality that we cannot master or control; it indicates where we must eschew the pursuit of new knowledge and apply moderation and restraint to our technoscientific and political ambitions.[14]

THE END OF ETHICS
IN A TECHNOLOGICAL SOCIETY

Any sufficiently advanced technology is indistinguishable from magic.
— Arthur C. Clarke, as quoted in an advertisement
for Apple Canada, Inc.

The more scientific progress accumulates ready-made combinations of signs, the more the mind is weighed down, made powerless to draw up an inventory of the ideas which it handles. Of course, the connection between the formulas thus worked out and the practical applications of them is often itself too completely impenetrable to the mind with the result that it appears as fortuitous as the efficacy of a magic formula.
— Simone Weil, *Oppression and Liberty*

The expansion of the will to power from the realm of phenomena to that of substance, or the attempt to operate in the realm of substance pragmatically as if it were the realm of phenomena – that is the definition of magic. The interrelation of science and power, and the consequent cancerous growth of the utilitarian segment of existence, have injected a strong element of magic culture into modern civilization.
— Eric Voegelin, "The Origins of Scientism"

Technology: A Canadian Preoccupation at the End of Canada

"Technology" is a ubiquitous term at the beginning of the twenty-first century. Nevertheless, its meaning is not perfectly clear, and its central importance in our self-understanding and self-definition in the modern age is only beginning to be appreciated. Often we equate technology with machines of various sorts: cars and computers, televisions and DVDs, nuclear power plants and laser printers. We assume that these machines may make us more powerful, more comfortable, more productive, and more liberated. In this sense, technologies are understood as tools that we can use well or badly depending on the good or bad ends to which we use them. Cars can be used for transportation, for fornication, or for murder. DVDs can be used for appreciating cinema classics or for indulging a taste for violent, degrading pornography. Nuclear fission can be used to power a city or vaporize it. Technology, understood as a tool, is purely a means to an end. In itself, it is ethically neutral.

This apparently obvious instrumentalist view of technology has, until recently, remained unquestioned in modern societies. Yet somehow it is also combined with the less obvious assumption that technology is more than the sum of the tools that we use; along with scientific research, it can provide the all-embracing answer to the political, social, and economic difficulties that the human race confronts. A number of contemporary thinkers have criticized this assumption. Among others, Lewis Mumford and Langdon Winner in the United States, E.F. Schumacher in England, and Jacques Ellul in France have rejected both the instrumentalist view and the ideological assumption.[1] They have suggested that we should understand technology more as a system than a tool. For them it is a network of interrelations, the elements of which – the acting factors – have "a sort of preferential disposition to combine among themselves rather than with outside factors"[2] and to dynamically modify the other elements through feedback structures. As such, technology must be studied within the context of political science, media theory, and social ethics.

Perhaps because they have lived closest to the most fully realized and pervasive technological society on earth but have not totally identified with it, Canadian thinkers have taken it as their task to analyze the dynamo.[3] What Zygmunt Bauman has written of Scotland's role in understanding the economic changes taking place at the beginning of Britain's (and Europe's) industrial revolution may be applied to Canada's role in probing beneath the surface of the technological society: "The tendencies at work in the centre are as a rule most promptly spotted and most clearly articulated on 'the fringes.' Being at the outskirts of the civilizational centre means being near enough to see things clearly, yet far enough to 'objectify' and so to mold and condense the perception into a concept."[4]

Harold Innis in the forties and fifties explained how every technique blinds its users to the cultural biases that it creates.[5] In the sixties Marshall McLuhan extended Innis's insights into a full-blown media theory, summarized in his aphorism "the medium is the message."[6] Every medium can be understood as an extension of one of the senses of the human being who uses it. The telephone is an extension of the ear; the automobile is an extension of the foot. Each medium changes the sensorium of the body and the social organization of the body politic, even as it numbs its user to its effects. In focusing on the message, we become blind to the medium. "The last person you should ask to explain the properties of water," McLuhan quipped, "is a fish." Ursula Franklin, like Innis and McLuhan a professor at the University of Toronto, continued this thematic discourse in the 1989 Massey Lectures entitled "The Real World of Technology." Echoing Heidegger, she pointed out that "technology has built the house in which we all live."[7]

Innis, McLuhan, and Franklin, for all that they have added to our comprehension of the effect of technology as a system on human culture and society, tend to see its role and effects as continuous and constant throughout human history. They do *not* see modern (technological) society as *qualitatively different* from other societies that preceded it. Their argument goes something like this: All human beings have used tools of one sort or another, to hunt or fish or pray or harvest or make pottery. And all human societies have passed on their tools and production methods and religious rituals (and thus their technical systems) to the generations following them. The rise of science has changed our tools and methods, but these are changes of degree, not of kind.

According to Franklin, for example, through most of recorded history our tools and methods have been of two distinct types: the holistic and the prescriptive. Holistic technologies lead to specialization by product, but they leave the artisans in complete control of the process: "Their hands and minds make situational decisions as the work proceeds, be it on the thickness of the pot, or the shape of the knife edge or the doneness of the roast."[8] Prescriptive technologies, on the other hand, lead to specialization by process. "The making or doing of something is broken down into clearly identifiable steps. Each step is carried out by a separate worker, or group of workers who need to be familiar with the skills of performing that one step."[9] Franklin emphasizes that prescriptive technologies did *not* emerge with modern science. They were operative when the pharaohs built the pyramids in Egypt in the third millennium BCE and when the artisans of the Shang dynasty cast in bronze in China in the twelfth century BCE. Franklin does acknowledge that "the categories of holistic and prescriptive technologies involve distinctly different specializations and divisions of labour and consequently they have very different social and political implications."[10] But these implications can be drawn about ancient societies as well as about our modern world.

Franklin points out that, although holistic and prescriptive technologies have been used through most of recorded history, the latter required a major social invention. This took place millennia before the development and application of modern scientific method. Literacy, record keeping, and standardization of measurements were essential for precision, prediction, and control; experimental science was not.[11] For this reason, Franklin argues that science is not and has not been "the mother of technology. Science and technology have parallel or side-by-side relationships; they stimulate and utilize each other. It is more appropriate to regard science and technology as one enterprise with a spectrum of interconnected activity than to think of two fields of endeavour – science as one and applied science and technology as the other."[12]

She admits, however, that scientific method has transformed applied science and technology: it provides a way of "separating knowledge from experience ... It provides a way to derive the general from the particular, and then, in turn, allows general rules and laws to be applied to particular questions."[13]

And so the application of scientific method to more and more areas of human life has meant that prescriptive technologies have become progressively more dominant since the rise of empirical science and the industrial revolution. They have transformed our society beyond recognition. Prescriptive technologies, Franklin points out, come with an enormous social mortgage. "The mortgage means that we live in a culture of compliance, that we are ever more conditioned to accept orthodoxy as normal, and to accept that there is only one way of doing 'it.'"[14]

It was Innis's merit as a social scientist that he set about, before World War II, to describe the mortgage that Canadian society held as a result of its economic dependence on the fur trade, the cod fishery, the railway, etc., and the prescriptive technologies that those endeavours demanded for participation in the French and British empires. Innis believed that one could study the techniques of work and of communication as they developed along the St Lawrence in the nineteenth century in the same way that one studies their function along the Nile in Egypt during the second millennium BCE. Prescriptive technologies were at the heart of both, and their study is the key to understanding the political economies of their respective societies.

McLuhan, following Innis, examined in a formal (and less disciplined) way the techniques of work and communication with a view to understanding their social effects. His approach was not that of a social scientist. As a literary critic and James Joyce scholar, he learned from Eric Havelock and Walter Ong that the most important cultural changes came about as a result of "transformations of the word" or media.[15] Ong divided history into three distinct phases. First, there existed *oral-aural* societies: tribal or pre-literate communities where direct, face-to-face communication was the only kind possible. Oral traditions and myth constituted human culture. Second, there were *historical* societies, which emerged after hieroglyphics, script, and the alphabet were invented and records began to be kept. Later, as papyrus and manuscripts became commonplace, the centralization of political power became possible. The Persian, Greek, and Roman empires of the "ecumenic age" resulted.[16] Eventually, at the beginning of the modern age the printing press, the prototype of mass production, gave rise to the "Gutenburg galaxy,"[17] whose tremendous social consequences included the homogenization of European languages within large geographical areas and the emergence of the nation state.

Third, then, *post-literate* societies – where electronic media predominate and affect every aspect of social organization – have come to the fore since the invention of the telegraph in 1844. Neither Ong nor McLuhan relates this invention to the rise of science, nor do they attribute any particular importance to the development of the scientific method. And contrary to common sense and historical evidence, they would have us believe that the effects of electronic media have been simply to decentralize authority, to minimize the importance of prescriptive technologies, and to reverse the homogenizing tendencies of print culture.

Although their approaches are very different, both Franklin and McLuhan share the view that the most important changes in the modern world have come about as a result of the development of electronic media. Franklin says that "it was essentially during the last 150 years that the speed of transmission of messages truly changed. This, in turn, so completely changed the real world of technology that we now live in a world that is *fundamentally* different." Electronic media, she continues, have led to the creation of "a host of pseudorealities based on images that are constructed, staged, selected, and simultaneously transmitted."[18] As well, she acknowledges that the human capacity for deception and illusion has also been enhanced in the age of instant information. However, Franklin does not link all of these negative effects to the emergence of science itself. Rather, she focuses on the diverse uses of modern science; she speaks as if science were one technique among many. It too is a technique that can be used well or badly.

Franklin contends that in the modern world science has been used badly in two specific ways. First, as we have already noted, it has increased the power of prescriptive technologies, which create a culture of compliance and destroy human autonomy. Second, "scientific constructs have become *the* model of describing reality rather than one of the ways of describing life around us. As a consequence there has been a very marked decrease in the reliance of people on their own experience and their own senses."[19] She also acknowledges that technology seems to have become self-augmenting, to use Ellul's term;[20] it has developed a momentum of its own. This was brought home to Franklin as a result of her experience as chairperson of a committee whose mandate was to formulate a blueprint for Canada as a conserver society.[21] "The convincing and urgent case for not proceeding with global technological expansion along the then established pattern was made ... Nevertheless, [she wrote in 1989] there has been no change in direction ... but an acceleration of technological expansion along lines known to lead to greater and more irreversible problems."[22]

Interestingly, Franklin accounts for this global technological expansion in terms of a failure of governance. She assumes that a technological society is still under the control of government and business interests and that they can make political judgments about the direction of technological development. She may be wrong on both counts. The role of experts in a technological society limits and sometimes eliminates the power of elected officials and managers. Should the acceleration of technological expansion and the degradation of the environment over the past two decades (in spite of the emergence of the new ecological consciousness) not lead us to question our assumptions about governance in the modern world?

Willem Vanderburg, a colleague of Franklin, has, after a lifetime of study, drawn exactly this conclusion. *The Labyrinth of Technology* represents his attempt as an engineer to present a new preventive approach to technological development. Instead of introducing end-of-pipe solutions to our environmental problems, he would have us avoid them in the first place. The technical approach to life abstracts everything from its human, societal, and biospherical contexts, separates knowers from doers, and tends to eliminate self-regulated activities. Vanderburg proposes that we should pay as much attention to contextual as to performance values, and thus consider the effects of techniques on society (and the individual human beings who make it up) as well as on the biosphere. In his ideal world, the preventive approach is essential if our technological and economic development is to achieve sustainability.

However, at the end of his analysis, Vanderburg admits that his proposal will never be adopted. He wakes up to the realization that technique will go on undermining human consciousness and cultures because we lack "a critical awareness of how much the world has changed in the last half of the twentieth century."[23] Vanderburg concludes that "modern technology is now regulated on its own terms." We now lack "a genuine set point ... by which technology and economic growth can be regulated."[24] The problem is not that we have "an ingenuity gap" but that we lack any ethical foundations upon which to evaluate technological development.[25]

Vanderburg accounts for this by showing how the development of technology-based connectedness leads to the desymbolization of traditional culture and experience. Symbolization is essential for the development of what he calls a lived milieu. In pre-history this lived milieu was nature; in historical times it became political society. Humanity's first two mega-projects involved the creation of language and myth in oral-aural cultures and the creation of political symbols[26] and literacy in historical societies. In both cases, the lived milieu allowed for the creation of "an entire symbolic universe that encompasses the unknown as details that remain yet to be discovered and lived but that cannot call the present into question."[27] For the individual brain-mind, "symbolization is integral to the living of a human life."[28]

In the third mega-project, "technology is creating a new life-milieu that includes, but is not limited to, the modern city. The web of technological means is used in virtually every daily-life activity, to the point that they interpose themselves between us and others, between us and much of what happens in our society and the world, and between us and nature."[29] The integration of the brain-mind into a desymbolized culture is made more difficult, and culture-based connectedness, which "weaves the world," is under siege.

This is precisely why we must go beyond Innis's, McLuhan's, and Franklin's respective analyses of technology, which presume a continuity between pre-modern societies and scientific – or perhaps, more accurately, scientistic[30] – societies. The novelty of research science and technology (both the term and the reality) is denied or downplayed. And Innis's, McLuhan's, and Franklin's insights can be used to induce us to accept uncritically the implementation of computer technology as one more language.'[31] We are proposing that we take seriously George Grant's argument that "technology" defines modern society and accounts for its radical newness:

When technology is used to describe the actual means of making events happen, the word reveals to us the fact that these new events happen because we Westerners willed to develop a new and unique co-penetration of the arts and sciences, a co-penetration that never before existed. What is given in the neologism – consciously or not – is

the idea that modern civilization is distinguished from all previous civilizations because our activities of knowing and making have been
brought together in a way which does not allow the once-clear distin-
guishing of them.[32]

Western society has been inspired by a faith that by means of this
co-penetration we can master nature and human nature and
thereby overcome hunger, disease, labour, and war. This has meant
that the "demands of technology are themselves the dominating
morality."[33] The technological imperative has opened every aspect
of human life to restless transformation. The assumption is that it is
always ethically acceptable to experiment to find out whether we
can do something, and if we can, we ought to. But the adoption of
the technological imperative has meant the liberation of means
from ends. The purpose of this book is to explore what this has
meant in such spheres of human life as the economy, the environment, energy production, war, and human reproduction.

1

Technology, Religion, and Progress: The Beginning and the End of Optimism

The origins of Western faith in technology are obscure. Some find them in the Hebrew scriptures' emphasis on human dominion or mastery;[1] others find them in Augustine's (and the Western Christian Church's) emphasis on the role of the will.[2] Some find them in the ninth-century thought of John Scotus Erigena, with his new, positive view of the "mechanical arts";[3] others find them in the Reformation rejection of philosophy, and the development of the Protestant ethic and the spirit of capitalism.[4] Political philosophers find them in the Renaissance projects of Bacon, Descartes, and Machiavelli.[5] Without pinpointing its origins, we can state that faith in technology had received clear expression by the time of the Enlightenment, when the doctrine of progress had supplanted the Christian doctrine of providence. The Biblical understanding of time[6] was either militantly rejected, slowly transformed, or secularized.[7]

The traditional Christian conception of providence assumes the linear understanding of time symbolized in the literary framework of the Old and New Testaments. Time has a beginning, a middle, and an end. The beginning is creation, as described in Genesis. The middle is *Heilsgeschichte* or salvation history,[8] the subject of innumerable recountings, artistic depictions, and theological analyses from the time of the Fathers of the Christian Church to the present. And the end, though yet to come, is in some proleptic sense known from the last book of the Bible, Revelation. Salvation history begins with the election of the Jews in the call of Abraham, Isaac, and Jacob and continues with Moses' reception of the Torah and the preaching of the Hebrew prophets. For Christians, the culmination of this history was announced by the last of the prophets,

John the Baptist. The centre of history is the life, death, and resurrection of Jesus, the Christ, the Messiah, the Incarnation of God. Salvation history continues in the life of the Church, or the Body of Christ, to use Paul's terminology. It will come to a close at the apocalypse, the *parousia* or return of Christ at the end of time.

The Christian doctrine of providence brought together this linear conception of time, the eschatology of the New Testament, and the natural law tradition derived from Greek philosophy and mediated to the Christian Church Fathers by the Stoics.[9] This synthesis, achieved initially by Augustine (in *The City of God*)[10] in the fifth century, combined an orientation to the future as the locus of human fulfilment (the coming of the kingdom with the return of Christ at the end of time) with a belief in eternity (as the divine realm of goodness totally beyond time). This world or this age (*saeculum*) achieves its ultimate significance only in relation to the other or the next. The city of man has no meaning except in relation to the city of God. The next world is to be realized both in the future and in eternity.

With the recovery of the writings of Aristotle (particularly by the Arab philosophers in the eleventh and twelfth centuries) and the general acceptance of his more clearly articulated notion of natural law, medieval theologians modified this synthesis.[11] Thomas Aquinas developed a Christian natural law ethic, which, he argued, was immutable because it was rooted in humanity's relation to God, who is eternal. The eschatological character of Christian faith, along with its orientation to the future, was overshadowed by the philosophical and metaphysical legacy derived from Greek thought. This medieval synthesis became unstable in the fourteenth century with Occam's nominalism, and it collapsed under the pressure of the Protestant Reformation and the Renaissance. The Reformation re-emphasized the Hebraic (specifically, the Jewish apocalyptic) element in the origins of Christianity and attacked the Hellenic (specifically, the Catholic) conception of natural law. Renaissance thinkers emphasized the creative powers of humanity, which could transform history from within, whether by magical (alchemical) operations performed on nature, as Paracelsus would have it, or through scientific experimentation, as Francis Bacon proposed. George Grant explains that

by the seventeenth century, both the theologians and the scientists wished to free the minds of men from the formulations of medieval Aristotelianism, though for different reasons. Because of our present education, the rejection by the 17th century scientists of the traditional doctrines is well known. They criticized the medieval teleological tradition with its commitment to substantial forms as preventing men from observing and understanding the world as it is. The criticism by the theologians is less well known and less understandable in an age such as ours. The theologians attacked the medieval teleological doctrine as the foundation of what they called "natural" theology, and that theology was attacked because it led men away from fundamental reliance on Christian revelation.[12]

The Reformation attack on natural theology was reasserted in Karl Barth's twentieth-century critique of philosophy and religion as forms of idolatry, that is, attempts by human beings to rise to God by the unaided use of reason. It counselled a return to the Bible as the sole source of Revelation, a reaffirmation of its linear conception of time, and an acceptance of its future (or eschatological) orientation. Having rejected the medieval account of science, however, this Protestant return to the Bible was combined with "an openness to the empiricism and utilitarianism in the English edition of the new sciences."[13] The history of the rise of science in the West (and the role of luminaries like Descartes and Bacon) is well known, although it is not as unambiguous as is commonly thought. It set the stage for the Enlightenment attack on Christian doctrine[14] and the American and French revolutions. The effects of these revolutions continue to this day, but they pale in significance when compared with the transforming power of the industrial revolution, which has become global in its consequences.

With the Enlightenment came the explicit denial of an otherworldly transcendence, whether in eternity or at the end of time.[15] There emerged what George Grant has called the history-making spirit, dedicated to fulfilment in this world only, through the elimination of evil. Human beings were no longer called upon to do good to merit a heavenly reward but were to work toward the creation of a perfect world, a utopia, or, at least, "to leave this world a better place" for future generations.

As belief in God was driven from men's minds, it was not replaced (as it was in the classical world) by a rather sad humanism (the attempt to live as pleasantly as one could in a meaningless world); rather it was replaced by an optimistic humanism, by a belief in progress. Time is still oriented to the future, but it is a future which will be dominated by man's activity. The idea of human freedom merges with the Judeo-Christian hope and produces the idea of progress. This means an entirely new kind of humanism. For a humanism arising in a Christian setting was bound to be quite different from one which had arisen from the archaic religious cultures. It was a humanism of project and reform. It was a humanism which put science and technology at its center, as the means of redemption.[16]

Science and technology, Enlightenment humanism claimed, offered the means to eliminate the evils that had distorted human life from time immemorial: labour, scarcity, disease, and war. That labour, scarcity, disease, and war were evil was self-evident (although it was not self-evident that they were the only or the most important forms of evil). That they could be eliminated was not an unfounded hope. The rise of the physical sciences, the development of the steam engine and the factory system, the increasing productivity of agriculture as it was mechanized and "chemicalized," the advances in medical knowledge and hygiene, and the improvements in transportation and communication were all prefigured in the early stages of the modern era, in the late seventeenth and early eighteenth centuries. This led to the unspoken hope that the human race would also be able to eliminate the causes of strife in the hearts of human beings and in the relations of nations and societies. Liberty, fraternity, and equality would all be achieved with the emergence of an economy of plenty, thanks to the development of science and technology.

It should be clearly noted, however, that in certain basic respects this revolutionary hope was opposed to the traditional Christian doctrine that in Adam, all of humanity had fallen and every human generation was equally corrupt and inclined to evil. Perfection could be attained only by the individual soul at death and by the human race at the end of, not within, history. The Enlightenment thinkers were much less pessimistic about life in what Christians called "this vale of tears." They asserted that humanity was not naturally depraved but unenlightened, and that ignorance and superstition could be eliminated through education if the illusions of religion were destroyed. It was clear to them that the proper end of man was not some transcendent, beatific vision but the good life here on earth. This good life would be achieved through scientific and technological progress.

Humanity must move onward and upward into the light.[17] This movement into the putative light has required the transformation of our very conception of ethics in the modern period.

From the time of the Greek philosophers, ethics had been understood as an attempt to articulate the demands of justice both as they exist in a specific society and as they are generally conceived. The Enlightenment project and technology radically changed our understanding of these demands. The history-making or Promethean spirit of modern man has led us to think of justice in terms of the elimination of the external manifestations of evil (labour, scarcity, disease, and war) from the world. For the ancient and medieval philosophers, the demands of justice were to be articulated in the face of these vicissitudes. For the moderns, the demands of justice required a plan for their elimination. Modernity, in fact, understands ethics in terms of this project, which refuses to accept any limitations that have been placed on humanity. It understands ethics in light of the future rather than *sub specie aeternitatis*. It rejects the doctrine of natural law, which until the modern period gave a clear orientation to Western societies and a clear sense of limit to its members.

The doctrine of natural law asserts that there is an order in the universe and that right action for human beings consists of attuning themselves to it.[18] That order is related to the order of the natural environment (the material world), but it cannot be equated with it. Human beings can discern a universal order because they participate in it through the life of reason. The natural law is therefore not to be confused with the laws of nature. The laws of nature can be discovered through scientific experimentation, which reveals the necessity and chance that rule the operations of matter. But human beings, because they participate both in material nature and in reason, cannot discover their own nature by examining matter that does not participate actively in the life of reason. An examination of material nature can reveal its laws to humans, but it cannot reveal the meaning or purpose of human freedom. According to the doctrine of natural law, human meaning and purpose can, however, be discovered by philosophical reflection. The classical and Christian traditions asserted that metaphysical knowledge is attainable because the proper ends of human action can be discovered by reason, and the passions of humans can be ordered in light of those ends. Classical ethics assumes this account of reason.

16

This view has, of course, been rejected by modern political philosophers from Machiavelli to Hobbes and Locke, from Rousseau and Marx to Mao Zedong, from Feuerbach to Nietzsche, Heidegger, and Foucault. With the rejection of the doctrine of natural law, a distinctive orientation toward virtue and a sense of limit has been lost. What has emerged is a new understanding of freedom, which was articulated first in the Renaissance. Modern freedom is identified with creativity and is viewed as self-evidently good, not merely the necessary condition for the development of virtue but the end of human action. One expression of this sense of freedom is the existential individualism of Jean-Paul Sartre.[19] Human beings are not only creative; they are self-creative. They create themselves in time, and if Sartre is correct, they are nothing but what they create themselves to be. This is what he means when he says that a person's essence is her freedom and her existence precedes her essence. There is no order in the universe that precedes or limits a man's or woman's self-creation, and there is nothing therefore that can orient it, because outside the order that humans create, there is nothing but an absurd universe totally unresponsive to our quest for meaning.[20]

With the development of the modern conception of freedom as self-creativity has emerged the philosophical dilemma that is illustrated in virtually every moral issue we confront publicly and privately today. Abortion, euthanasia, reproductive technologies, genetic manipulation, environmental degradation, and weapons research all present us with one question: What are the limits to our putative self-creativity? Can human beings degrade themselves through their collective self-creation?

The natural law tradition has been criticized out of public existence because it seemed to accept certain evils as inevitable and ineradicable. It appeared to counsel passivity in the face of the negative aspects of human life. At least until very recently, the natural law tradition was deemed an immoral morality by those held by the progressive hope, for it was not animated by a desire to eradicate obvious evils. On the other hand, the history-making spirit (with its belief in human progress) expressed a brash confidence – some would say an arrogant assertion – that those evils could be eliminated. But it has shown itself to lack any sense of limit as to what humans may justly do in their passion to make history or in their attempts to wipe out corruption or eliminate evil. Paradoxically, in its search for utopia the history-making spirit seems to have unleashed the most horrendous atrocities. According to Gil Elliot in *Twentieth Century Book of the Dead*,[21] the last century saw over 100 million people exterminated or displaced, most of them as the result of utopian plans to create a better world through one "final solution" or another.[22]

This philosophical dilemma has given rise to George Grant's perplexing query: "Are there any limits to history-making? The question must be in any intelligent mind whether man's domination of nature can lead to the end of human life on the planet, if not in a cataclysm of bombs, perhaps by the slow perversion of the processes of life."[23] Seven years after he first asked this question, Grant abandoned his own Hegelian optimism and came to an unpleasant conclusion. Having lost all hope that North America could develop a genuine synthesis of Christianity and modern science, he argued that technology "inhibits the pursuit of other ends in the society it controls. Thus its effect is debasing our conception of human excellence."[24]

In the 1960s Grant's pessimism was barely tolerated among Canadian or American academics, for it went against the spirit of technological optimism that marked the phase of post-Depression and post-war reconstruction.[25] However, by the end of the 1970s pessimism had become the new realism. Robert Heilbroner, the renowned American economic historian, articulated this pessimism for an American readership. He bluntly asked the question percolating to the top of all thoughtful minds: Is there hope for humanity?[26] Heilbroner was not asking, as medieval or reformation theologians had, about the possibility of sustaining the theological virtue that charted the human course between presumption and despair about eternal salvation. Nor was he inquiring about the possibility of creating a perfect world here on earth, as Enlightenment philosophers had two centuries before him. He was calling into question the very possibility of humanity's physical survival beyond the twenty-first century. And the answer Heilbroner gave was bleak: there is no hope for human survival. In the face of the external threats that we confront, our species' survival is not in the cards.[27]

Given the successful landing on the moon in 1969, why did so many affluent people begin to feel that the earth was more like the *Titanic* than a spaceship, and that since they could do little to prevent the ship from going down, they might just as well drink up all the champagne on board? Heilbroner linked this change of mood to three external threats. The first threat was called the population explosion.[28] Although the global population in 1974 was only 3.6 billion, it was projected that by the year 2025 the planet would have to support over 10 billion human beings. This task would not be so daunting were it not clear that the tremendous increase in food production that enabled the planet to provide sustenance (however inadequate in specific locales) had been achieved through the use of vast quantities of fossil fuels.

Heilbroner saw this increasing global consumption of oil, coal, natural gas, and nuclear energy as the cause of the second external threat to our survival, namely the degradation of the environment.[29] In 1974, he was not alarmist about any of the forms this degradation would take: the greenhouse effect and the warming of the atmosphere due to carbon dioxide emissions; the depletion of the ozone layer due to CFC emissions; acid rain due to sulphur dioxide emissions; the pollution of the air and water by industrial chemicals, pesticides, fertilizers, and fossil fuels as well as ionizing radiation. He thought that we had about "150 years before the atmosphere would warm up appreciably."[30]

By 1979, however, Heilbroner saw that this was overly optimistic. He wrote:

According to current scientific estimates, the amount of CO_2 in the air is expected to double by 2020. This addition to the window pane within our atmosphere would be sufficient to raise surface temperatures on the earth by some 1.5 to 3.0° ... Among the projected effects of a rise in temperatures of 1° to 3° in our planetary greenhouse would be the further unlocking of vast amounts of water congealed in our polar icecaps. This could eventually bring sea levels above the level of land in populous delta areas of Asia, the coastal areas of Europe and much of Florida.[31]

He related environmental degradation, in turn, to the third external threat to human survival: resource depletion, particularly the depletion of non-renewable fossil fuels. However, in 1979, he made no mention of peak oil, the importance of which will be elaborated later.

The combined effect of Heilbroner's three external threats was an increased possibility of wars, particularly wars of distribution. The four-fifths of the global population forced to survive on two-fifths of the world's resources could easily conclude that they have little to lose by entering into such wars, since many would be close to starvation in any case. In less developed countries, preparation for such wars exacerbates the starvation, of course. Combine this militarization with the horizontal proliferation of nuclear weapons, and one can only expect an increasing number of threats by third world nations to use them.[32]

Although the vertical proliferation of nuclear weapons among the superpowers (which was Heilbroner's concern in the 1970s) has abated since the fall of the Berlin Wall and the end of the Cold War, the dependence of "developed" societies on third world nations for the energy (and other) resources necessary to the maintenance of their standard of living means that wars of redistribution remain possible. (The protracted crisis in the Middle East, the Iranian threat in 2007 to develop nuclear weapons, and the renewed arms race between India, Pakistan, and China are taking place against this background.) Wars between middle powers are perhaps more probable than ever.

Heilbroner argued in *An Inquiry into the Human Prospect* that each of these external threats to mankind is, at least indirectly, the result of the development of science and technology.[33] Modern medical, hygiene, and public health measures have combined to lower the death rate in both developed and less developed countries. But the less developed countries have maintained their high birth rates, and this has led to burgeoning populations in all but a few countries. The Westernization of the world through the export of Western scientific methods, technology, and consumption patterns has led to the environmental degradation and resource depletion that pose the second threat. And the size of research and development in the weapons industry, which keeps somewhere between one-half and four-fifths of all scientists employed (depending on who does the reporting), makes the weapons industry virtually impossible to control or dismantle.[34]

The external threats to our survival are directly the result of the economic growth that has been the chief goal of both capitalist and communist societies for the past century. Another question Heilbroner therefore posed was: Can either capitalism or socialism meet the challenges that economic growth has produced? And the answer he gave was, again, no. Both systems are committed to

the industrial system, which imposes common values (like productivity, efficiency, and indifference to the health of the environment) on their populations.[35]

Neither capitalism nor socialism, in spite of their apparent differences, can easily manage the adaptation of an industrial society to a
steady-state economy, for "the mode of production must be abandoned in a mere flash of time, as historic sequences are measured."[36]
And yet, Heilbroner argued, such an adaptation is absolutely necessary because we are neither able to sustain growth, owing to resource
depletion, nor able to tolerate it, owing to environmental degradation and the heating up of the atmosphere. What made the human
prospect so grim for Heilbroner was that the required adaptation
would clearly demand drastic curtailment of the types of freedom
that those brought up in democratic, capitalist societies have come
to assume as their birthright. This in turn would necessitate the
emergence of an authoritarian, if not a totalitarian, regime run by a
truly charismatic leader who would be able to implement some of
the solutions that Heilbroner proposed in his last chapter.

The vagueness and the impracticality of Heilbroner's proposals
made him pessimistic, yet they also allowed him to see a ray of hope:

The human prospect is not an irrevocable death sentence. It is not an
inevitable doomsday toward which we are headed, although the risk of
enormous catastrophes exists. The prospect is better viewed as a formidable array of challenges that must be overcome before human survival is assured ... The death sentence is better viewed as a contingent
life sentence – one that will permit the continuance of human society,
but only on a basis very different from that of the present, and probably only after much suffering during the period of transition."[37]

And so Heilbroner made some proposals. He recommended the
"gradual abandonment of the lethal techniques, the uncongenial life-
ways, and the dangerous mentality of industrial civilization itself."[38]
(This obviously referred to weapons of war: nuclear, chemical, and
perhaps even conventional.) But Heilbroner did not state whether he
considered other common elements of modern life like nuclear
power generation, pesticides, automobiles, or airplanes "lethal." He
then recommended a return to the parsimonious attitudes that have
virtually disappeared in a consumer society: "Resource consuming
and heat generating processes must be regarded as necessary evils, not

as social triumphs, to be relegated to as small a portion of economic life as possible."[39] Third, Heilbroner suggested that we would have to minimize the ethos of science and the work ethic and reintroduce "tradition and ritual, the pillars of life in virtually all societies other than those of an industrial character."[40] We would have to live in a society where public values would take precedence over the private, and a new contemplative spirit would replace the drive of industrial society. Heilbroner did not suggest a return to the ethics of natural law and an abandonment of the history-making spirit. His analysis of the modern dilemma was that of an economist, not a philosopher.

Heilbroner's proposal, however, echoed the mysticism of the German philosopher Martin Heidegger, who irrationally asserted that "only a god can save us."[41] In the postscript to the inquiry "What Has Posterity Ever Done for Me?" Heilbroner made it clear that in his view there is no *rational* basis for any sane person to make sacrifices for future generations, particularly if it is doubtful whether those sacrifices will have their desired effect. He argued that what was required to legitimate and motivate those sacrifices, that is, to defeat the "danceband on the *Titanic*" mentality prevalent in developed societies, was "a religious affirmation welling up within us as we careen toward Armageddon."[42] He recommended a turning away from our "Promethean spirit" and an acceptance of the "example of Atlas, resolutely bearing his burden."[43] Enlightenment optimism seems to have been transformed into mythic endurance.

Much of Heilbroner's pessimism has been borne out in the last twenty-five years, as the global community has attempted to deal with his predictions regarding poverty and malnutrition as well as climate change. These will be explored in the following chapters.

2

Technology, Poverty, and Malnutrition:
The End of Distributive Justice

In the last decade of the twentieth century the annual output of the global economy grew by an estimated 25 per cent. The number of people living on less than one US dollar per day hovered at around 1.2 billion over the same period. And while the richer countries showed steady growth in their per capita income figures, more than eighty of the poorest countries had per capita incomes lower in 2001 than they had been a decade earlier.[1] "In 2001, the World Bank reported that 1.1 billion or one fifth of the population of the world's poor countries lived on less that what one dollar a day would buy in the United States. About 2.7 billion people or over half the developing world's population lived on less than two dollars per day."[2] Meanwhile, as Thomas Homer-Dixon pointed out, in 2004 there were 587 billionaires "with a combined wealth equivalent to 20% of the annual economic output of the U.S.A."[3] This at a time when we have more international cooperation on trade and development strategies than ever before.

We have sophisticated international bodies to address economic problems and trade disputes. We have free and open markets; indeed, at the behest of financial experts and a global business elite, governments around the world have deregulated their economies and liberalized trade. We have an unprecedented array of technical means at our disposal. However, in spite of brash statements made by proponents of globalization and the conventional wisdom of opinion-makers about the incredible economic growth in China and bright prospects for India, careful studies seem to indicate that the gap between rich and poor is growing ever wider both within and between the world's nations. In his groundbreaking 2005 study *Worlds Apart*,

Branko Milanovic, a lead economist at the World Bank, exploited its vast database on household incomes and expenditures and found that "inequality between individuals stayed roughly constant, and extremely high, in the last two decades of the twentieth century." On the basis of his reading of Milanovic, Homer-Dixon concludes that "when we look at inequality between individuals, we find that widening inequalities inside China and India have counterbalanced gains from China's overall growth. We also find definitively that we now live in a world without a middle class: over 77 percent of the world's people are poor (with a per capita income below the Brazilian average), while nearly 16 percent are rich (with incomes above the Portuguese average), which leaves less than 7 percent in the middle."[4]

What is perplexing in all this is that the consensus among expert economists favours staying the course; we are told to consider the success stories like the booming "Asian tiger" economies.[5] We are told that we need more trade liberalization, more globalization, a freer environment for the operations of the transnational corporations that dominate the world economy. But when, and in terms of what criteria, do we judge whether the program actually works? And when do we start to seriously consider what kind of social order is produced if and when it does work?

In this chapter we shall observe how the history of colonialism in the modern era unfolds within the broader history of the rise of technique and how both have resulted in greater and greater inequities over time, in spite of all rhetoric to the contrary.[6] For example, one repeatedly observes evidence of what we have been calling "technical necessity" – the imperatives determined by the instrumental logic of technical systems – in the official language of the World Bank and the International Monetary Fund (IMF) in their literature on development. The tone of this discourse is adopted by officials of the World Trade Organization and the G-8, most notably when they are responding to their critics. What becomes clear is that these officials and their critics are not speaking the same language. The latter appeal to ethical imperatives, the former to the procedural logic of monetary policy and economic technique. The global economic elite's commitment to technique is made before all consideration of goals, appropriate means, and ethical standards. And, as we have argued, technical necessity, insofar as it overrides ethical reflection, amounts to nihilism. As with the issues that we will explore in later chapters, we must see that what is actually at stake in our acceptance of the language of technical necessity, whether in the form of medical science or of neo-liberal economics, is our very capacity to reflect on what we do.

Ethicists like Robert Stivers and Ian Barbour have argued that the liberal Protestant tradition has the conceptual resources to reorient society and to meet the external challenges outlined by Heilbroner and summarized in the last chapter. Those resources have been developed in the meetings of the World Council of Churches over the past forty years. The ideals of justice, participation, and sustainable sufficiency have been articulated, and proposals have been made for more appropriate global economic development that can remedy widespread hunger, the social and political alienation caused by technology, the depletion of our resources, and the destruction of the ecosystem. Interestingly, in their discussion, technology has moved from being simply part of the solution to also being a part of the problem.[7]

The World Council of Churches' discussion of poverty and malnutrition in less developed countries has shared the assumptions accepted by most development economists since World War II regardless of their ideological bent. Barbara Ward Jackson articulated these assumptions when she suggested in a spate of books written in the sixties and the seventies[8] that we should not ask why the third world is poor. Rather, we should reverse the question and ask why the first world is rich?[9] Like those who hold to what we have called the "mastery thesis," she suggests that the reasons are rooted in Western culture and biblical religion, which gave rise to the industrial revolution and the economic development of the North Atlantic region in the eighteenth and nineteenth centuries.

This account points, first, to the historical and cultural ramifications of those passages in Genesis that speak of humanity's lordship in creation: "Be fruitful and multiply, fill the earth and conquer it. Be master of the fishes of the sea, the birds of the heaven and all living animals on the earth."[10] This emphasis on human dominion over creation, combined with a belief in a radically transcendent God, leads to the dedivinization (or demythologization) of creation, or the "disenchantment of the earth" to use Max Weber's phrase.[11] This disenchantment has its origins in the movement from an order based on cosmological myth to an order based on a historical covenant of the people with Yahweh, the Lord of Creation.[12]

Second, there is in both Judaism and Christianity (as well as in Islam) an eschatological emphasis on the future as a time of fulfillment. This has been transmogrified in the modern period, as we have seen, into a belief in progress. The result in the West is that we generally see ourselves as not only free but required to manipulate the natural environment in the interests of our human future. We think of ourselves as creators of the future. Experimental science is the most important means we have devised to create it. Experimental science arose in the North Atlantic region and not in India or China, two rich civilizations that invented many sophisticated techniques (gun powder and the printing press, for example) long before they were developed in Europe. Research science entailed a new approach to medicine that had enormous social consequences, first for Europe and then, with European imperialism, for the rest of the world. These consequences are often summarized under the rubric of modernization. The industrial revolution included the transformation of medicine and hygiene, agriculture, education, transportation, and communications. These all laid the groundwork for an acceleration of economic growth and the great "transformation" described by Karl Polanyi some sixty years ago.[13]

Improvements in medicine, hygiene, and public health led to a population explosion in Europe in the nineteenth century: between 1815 and 1914, Europe's population increased from 180 million to 460 million, in spite of massive emigration to the Americas.[14] Because population growth tailed off in developed countries in the twentieth century, the explosion itself is rarely noted or appreciated. The reasons for it are obvious in retrospect: the birth rate remained relatively high while the death rate (and specifically infant mortality) declined dramatically beginning as early as 1760 in Great Britain.[15] Population growth, combined with the mechanization of agriculture (which enhanced its productivity and created rural unemployment), led to the migration to the cities of masses of people in search of work. Those who moved to the cities were forced to accept poor pay, long hours, and difficult working conditions in the new factories (textile, industrial, etc.) or in domestic service. (This accounts for the expansion of bourgeois comforts, which initially relied less on new machines than on a large servant class to maintain standards of domestic ease.)[16]

The development of the railway and electronic means of communication – the telegraph was invented in 1844 and the telephone followed quickly – meant that production facilities were no longer limited to local distribution of the goods (whether agricultural or industrial) that were produced. Technical scale and technical efficiency, both of which increased the cost-efficiency of production, began to determine the size of factories. In England, Holland, and Germany, from about 1760 on, the merchant class was able to make substantial profits on the backs of a poorly paid proletariat, and, motivated by the Protestant ethic, it was more inclined to reinvest these profits in new factories than to spend them on consumption or in riotous living. In nineteenth-century England, this led both to the concentration of wealth in the hands of the few, which Marx so much deplored in the economic analysis of *Das Kapital,* and to the grinding poverty and child labour that Charles Dickens described in novels like *Oliver Twist.*

It was not until the late nineteenth and early twentieth century that some of this new wealth trickled down and contributed to the formation of a new middle class.[17] According to Barbara Ward Jackson, three factors were influential in this development. First, there was the universalization of the franchise in England and other parts of Europe. With the vote, the working class was able to form a political party that articulated and fought for its interests in Parliament. Second, the labour movement formed unions, which through collective bargaining and strikes could limit the power of the owners and force them to share a portion of their wealth with those whose labour produced it. And last, there was the realization that a middle class provided a new market for the goods and services produced if workers were paid enough to purchase them. Henry Ford is credited with realizing that there would be no demand for the Model T unless the wages of the workers in his assembly plants were increased. It was in his own interest, therefore, to pay his employees better. Thus began what John Lukacs has called "the automobile century."[18]

At the same time that the middle class was emerging in Europe and North America, poverty and malnutrition were increasing in less developed (third or fourth world) countries. This was largely the result of colonialism, which began with the Spanish and the Portuguese when they were sea powers in the sixteenth and seventeenth centuries, continued with the Dutch, French, and the British in the eighteenth and nineteenth centuries when industrial power became crucial, and was transformed by the business acumen and technological expertise of the Americans in the twentieth century. Colonial expansion drew the countries of the south into the orbit of the incipient modernity of the western European powers. It was an arrangement that would benefit the latter at the expense of the former.

To be sure, the colonial powers did introduce some modern medical and public health measures, which resulted in the demographic changes that have been called, mistakenly we believe, the "population bomb."[19] However, they neglected to create an industrial system or infrastructure adequate to the needs of the colonized populations but were content to use foreign countries as their source of raw materials, particularly minerals, and as a market for their own manufactures. They developed transportation and communication networks only with a view to facilitating these exports and not to serve the colonies themselves. Poverty and malnutrition in the colonized countries were thus exacerbated by the combination of population growth and the incoherence of their economies.[20]

During the colonial period, that is up to about 1950, poverty in the third world was legitimated in the "developed" world by what Gunnar Myrdal, the Nobel prize winning economist, called the Colonial Theory.[21] This theory stated bluntly that the native populations of Asia or Africa or Latin America had a tendency toward idleness and inefficiency, which was rooted in their backward social system as well as their racial inferiority. Their health suffered because of their generally hot climates, which helped explain the low productivity levels. They were, according to the theory, caught in a double bind: malnutrition and poor living conditions made them less healthy and less productive, and their lack of productivity kept them poor and malnourished. The Colonial Theory concluded that little could be done to improve the conditions of the poor, and that therefore little should be done; certainly there was no need on the part of the generally wealthy northerners to incur any sacrifices on their behalf.

After 1950, according to Myrdal, Protest Ideology replaced the Colonial Theory as the colonies declared their independence one by one.[22] Neo-colonialism and economic dependence on the former colonial powers replaced the political dependence of the pre-World War II period. The Protest Ideology was put forward by both the new governments and the old colonizers. It rejected the central tenets of the old theory. It denied the importance of climate, race, social structure, cultural attitudes, or political institutions in the underdevelopment of the new nations. Religion and culture were not regarded as impediments to rapid development, which, it was argued, could be fueled by the transfer of technology from the developed to the less developed countries. Optimistic economic projections, like those of Walter Rostow,[23] were made by think-tanks in first and third world countries. Everyone was content to believe that development would not require any sacrifices of the economic elites in either the first or the third world. The poor could get rich without the rich getting any poorer. This was a consoling thought for the multinational corporations based in Europe and the United States, as well as for their contacts among the elites of the third world. It meant not only business as usual but more business.

It was in 1949, on the eve of this shift in the character of north-south relations, that the concept of "development," as it is now widely understood, was first used by Harry Truman. Wolfgang Sachs points out that this concept has meaning only in the context of what continues to be a network of neo-colonial relationships between north and south. "Development" includes under one rubric two aspects of the colonial relationship that formerly – under the British, for example – were distinct: the paternalistic mission of moral improvement, the so-called "white man's burden," and the large-scale economic mobilization of labour and resources.[24] The concept of development could baptize what was often little more than good old-fashioned greed with the spirit of missionary zeal. As Sachs suggests, "Development was the conceptual vehicle that allowed the USA to behave as herald of national self-determination while at the same time founding a new type of world-wide domination: an anti-colonial imperialism."[25] By way of development, which involved the transfer of technology and economic means, the practical reality of domination could be reconciled with the ideological pseudo-reality of salvation.

The great optimism of the post-war period, an optimism linked to a burgeoning of technological means, prevented any insight into how the imposition on the third world of the technical imperative involved with Western capitalist development was a part, if not the very essence, of their problems. So the various proposals for technical solutions – both those that relied on technology transfer and those that required the implementation of economic strategies generated by economists and development "experts" – were made without the least sense of irony. A classic example of this is John F.

Kennedy's "Alliance for Progress." In his address to Congress in 1961, Kennedy observed: "Throughout Latin America millions of people are struggling to free themselves from the bonds of poverty, hunger and ignorance ... To the North and the East, they see the abundance which modern science can bring. They know the tools of progress are within their reach."[26] Many, if not most, of those Latin Americans "struggling to free themselves" would have identified their bondage with the imperial power of America itself, but Kennedy's rhetoric presented to third world peoples the possibility of a prosperous, US-sponsored liberal-capitalist utopia as an alternative to revolutionary change. This vision gained momentum when a profusion of capital in the Western financial world in the late 1960s and 1970s resulted in massive development loans being made available to third world countries. A great many impressive high-tech mega-projects in infrastructure development were, with the help of Western capital, initiated during those years.

But, alas, the bust was not long in coming for many of the third world economies. As a result of rising interest rates and changing economic conditions on a world scale, countries like Brazil that were believed to have shown such early promise, and that had involved themselves deeply with lending institutions, shortly found themselves in dire straits. The shanty towns on the outskirts of Brasilia became the bleak and disturbing icon of the debt-ridden third world.

By the late 1970s it started to become clear that a simple "transfer of technology" to third world countries was not the easy solution to poverty and malnutrition. The hope that with more technological hardware and expertise, and a sum of loan capital to get things started, the third world could be helped to "catch up" with the first was deflated and often replaced by indifference. Accordingly there was a tendency in developed countries either to give up on some former colonies or to blame the victims. Garret Hardin urged the adoption of a triage method, whereby some national economies would be abandoned and allowed to collapse because more good could be done if the wealthy West concentrated its aid efforts on the more successful countries.[27] Third world societies were urged to follow the Chinese model and put population policies in place that would move them toward zero population growth. In 1976, a spate of articles appeared in the popular press that urged developed countries to link their foreign aid to this policy. Some writers went so far as to argue that all foreign aid should be for birth control.[28] The less developed countries were, at the same time, blamed for global (and even domestic) ecological problems, which, it was implied, were chiefly the result of population growth (and immigration). The advanced industrial system was thereby relieved of blame or responsibility for both the poverty of third world countries (as if poverty were not itself a byproduct of colonial exploitation) and the environmental problems of the first (as if the modern industrial system's increasing drug-like dependence on fossil fuels and chemicals had nothing to do with this).

But the debt crisis of the late 1970s and 1980s was also the occasion for the economists' most ambitious forays out of the think-tank and into the real world. Solving the debt crisis would require even more involvement from the technicians than did issuing and administering the loans. Harsh medicine would have to be administered by the IMF but it would all be for the best. Loans would be made available to help indebted states with their crushing interest payments, but only on condition that certain fundamental changes were made in their economies. These changes would be prescribed on a case-by-case basis by the World Bank and the IMF. The changes included reorienting economies further toward an export bias to generate more foreign capital. This often meant moving toward dependency on the production of a single crop or commodity. The so-called Structural Adjustment Plans (SAPs) also required governments to cut spending, which usually meant gutting education and health care. Governments were also required to reduce tariffs, devalue local currency, reduce wages, and privatize public corporations. Having no alternative, many countries were forced to agree to these conditions. By the end of 1992, 267 structural adjustment loans had been approved.[29] But many studies, including one conducted by an IMF economist, found that the SAPs usually did not work. In fact, a comparison of a number of countries that agreed to stabilization and adjustment plans with those that didn't shows that between 1973 and 1988 the latter actually experienced more growth.[30] In this case, it would seem, the best therapy was to stay away from the doctor.

Walden Bello examines the case of Chile. Up until 1971, Chile's average annual growth in gross domestic product was between 4 and 4.5 per cent. During the years of the Pinochet regime (1974–89), Chile's economic policy was influenced by some University of Chicago-educated economists who, with great technical efficiency and enthusiasm, put structural adjustment policies into effect. Chile's annual economic growth rate promptly dropped to 2.6 per cent. The country suffered two major depressions in the decade after Pinochet came to power. And, perhaps most telling of all, the share of national income going to the poorest 50 per cent of the population dropped from 20.4 to 16.9 per cent, while the percentage going to the rich rose from 36.5 to 46.8.[31]

There are many similar examples of countries whose economies have been, from the point of view of their struggling populations, all but destroyed by the misguided meta-strategies of the World Bank and the IMF. And it would be too simplistic to suggest that these institutions, and their staff, press on with their agenda only because they serve the interests of a small, greedy corporate elite. There is good reason to believe that many economic experts are quite genuinely committed to the theory. They simply don't read the facts the same way. As Herman Daly, himself an economist, observes: "My major concern about my profession today is that our disciplinary preference for logically beautiful results over factually grounded policies has reached such fanatical proportions that we economists have become dangerous to the earth and its inhabitants."[32] There are some notable exceptions; Daly, who at one time used to teach the doctrine of deregulation and free trade, is one of them. And Ravi Kanbur, the Cornell University economist who was initially the primary author of the World Bank's World Development Report for 2000–01, sparked a battle within that institution by making the fairly understated claim that market liberalization was not itself a sufficient strategy with which to address issues of poverty.[33] In the end, Kanbur resigned his position in protest.[34]

And there have been comprehensive proposals for an entirely different model of development that does not presume that it is desirable or even possible to continue to draw the third world further into the orbit of high-tech Western capitalism. In his 1973 book *Small Is Beautiful*, E.F. Schumacher argued that the transfer of advanced technology would exacerbate the problems of less developed countries. Schumacher did exploratory calculations to show that the modernization of their entire economies was not only misguided but impossible.[35] Long before third world countries would be modernized we would run out of cheap and simple fossil fuels. Schumacher went even further than this, however; he claimed that the modern industrial system was beginning to make the developed world poor. Unfortunately, a society that equated growth in the gross national product with an increase in economic well-being was unable to hear his message.

Schumacher contended that even developed countries were becoming poorer because they were using up their capital, which, once depleted, would be gone forever.[36] We were, he explained, consuming our fossil fuels (oil, coal, natural gas), and in the process using up the tolerance margins of nature. Schumacher saw that the polluting of the atmosphere, the waterways, and the land could not continue indefinitely without destructive consequences for the polluters themselves. He argued that economics gives us a fragmented view because it does not distinguish between primary and secondary, or renewable and non-renewable, resources. It leads us to think that labour is a necessary evil to be reduced to a minimum. The result is that we measure our standard of living by consumption. Profound inequities, endemic violence, and social alienation are symptoms of the breakdown of social bonds in a consumer society. In fact, it has been noted by such thinkers as Jacques Ellul that technical necessity demands, along with mass consumption, the destruction of even the most elementary bonds of social solidarity. These bonds of solidarity often also formed the basis of a complex economic fabric in which a culture of frugality survived by using various time-tested patterns of subsistence. As Wolfgang Sachs observes, "the culture of growth can only be erected on the ruins of frugality, and so destitution and dependence on commodities are its price."[37]

In 1974 Schumacher saw that the third world faced a unique set of problems: the transfer of technology and development of a modern sector in the major cities created a dual economy.[38] Fifteen per cent of the population lived in these cities, which were relatively wealthy because they were plugged into the global economy and received the aid and the investment of the first world. But the 85 per cent living in the rural areas and small towns received none of this aid or investment and suffered mass unemployment or underemployment, malnutrition, and poverty. When possible, the rural poor would migrate to the cities (Sao Paolo, or Mexico City, for example) in search of a better life. As Schumacher predicted, this mass migration put tremendous pressure on the cities and led to a mutual poisoning of the city and the countryside. The cities become polluted and congested while the villages and towns become demoralized and depopulated. Schumacher argued that, to be effective in combating these trends, foreign aid must bypass the cities and be used to create small work-places that have relatively simple production methods, use raw mate-rials that are ready to hand, and produce goods and services that are needed locally. Intermediate technology would make rural develop-ment possible. That is, aid should be used to introduce tools, prod-ucts, and processes that are appropriate for a society where there is a scarcity of work, not a scarcity of workers. Intermediate technology would increase the efficiency of the workers so that they could see the efficacy of their labour. Schumacher's development plans were devised to maintain human scale and maximize participation in the economy rather than allow technical scale and the maximization of productivity to determine the shape of society.

Schumacher was adapting the suggestions of Gunnar Myrdal, who had recommended that third world development should focus on labour-intensive agricultural expansion that would increase em-ployment and guarantee that the populations could feed them-selves.[39] But Myrdal saw that both third world elites and first world managers of multinational corporations would oppose the reforms required. Policies addressing inequality in societies that have virtu-ally no middle class have been opposed by domestic elites at every turn, although these reforms are always on the agenda in less devel-oped countries.[40] Educational reform, focusing on the teaching of literacy and practical skills in elementary schools, remains a good idea whose time has not been allowed to come.[41] And, most impor-tantly, little has been done to counter the neo-colonial mechanism that encourages first world countries to link up with the privileged and reactionary groups inside third world countries who are well served by the global economic system.[42] The World Bank, the IMF, and aid agencies themselves seem to have reinforced this mecha-nism, which virtually guarantees that money for development stays in the cities and is linked to the economic plans of the domestic elites who function as the local agents of foreign capitalists, multi-national corporations, and first world governments.

Those committed to a neo-liberal free enterprise ideology often ignore the salient facts. Statistics show that since 1950, in every re-gion but Africa food production has kept ahead of population growth.[43] Malnutrition is generally the result of the failure to dis-tribute the food to those who need it most but who have the least ability to pay for it. Also, there is no correlation between the density of population of an area and the hunger of its inhabitants. We know that population and malnutrition decline when social arrangements beyond the family offer economic opportunity. Economic opportunity and food production are enhanced by a *local* market economy. A *global* free market, on the other hand, inevitably favours agribusinesses, which have the capital to buy up the land and hire tenant farmers to produce crops for export. They alone can afford the machinery, chemical fertilizers, pesticides, and fossil fuels required to industrialize agriculture and produce cash crops for export. But this invariably leads to greater dependency of the poor countries on the rich. Export-oriented agriculture means that less developed countries are producing food for the more developed countries and are forced to buy food from other countries with the foreign currency earned. Often this means that their own populations cannot afford imported food.

Here we can see the essential bind. The emergence of the "global economy" has perhaps begun to make evident what has long been a fact. Third world societies, as indeed Schumacher argue, are not in need of modernization. They are generally not pre-modern, even if what we mean by "modern" is defined in terms of technological development. The technological system is global, but its control centre is the developed West. The period of colonialism was one in which the social orders of societies in every corner of the globe were effectively *reordered* to accommodate the demands of Western technological development. Those who marvel at the emergence of a high-tech, post-industrial economy fail to notice how the great factories that have disappeared from our cities have simply re-emerged in the maquiladoras and free trade zones of third world countries or in China, where labour and resources are cheap. The poverty of the third world is as much a phenomenon of technological development as the computer and the automobile.

Other thinkers, in addition to Schumacher and Myrdal, have attempted to put forward more balanced assessments of the issues behind the plight of the third world and, in some cases, proffer their own modest proposals for more just and well-integrated development strategies. One thinks of Frances Moore Lappé, Susan George, and Jim McGinnis.[44] One thinks also of the noted environmentalist Barry Commoner, who argued strongly that the only morally acceptable solution to the problem of poverty is economic development.[45] Draconian population control programs may work in certain circumstances, but they put the cart before the horse.

People will willingly restrict the size of their families if they have a sense of economic security and confidence in the future. This is clearly what has happened in the developed countries, which have generally reached zero population growth without any governmental controls. But Commoner insisted that economic development in third world countries must not follow the Western pattern; it must be ecologically benign. "Economic development can proceed without a concomitant decrease in environmental quality if it is based on an appropriate, ecologically benign production technology. For example, crop production can be increased without incurring the environmental hazards of conventional chemical agriculture by practicing organic farming instead."[46]

This kind of economic development will require the support of first world countries and the donation of its most environmentally sensitive solar technologies. In making this suggestion, Commoner demonstrates the difference between his approach and that of Schumacher. He wants the first world to allow the third world to skip over the most environmentally destructive phase of economic development (the nineteenth and twentieth centuries) and to move right into the future by using such devices as the photovoltaic cell to meet its energy needs. "The only remedy, I am convinced, is to return some of the world's wealth to the countries whose resources and peoples have borne so much of the burden of producing it – the developing nations. Such colonial reparations ought to be paid not only in goods but, more usefully, in the means of producing them. And the productive processes should be those that correct both the environmental and economic defects of the technologies that have enveloped the global ecosphere in pollution."[47] Paradoxically, Commoner's proposed solution to the problem of poverty is based on his judgment that *new* Western technologies can enable third world countries to bypass the problems created by the old. For its implementation, this solution will require one more revival of the Enlightenment faith in progress. But isn't that where we came in?

The basic problem is that the Enlightenment faith is now carried by multinational corporations who have a vested interest in old technologies that are based on fossil fuels – in short, the petrochemical industries. And the power of multinational corporations is not limited to economic power. Their power is also cultural and ideological. This kind of power derives largely from the fact that they represent the highest unfolding of the potentialities of technique. They are malleable social ensembles; they form cultures without roots, traditions, or prior commitments. In fact, Jerry Mander has argued that the corporation is itself a form of machine. "The corporation," he claimed, "is not subject to human control as most people believe it is; rather, it is an autonomous technical structure that behaves by a system of logic uniquely well suited to its primary function: to give birth and impetus to profitable new technological forms, and to spread techno-logic around the globe."[48] The humanistic rhetoric of corporate public relations is evidence of the extent to which these organizations/machines embody the contradictions that have been part of the technological enterprise from the beginning. However, to be sure, there is nothing in the logic of that enterprise that obliges its agents to concern themselves with justice.[49]

In recent discourse, development has become almost a synonym for justice. But development is by no means a neutral concept, as is often assumed, to be filled by whatever notion of justice or equity we choose to apply. According to Wolfgang Sachs, "development" is the conquest of society by the market – it thus reflects onto the south a process that has already occurred throughout the north. The extension of this conquest was part of the colonial project from the beginning. As Sachs writes, "the ideals and mental habits, patterns of work and modes of knowing, webs of loyalties and rules of governance in which the South's people were steeped were usually at odds with the ethos of an economic society."[50] That ethos emerges out of the ascendency of technical necessity, where the "science" of economics provides the mathematical matrix by which the efficiency and efficacy of our technique is quantified and assessed – it is the *ethos* of a civilization that has already abandoned *ethics*.

This helps to explain why the various proposals for different models of development have gone not only unheeded but generally unconsidered. In a 1991 article entitled "Towards Development Ethics," D. Crocker suggested that "we need critical and explicit reflection on the ends as well as the means of development, on the *what* as well as the *how*. Given that the non-normative sense of development can easily be confused with the normative senses, it is often best to speak of 'authentic' or 'good' development as the theoretical and practical goal of development ethics."[51] We have, in this chapter, reviewed a number of comprehensive proposals for "authentic" development; we have also noted the evolution of various frameworks for analysis and development policy in the post-war period. It does seem odd that after half a century of "development" we are still hearing calls for some kind of normative framework. But perhaps it is not so strange if we take seriously Ellul's analysis of technique. As he has observed, "the power and the scope of present technical means completely dominate the sphere of our thought and life."[52]

We have seen that the technical system is about the proliferation of means; the ends are considered only in light of the newly acquired possibilities. Given Mander's observation that both the corporations currently dominating the global economy and the global trade deals that facilitate corporate control are, themselves, technical forms, it is not surprising that proposals calling for a re-evaluation of our priorities are simply swallowed up in silence and apathy. What development has so far accomplished is a situation in which 20 to 30 per cent of global trade is carried on by large corporations and their subsidiaries. What is officially called "trade liberalization" is in reality the opening of an environment in which that trend is likely to continue and in which there will be less and less opportunity for public input and reflection. The large and angry crowd of protesters gathering outside of makeshift fortresses in which bodies like the World Trade Organization meet is an indication of a certain public sense of alarm, but it remains to be seen whether that concern will grow and effectively check the burgeoning power of the global technical system. Ellul observes that "fundamentally, man is alienated within the technical system that substituted technical fatality for the former fatality of nature."[53]

We have been arguing that the nature of our commitment to technology undermines our capacity for moral reflection. Our commitment to programs that are essentially defined within the horizon of technical necessity indicates a failure to think about the obligations put on us by any commitment to the good. Indeed, the assumption that justice between the peoples of the north and the south can best be worked out under the rubric of "development" is one that seems to exclude moral reflection on the past and future of north-south relations. Sachs has suggested that "the lesson to be drawn from 40 years of development can be stated bluntly: the issue of justice must be delinked from the perspective of 'development.' In fact, both ecology and poverty call for limits to development."[54] We have argued that the institutions arising within the era of development, neo-colonialism, and globalization – e.g., the Bretton Woods institutions (the World Bank, the IMF) and the multinational corporations – are essentially technical phenomena. As such they are, in a sense, post-ethical. If we are to begin to rethink, on an ethical basis, the nature of our relationship to the peoples of the third world, we will have to first rethink our fundamental commitment to technology – and in the developed world of the twenty-first century, that necessarily involves every aspect of our lives. It also involves our concern for the environment, which we will examine in the next chapter.

3

Sustainable Sufficiency is Not Enough: The End of Environmental Ethics

In the first decade of the twenty-first century we find ourselves in the midst of a global ecological crisis: it is estimated that we are currently losing 50 million acres of forest annually (an area the size of England, Wales, and Scotland combined);[1] carbon dioxide levels in the atmosphere are higher now than at any time in the last 650,000 years, leading to alarming increases in average atmospheric temperatures – as of 2005, the hottest year on record was 2005;[2] in 2001, the Intergovernmental Panel on Climate Change, an international body of scientists who review and report the latest findings, predicted that global temperatures would rise by between 1.4 and 5.8° centigrade in this century, a figure that is now widely viewed as conservative;[3] in 1998, 3000 square kilometers of Antarctic ice shelf broke up and melted, and in February 2002 the 2,250-square-kilometre Larsen B ice shelf also broke up, heightening concerns that rising ocean water levels could swamp many of the world's coastal regions in this century;[4] in 2001, the government of Tavalu in the South Pacific signed a deal for New Zealand to take in its refugees as its islands disappear under water;[5] alarming rates of aquifer depletion and loss of arable farmland to degradation and development mean that, in this century, many regions of the world will find themselves unable to support their populations; over the last half of the twentieth century, the global fish harvest rose from 19 million to 90 million tones and, as of the year 2000, thousands of species were on the brink of extinction.[6]

Each of these trends, by itself, is alarming, but what is more troubling are the synergistic effects – the combined results of, for example, deforestation and climate change – that are occurring with greater frequency and are increasingly difficult to predict. For example, as average global atmospheric temperatures rise, massive areas of permafrost in the far north begin to thaw, releasing billions of tonnes of gases into the atmosphere and thereby accelerating the rate of climate change. This kind of process is being referred to as "positive feedback," and it is widely held that such effects will play an ever greater role in thedynamics of climate change.[7] The gradual degradation of the global environment is without a doubt one of the single most pressing ethical challenges for the humanity in the twenty-first century. The public's willingness to acknowledge the seriousness of the crisis – which still well outstrips its willingness to do much about it – is perhaps reflected in the success of former US vice-president Al Gore's Academy Award-winning documentary *An Inconvenient Truth*. In the best-selling book of the same title, Gore writes: "Today, we are hearing and seeing dire warnings of the worst potential catastrophe in the history of human civilization. A global climate crisis that is deepening and rapidly becoming more dangerous than anything we have ever faced."[8] What makes the prospects seem so bleak is that it is the well-entrenched patterns of consumption and production within the developed world that are the main source of the problem.

Over twenty years ago Robert Stivers described the developed world as an eight-cylinder Cadillac roaring down a superhighway and ignoring the problems emerging around it. The gas guzzler is in need of repair, the pavement is deteriorating, pollution is becoming a problem for those living on the edge of the road, gas stations are raising their prices, and many are saying that it is time to put on the brakes.[9] The natural tendency is, however, to continue with the same pattern of economic development that produced the automobile and the superhighway. Technological optimists like Herman Kahn and Julian Simon[10] argued then that the only way to solve the problems of poverty, resource depletion, and pollution was through *more* economic development and technological innovation. And they had faith that the free market system and the enterprise of its participants would provide a bright future for the globe. Reagan and Thatcher expressed such a faith in "trickle-down" (supply-side) economics for the English-speaking middle classes in the 1980s; more recently, the torch has been carried by the likes of George W. Bush, Tony Blair, and Stephen Harper.

Others have been more skeptical about the ability of corporate capitalism to solve the problems that unbridled economic growth has created. They have argued that a new orientation is required. As moderates, they are committed to technological and structural change but do not believe that any radical shift in values or life-styles is required. Economic development should continue, although the type of economic development should change. We might place environmentalists like Amory Lovins or Barry Commoner in this category.[11] A "soft energy" path that relies on solar, wind, and co-generation power rather than coal, oil, or nuclear power clearly requires as much technological innovation and perhaps as much capital investment as a hard path, but it is more parsimonious in its exploitation of resources and less destructive in its effects on the environment. Some Christian ethicists espouse this approach but combine it with a personal religious commitment to responsible consumption and wise stewardship of natural resources. The World Council of Churches itself seems to have placed itself in this camp. The most articulate Christian expression of this point of view has been produced by Herman Daly and John B. Cobb Jr.[12] Their proposals are more imaginative but they do not differ substantially from those contained in the 1986 report of the UN-sponsored Brundtland Commission.[13]

It was Brundtland who first popularized the term "sustainable development"; the concept was also the guiding principle for *Agenda 21*, the document that articulated the principles of the 1992 United Nations Conference on Environment and Development in Rio de Janeiro.[14] There is a great deal of debate among environmentalists about the meaning and ultimate usefulness of this concept. Many object to it because it implicitly ignores the urgency of the environmental crisis. As Leslie Paul Thiele suggests, "by loudly celebrating the promise of economic growth while paying only lip service to environmental preservation, the language of sustainable development often gains political currency at a substantial ecological cost."[15] Others have maintained that notions like "responsible consumption" and "sustainable sufficiency" are used to legitimate the global economic status quo, that is, to defend the privileges of the rich, developed nations and condemn less developed nations to continued poverty. In 1979 C.T. Kurien pointed out that the lifestyles of the poor of the third world are no threat to the ecosystem either at present or in the foreseeable future, and preoccupation with the environment could be viewed as a first world ploy to restrict the economic growth that many parts of Asia, Africa, and Latin America require for their simple survival. Why should these nations take seriously the first world's supposed concern for future generations when they seem unable or unwilling to do anything for malnourished people suffering now in foreign lands? Kurien told the World Council of Churches assembled at MIT:

If you claim to be concerned about the unborn humanity that you cannot see but show no regard for the humanity that you can see all around you, then you are a liar. It is a small affluent minority of the world's population that whips up a hysteria about the finite resources of the world and pleads for a conservationist ethic in the interests of those yet to be born; it is the same group that makes an organized effort to prevent those who now happen to be outside the gates of their affluence from coming to have even a tolerable level of living. It does not call for a divine's insight to see what the real intentions are.[16]

More recently, Wolfgang Sachs has suggested that much of the current rhetoric around global ecology management implicitly involves yet another in a long line of attempts to pin the blame on the third world victim: "A storyline is being developed in which effects are reinterpreted as causes; one reads of environmental dangers, poverty and destabilization not as part of the global effects of the North, but as having their origins in the South."[17]

Nevertheless, as industrial civilization has spread like an oil slick across the globe and our ecological problems have deepened to the point of crisis, a debate about whether we should opt for an expanding or a no-growth economy has begun. It should be noted that the debate has been purely theoretical; no government of any nation has seriously asked whether economic growth is good. But in the 1970s Herman Daly insisted that this question had to be posed.[18] He argued at MIT that our problem is not that we are running out of non-renewable resources (like oil) but that because of the precipitous rate at which we are consuming non-renewables, we are destroying the capacity of the renewable resources (like the forests or fisheries) to regenerate themselves.[19] Our rapid consumption of yesterday's sunshine (fossil fuels) has allowed us to reach and sustain a combined level of population and per capita consumption that could never be sustained with the use of renewable resources alone. But in the process our energy consumption is jeopardizing our ability to harvest tomorrow's sunshine. Atmospheric heating, acid rain, ozone depletion, air and water pollution, and so on may mean that we have already maximized our agricultural seafood production. Daly's conclusion was that we must define limits to our global and local sustainable yield throughput and then learn to live within those limits.

To bring this abstract theorizing down to earth, we might consider the generation and consumption of electrical power in industrialized societies. Between 1945 and 1975, consumption doubled every ten years in most developed countries as people learned to "live better electrically."[20] By 1975, although the population had only doubled, it was using eight times as much electricity as at the end of World War II. Since then, the rate of growth has declined appreciably, largely because of a slowdown in the increase of demand (to between 2 and 4 per cent per annum), which was not predicted by utility companies. Nevertheless, power producers, nuclear associations, and politicians still argue that we won't be able to meet the increasing demand for electricity in the future. Economic growth will require more electricity. Daly suggests that a more realistic way of managing an economy is to determine how much economic growth and energy consumption are desirable and possible (and these are never the same), and then limit growth and consumption.[21]

Daly's argument for the moral necessity of limiting economic growth amounts to a practical critique of utilitarianism and materialism.[22] "The greatest good of the greatest number" is an impossible ideal when translated into the modern economics of greed; the greatest amount of goods for the greatest number of people is a form of double maximization. One can either maximize the number of people who will receive the limited number of goods we can produce or maximize the goods that a limited number will receive. But one cannot do both at the same time. Economics is not called the dismal science for nothing; it must deal with *scarce*, that is to say limited, resources. But there is an even more basic problem with the utilitarian formula. It assumes that the acquisition or production of more goods or services is always good for the individual as well as for society. It has not encouraged a discussion of what the "good life" is, nor has it attempted to define it. What has Athens to say to Wall Street, or Jerusalem to Madison Avenue? Nothing. Keep on producing. Keep on advertising. Keep on consuming. Daly concludes that utilitarianism inevitably leads to a type of mania for growth that has become the mark of a consumer society. Utilitarianism does not allow the question of limits to growth to arise; there can be no answer to the query of how much is enough. More is automatically better than less.

This was Julian Simon's basic assumption in his popular book *The Ultimate Resource*, written in the early 1980s. Simon was fundamentally opposed to the limiting of any type of growth, particularly population growth, by governments. He believed that the globe could support many more people than it did then and that individual couples are in the best position to decide whether they wish to have more children; there is no connection between population density and poverty. People, with all their industry, creativity, and ingenuity, are the ultimate resource. Economic growth can be expected to provide everything they need. Economic history shows that whenever a resource becomes scarce, new methods are developed to increase the supply, or substitutions are discovered.

In one classic example of his argument, Simon claimed that the supply of fuel is infinite.[23] And with regard to pollution, he took the attitude that the quality of the environment was improving thanks to pollution-control devices. The proof of this was that the lifespan in developed countries continues to increase. Simon placed his faith in the market: it will allocate resources and encourage ingenuity so that all the problems can be solved. Technological innovation will have a major role to play in eliminating environmental problems if economic growth allows for it.

We do not propose here to consider the specifics of Simon's claims, which, although clearly misleading overall,[24] have been shown to be true in some respects in the developed world. Like Herman Kahn, who reveled in the accomplishments of corporation capitalism, Simon tended to ignore the negative consequences of the concentration of tremendous amounts of capital and, by extension, political power in the hands of relatively few multinational companies, and of the systematic elimination of competition from vast segments of the economy. He wrote as if the small-scale laissez-faire capitalism of the nineteenth and early twentieth centuries was still dominant. He also ignored the role of the mass media in creating markets by advertising. When huge corporations expand their economic influence by moving capital between countries to take advantage of cheap labour, tax incentives, and lax pollution laws, so-called free enterprise is not quite so free as Simon would have had us believe.[25] When the same corporations, including the military establishments, can buy up the expertise of the best scientists for their research and development efforts; and when, through advertising, corporations can create the markets for their products by fabricating needs in a largely compliant populace that averages over four hours of television viewing each day, Adam Smith's invisible hand has become an elbow. While there may be a "beautiful resource future" ahead for those countries with the capital to afford it, Simon and Kahn had difficulty convincing the poor of Africa or Latin America or South Asia that this future will be theirs. Nor could they easily show the developed world today that a beautiful future can avoid the grave ecological crises that Heilbroner predicted.

The alternative vision proposed by the World Council of Churches usually includes the "soft energy path" mentioned earlier. Amory Lovins was the first to use this term. Thirty years ago, he proposed a gradual changeover to renewable energy sources (solar, co-generation, wind and hydro, methanol) and a vast improvement in energy efficiency. Energy type would be carefully chosen on the basis of efficient end-use, and conservation (through insulation, for example) would always be preferred to increasing production and consumption. The socio-political advantages of the soft energy approach are, in Lovins' view, substantial.[26] In addition to decreasing the stresses on the environment, this approach would allow for the decentralization of energy production and would free capital for other types of economic development that have more benign consequences. Finally, it would eliminate the current dependence of Western countries, particularly the United States, on Middle Eastern oil, thereby breaking the connection between energy and war, a connection that has had grave consequences. Thirty years after President Jimmy Carter made this proposal, George W. Bush has acknowledged the American "addiction" to oil and proposed cutting back on the demand for Middle Eastern oil, which many Canadians fear will largely be replaced by Canadian oil from the tar sands of Alberta.[27]

Daly and Cobb elaborated the implications of the soft energy path within the general framework developed by the World Council of Churches. They have attempted to offer a coherent alternative to the "growthmania" that has dominated the discipline of economics since it began to separate itself from political (and moral) philosophy two centuries ago. The implications for the economy of the United States are carefully considered. These writers take seriously what Julian Simon ignores: the limited nature of even the "ultimate resource," whether it is thought to be "technology," "information," or "the human mind." Daly and Cobb state bluntly:

all talk about knowledge and the mind as an ultimate resource that will offset limits imposed by finitude, entropy, and ecological dependence seems to us to reflect incompetent use of the very organ alleged to have such unlimited powers. Surely knowledge can help us define limits and adjust to them in the most reasonable way. We can even learn to squeeze more welfare from the same resource flow, perhaps without limit. But that does not remove limits on the physical scale of the economy resulting from finitude, entropy, and ecological dependence.[28]

At the end of the Reagan years, in 1988, Daly and Cobb set out to realize a "paradigm shift" in economics that would reflect the needed reversal as the economy moved away from its dependence on fossil fuels (which has dominated economic development since the beginning of the industrial revolution)[29] to a reliance on solar energy as the ultimate natural resource. Although industrialism has enhanced our productivity as we have harnessed the energy of fossil fuels, it has also, in its quest to take advantage of the variable rate at which terrestrial energy can be used, broken down human community and mutual concern. Both capitalist and socialist societies have degraded the environment and disregarded humanity's links to nature, and they have jeopardized the future of all life forms on the earth.

Daly and Cobb therefore rejected a global economic system that bypasses and at times destroys the local culture.[30] They wanted to create an alternative economics that counters the "ideology of death" by which "we are destroying our own humanity and killing the globe." This ideology of death, they argued, has emerged through the fallacy of misplaced concreteness, which allows us, for example, to measure our economic success in terms of gross national product without asking what is being produced, to whom it is being distributed, or what the production process is doing to the worker or the environment. Instead, Daly and Cobb proposed the Measure of Economic Welfare, which would enable us to consider questions of optimal distribution and optimal scale and factor in all those "externalities" that detract from the common good. In conventional economics these externalities are not treated as real costs since no individual bears them. Unfortunately, as Daly and Cobb pointed out, it is the community and the environment that pay. Because of our blind optimism about the future – that is, because we have been held by the myth of progress – we have assumed that our industrial productivity could continue increasing indefinitely. But, Daly and Cobb warned, this is

little more than a wish, one whose empirical support from the last hundred years seems to be already coming to an end. As high-quality resources are depleted, and environmental services are weakened by pollution and habitat destruction, and as ever more powerful technologies seek to compensate for these losses, we witness greater technological risks (radiation, toxic waste, accidents), the costs of which, if included in the productivity calculation, would probably reveal a decline rather than an increase in productivity. If chemical companies were required to pay the full cost of cleaning up toxic wastes, would their productivity increase over the last decade not be negative?[31]

This same point was made from a slightly different angle by Barry Commoner in *Making Peace with the Planet*. He proposed a range of environmental reforms that would allow us to put an end to the war between the "technosphere" and the "ecosphere" and develop true respect for the laws of ecology. In the early nineties, he argued that our attempts to improve the environment by setting pollution standards and enforcing them through legislative means had failed miserably, and the health of the ecosphere had declined steadily.[32] The only areas where improvements were made were those where pollutants had been removed at source (for example, the elimination of lead in gasoline). Commoner's reforms would have required the virtual dismantling of the petrochemical industry, which has grown so rapidly in the post-war period, and "massively redesigning the major industrial, agricultural, energy and transportation systems."[33] In industry, he argued, dependence on plastic and synthetic materials, which has contributed to the trash problems of all developed countries, would have to be drastically reduced. In agriculture, the use of fertilizers and pesticides would have to be eliminated and a return to organic farming undertaken. As for transportation, reliance on the automobile, with its high-compression engines fueled by gasoline, would have to be terminated. Cars should be run on ethanol, methane, or photovoltaic cells instead (more recently, hydrogen has been seen as a possible alternative for the internal combustion engine).[34] Homes and workplaces should be heated by passive or active solar energy. The generation of electricity by nuclear power plants should be phased out.

Commoner proposed changes to the production techniques developed since World War II "in ways that eliminate, or very greatly reduce, their generation of pollutants without hindering their ability to produce the necessary goods and services."[35] These reforms, although difficult, were quite feasible from a purely technical point of view – if the will existed to undertake them over the next generation. To prove this, Commoner pointed (ironically) to the fact that "in less than forty years, we have managed to create a new ecological phenomenon – smog – by redesigning the automobile engine; algae-fouled lakes and seas by changing how crops are fertilized; and massive intractable radioactive wastes by reformulating military explosives and attempting to reorganize the electric power industry. If these technological changes have been made in so short a time, surely new changes comparable in magnitude, that undo their damage are possible as well."[36]

However, Commoner's proposed reforms required the development of politically suitable means "that bring the public interest in long-term environmental quality to bear on investment decisions."[37] And if distributive justice was to be achieved, they must be accompanied by measures that close the economic gap between the northern and southern hemispheres. They therefore required not only that the rich and the poor "make peace with the planet" but that we make peace with each other. Again Commoner offered a comprehensive solution: "We can end the environmental crisis by sharply reducing the commitment to militarism."[38] Worldwide military expenditures in 1990 were in excess of $1 trillion a year, or 6 per cent of total global production. If 50 per cent of this could be diverted to ecologically sound economic reform, the war with the planet could be terminated within a generation. With peace breaking out all over eastern Europe, Commoner was mildly optimistic that military spending among the superpowers could be cut and that economic reform could begin. But he concluded his book by noting that "the United States is still in the grip of the rigid taboo against even questioning – let alone changing – our commitment to exclusively private governance of production."39

Still, neither Commoner nor Daly and Cobb had any faith in the ability of free market capitalism to solve ecological problems. The market has demonstrated that it is able to allocate goods and services with economic efficiency, but the poverty and malnutrition of two-thirds of the globe show that it cannot be relied upon to distribute them justly. Similarly the market has demonstrated that it is able to create economies of scale that are efficient in terms of *production* but disastrous in terms of *ecological sustainability*. Neither the "commons" nor the future are, as we have seen, much considered by the market. "The market sees only efficiency – it has no organs for hearing, feeling or smelling either justice or sustainability."40 Daly and Cobb argued that a return to an understanding of economics as *oikonomia* was required. Such an understanding would refuse to make the market into an idol because it would realize that market growth does not always contribute to community welfare. It would realize that the market in itself cannot determine the optimal scale of the economy.

Since the early nineties environmentalists have become increasingly divided on whether the market system can ever be made sensitive to ecological realities. Leslie Paul Thiele traces this development in the history of the environmental movement, which he describes in terms of a series of four "waves." The first wave was characterized by a conservationist ethic; this was the period from the mid-nineteenth century to the 1960s that saw the establishment of many national parks and wildlife preserves. The second wave followed upon the serial publication of Rachel Carson's *Silent Spring* in the *New Yorker* in 1962 and was marked by a growing awareness of the ecological consequences of human activity and by efforts at containment. The next wave, from the mid-eighties through into the nineties, was defined by what Thiele calls co-optation: national organizations like the Sierra Club increasingly saw themselves as necessarily "realistic" political agents, cooperating with governments and corporations in ways that often left them alienated from their grassroots supporters and, as some would allege, increasingly without clear focus and vision.41 This kind of environmentalism has been absorbed by the marketplace, reflected in middle-class "healthy lifestyle" choices, like shopping organic, or in middle-of-the-road, corporate-friendly environmentalism; these developments, although perhaps salutary, can hardly be expected to forestall the impending crisis. The most recent, or fourth, wave is in Thiele's view more aware of the political and economic context of the environmental issues. Fourth-wave environmentalists are cynical about lifestyle environmentalism; they are increasingly aware of "the tension that remains between the preservation of nature and the demands of social justice but increasingly reject the antagonism."[42] This is why, more and more often, according to Thiele, one finds social justice activists and environmentalists side by side on the front lines against globalization.

Larry Rasmussen, in his *Earth Community, Earth Ethics*, is clear that globalization is driven by corporate, not democratic, power and cannot be renovated. "The sum of separate corporate decisions determines far more of what happens to people's lives and the environment than any public policies arrived at through democratic means and carried out by representative governments."[43] For Rasmussen, the global market system reflects "a materialist way of life" and by its very nature lacks the means to incorporate non-economic concerns. Like Daly and Cobb, Rasmussen hopes for far more fundamental change.

What, then, is required? Because the economy is not an isolated circular flow, the questions of economics, according to Daly and Cobb, must be related to the discussions of ecology, physics, chemistry, biology, etc. This means the question of the proper scale of the economy must be discussed. "Environmental degradation must be shown to result from the scale of the economy in general rather than only from the allocative mistakes that can be corrected while throughput continues to grow exponentially."[44] The development of what is called "biospheric thinking" is required. Daly and Cobb believe that it "can be integrated into and grounded by theocentrism in a way that does not neglect justice."[45] Biospheric thinking acknowledges the interdependence of all life forms without denying the uniqueness of humanity or the special vocation we humans have to exercise dominion over the earth. Such dominion must be understood in a kenotic or self-emptying way: the master understands himself as a servant; the ruler rules for the sake of the ruled.

In Daly and Cobb's view, this understanding of "dominion" has often been missed.[46] They agree with Lynn White Jr that the biblical call for dominion has been responsible for much cruelty and destruction.[47] Nevertheless, properly understood, it can provide a basis for a caring relationship to the future of the planet. The notion of stewardship can be revived.[48] "The best exercise of dominion now possible would be to make more space for other species to live their lives without human interference. This, in fact, is what many mean by renouncing dominion. But this policy would come about through human decision and would thereby reflect our dominion."[49]

Unlike Heilbroner, Daly and Cobb think that it is reasonable to be concerned about posterity even though it has not done anything for us:

Rationality, apart from belief in God, may indeed dictate indifference to the yet unborn. Since they do not now exist, they have no wants to be respected. But rationality that includes a rational belief in God has quite different consequences. God is everlasting, and future lives are as important to God as present lives. To serve God cannot call for the sacrifice of future lives for the sake of satisfying the extravagant appetites of the present. Believers in God know that the community to which they belong extends through time. One cannot discount a future that will be immediate to God. Belief in God grounds the ethical course that Heilbroner favours but does not know how to justify.[50]

Daly and Cobb do not, therefore, deny the destructive role that Christian theism (particularly in its Protestant form) has played in bringing about the ecological crisis that threatens the earth: "In varied forms it has supported anthropocentrism, ignored or belittled the natural world, opposed efforts to stop population growth, directed attention away from the urgent needs of this life, treated as of absolute authority for today teachings that were meant to influence a very different world, aroused false hope, given false assurances, and claimed God's authority for all these sins."[51] Nonetheless, they assert that Christian theism in its opposition to idolatry, its commitment to the whole of creation, and its concern for the future now offers a way to save the earth. Justice, participation, and sustainable sufficiency are ideals that, according to Daly and Cobb, can redirect the economy toward community, save the environment, and create a sustainable future.

Max Oelschlager, in his *Caring for Creation*, also makes a case for the importance of the Judeo-Christian narrative in developing an ethic of ecological concern. "Our culture is caught between a failed past and a future powerless to be born ... [T]he metaphor of caring for creation, springing out of our distinctive Judeo-Christian myth of origin, is the last, best chance for Americans to fashion a sense of community beyond the market and construct a sustainable society."[52] What Oelschlager shares with Daly and Cobb is an appreciation that the basic program of Enlightenment progressivism needs to be challenged. They see Judeo-Christian religiosity as representing some plausible competing claim in the hearts and minds of people in the modern West. But it is hard to know to whom Oelschlager is appealing. He appears to be trying to overturn the prejudice of an environmental movement that has been taught to pin the blame for the ecological crisis on biblical religion. This is a worthy undertaking. The critique of Judeo-Christian religiosity is a continuation of the Enlightenment project of replacing the religious narrative with a progressive scientific one. After all, this progressivist scientific humanism has cost the earth dearly over the last two centuries. It is thus the height of irony that environmentalists are so often willing to accept its version of history. But Oelschlager makes his case by appealing to a kind of postmodernist theory of narrativity and "the play of language."[53] And he invokes the pragmatism of people like Richard Rorty in support of his cause. These are strange allies. If the Judeo-Christian story is understood purely in terms of "the play of language," and thus in terms of its pragmatic rhetorical effectiveness, it is difficult to understand how it could be expected to hold out against that far more ubiquitous "language game" that boldly promises MTV, Gap clothing, and Starbucks coffee for the multitudes.

And this is the problem. We have not yet seen the end of the resiliency of that Enlightenment narrative. Every proposal for a technological fix, aimed at dealing with the problems technology has itself created, shows that there are yet many more tricks up the sleeves of the white labcoats and the Armani suit-jackets. As the atmospheric temperature continues to climb, it is not to fasting and Christian self-sacrifice that most of us are turning, but to the latest schemes of Shell and British Petroleum (corporations whose "economies" are larger than those of many of the world's nations). The latter already derives $200 million in annual revenues from the market – mostly in Europe – for photovoltaic cells. And, in 1997, Shell set up a subsidiary (Shell Renewables) with a five-year, $500-million development plan and claims to have invested $1 billion since 2000 in research and development in wind and solar energy.[54]

Many environmentalists point to these developments as small victories, and perhaps they are right. But what are the possibilities for a genuine shift of priorities when those priorities continue to be delimited by the narrow scope of the technological "imagination"?

For example, a number of corporations, including Shell, but also including Daimler Chrysler and Ballard Power Systems, have invested in the development of hydrogen fuel technology.[55] This technology has a variety of applications, but one promising scenario is that, in the near future, automobiles and buses could be designed to run on hydrogen. Hydrogen power is a relatively clean energy source, so this development holds out the hope for the reduction of carbon emissions and greenhouse gases. But there are a number of problems, the most obvious being that the electrolyzers used in the production of hydrogen require massive amounts of electricity. That means simply moving environmental problems from one sector to another.[56] The use of hydrogen fuel-cell motors would, nevertheless, on the whole work out to a credit on the ecological balance sheet. However, there are further problems. The most environmentally beneficial scenario for the development of hydrogen technology would involve fitting vehicles with direct hydrogen fuel cells, and that would require the development of adequate onboard hydrogen storage systems as well as a hydrogen fuel delivery infrastructure. All this would require a significant investment of resources and therefore a major commitment on the part of corporations and government. Onboard reformers that can derive hydrogen from gasoline, methanol, or natural gas are also a possibility. Deriving hydrogen fuel from natural gas would be the most environmentally salutary of these three options, but it poses further infrastructure problems. (This was part of the reason why the natural gas-powered internal combustion engine was not exactly a roaring market success.) So industry has generally opted to develop hydrogen fuel reformers that work with gasoline or methanol.

The trouble is that, from an environmental perspective, we are almost back at square one. The projected reduction in emission for this kind of vehicle is between 22 and 35 per cent, but as long as we continue to mass-market a fuel-guzzling fleet of SUVs while slashing public transit budgets, it is difficult to see how this development holds much overall promise. Since 2000 this point has been made with increasing intensity by what might be called "peak oil" theorists. As Colin Campbell has written: "Peak oil does not mean 'running out of oil,' but 'running out of cheap oil.' For societies leveraged on ever increasing amounts of cheap oil, the consequences may be dire. Without significant successful cultural reform, economic and social decline seems inevitable."[57]

Perhaps the most important popularizer of the tenets of peak oil is Richard Heinberg, author of *The Party's Over* and *Powerdown*. He first points out that the prediction made by research geologist M. King Hubbard in 1956 that North America would reach the peak of its oil production in 1970 and decline thereafter has been confirmed.[58] He agrees that the prediction of many oil and gas experts that we are rapidly approaching the peak of *global* oil production will be confirmed by steadily rising oil and gas prices over the next decade. We are at the end of cheap energy.

A number of responses to what some have called "the end of suburbia"[59] are possible for North Americans. Heinberg lists four. The first ("Last Man Standing") is to compete militarily, particularly in the Middle East, for increasingly scarce resources. Iraq, Iran, and Saudi Arabia take on immense importance. The second ("Waiting for the Magic Elixir") espouses a faith that techniques like hydrogen power will provide us with new and limitless sources of energy. The third, Heinberg's preferred option, is "powerdown," the path of self-limitation, cooperation, and sharing. To be effective globally this radical path must be undertaken by the US. Needless to say, Heinberg is not hopeful, and so he proposes a fourth option: building small communities of solidarity and preservation where skills like "food growing and storage, tool and clothing making, house and boat building, renewable energy generation" are developed.[60] Preservation communities will be protected by those whom they serve.

Heinberg doubts that we will choose the options of self-limitation and conservation. He agrees with Wolfgang Sachs' critique of development economics. Sachs points out that, since the 1970s, we have witnessed a series of marked improvements in fuel efficiency and automotive carbon emission, and thus a net reduction in the overall environmental impact of individual automobiles. "Yet the relentless growth in the number of cars and miles driven has canceled out that gain."[61] In our concern with eco-efficient gadgetry like hydrogen fuel cells, we have managed to overlook the real issues. The 1992 United Nations Conference on Environment and Development document, *Agenda 21*, for example, made no reference to the fact that the global population of cars was growing at a rate four times faster than that of the population of humans, and consequently no proposals to deal with that obviously important issue were put forward. *Agenda 21* took it for granted that the global environmental problem was one of management. For this reason, Sachs suggested that it might even be counterproductive to continue to abide the optimistic rhetoric of eco-efficiency.

The language of efficiency, even when couched in terms of environmental concern, is still an inherently reductionist technological language. It allows us to believe that the solutions to environmental problems rest in better, more comprehensive planning. The problem is that global biosphere management strategies may in fact further erode the much more humble and complex arrangements by which local cultures have lived – more or less within their ecological means – for millennia. Technocratic rationality cannot produce reasons for living a good and economically modest life. Sachs suggests that the notion of eco-efficiency tends to lead to "a hidden reductionism that turns ecological politics from a call for new public virtues into a set of managerial strategies."[62] There was a brief period when some people spoke seriously of the idea of "limits to growth," but this language has been displaced by the language of "global change" and "eco-system management." Sachs observes that "if there are no limits to growth, there surely seem to be no limits to hubris."[63]

Rather than making us suspicious of the project of Western technological science, the environmental crisis has in fact given a renewed impetus to the hegemonic "rationalization of the world."[64] Terms like "eco-system" and "biosphere" arise from a blending of two great, formerly antithetical, streams within modernity: romanticism and scientific rationality. Pictures of the blue planet, shot from high-tech cameras mounted on satellites and space shuttles, have, according to Sachs, become objects "of postmodern popular piety." The cover of the September 1989 edition of *Scientific American* displayed just such an image, along with the bold words: "Managing Planet Earth."[65] This recent concern for the biosphere has allowed corporate entities from Shell to the World Bank to reinvent and greenwash themselves. It has imbued the technological machinery of globalization with a new sense of purpose and a new motive for comprehensive planning. Sachs observes: "The threat to the planet's survival looms large. Has there ever been a better excuse for intrusion? New areas of intervention open up, nature becomes a domain of politics, and a new breed of technocrats feels the vocation to steer growth along the edge of the abyss."[66]

In fact, without some kind of "call for new public virtues," no amount of eco-efficient gadgetry is going to mitigate what, for the time being, appears to be our planetary fate. In the meantime the imperatives of the corporate-technological complex generally carry the day. Those who believe that the super-tanker can simply be redirected, and that the interests of corporations with their cadre of technicians and marketers can be made consistent with the aim of environmental sustainability, carry on the optimistic spirit of the Enlightenment. The real irony of our situation is that it may be the case that, with respect to that Enlightenment spirit, our only real hope is doubt.

Regardless, we may also be permitted some small hope that as fossil fuel sources run out, corporations and governments may be forced into developing *serious* alternatives – in which case we only have to hope that the oil runs out before the ozone.

4

Excursus on Nuclear Power: The End of Sustainable Sufficiency

"The energy industry is well aware of [ethics] and tries to factor them in. However, ethics have to be spread evenly and you can't burn benedictions in the boiler."[1]

– D.G. Andrews, Department of Nuclear Engineering, University of Toronto

"First come the eats, then morality."

– Bertolt Brecht, *The Threepenny Opera*[2]

As we have seen, since the first Earth Day in 1971 the environmental movement has attempted to bring to public consciousness the ambiguous ideal of "sustainable sufficiency."[3] In light of this ideal, energy experts have entered into a public debate about the advisability of constructing more and larger nuclear power plants in Canada and the United States. From the outset this debate has been about means, not about ends.[4] Those in favour of the proliferation of nuclear power plants believe that nuclear energy is an acceptable means to the good end of economic growth and technological expansion. They believe that nuclear energy is a sustainable energy source and that, in its many forms, it will guarantee that we have enough power in the future.[5] Those opposed to such proliferation maintain either that nuclear power has not yet proven itself to be a good means to that end or that it has already proven itself to be a bad means. That is, it has not yet proven – or cannot prove – itself to be safe. Anyway, opponents say, we can produce enough energy in other ways that *are* sustainable.

It is difficult for the average citizen, who lacks specialized knowledge, to make an informed judgment about the ethics of nuclear energy. The citizen is forced to rely on experts, and the experts have positioned themselves on both sides of the debate. For example, in December 1974 a group of twenty-eight leading US scientists (led by the Nobel prize-winning nuclear physicist Hans Bethe and by the long-time nuclear commentator and critic Ralph Lapp, as well as nine other Nobel laureates) published a short, sober letter concluding that "on any scale, the benefits of a clean inexpensive and inexhaustible fuel far outweigh the risks. We can see no reasonable alternative to an increased use of nuclear power to satisfy our energy needs."[6] On the other hand, more than two thousand biologists, chemists, engineers, and other scientists declared in 1975: "The country (US) must recognize that it now appears imprudent to move forward with a rapidly expanding nuclear power plant construction program. The risks of doing so are altogether too great."[7]

Let us briefly examine the main issues that have been involved in the nuclear energy debate from the beginning. There are four, each of which has a large technical component: the safety of nuclear reactors, the disposability of nuclear wastes, the security of the nuclear plants – and the plutonium (an essential ingredient of nuclear weapons) they create – in the face of terrorism or sabotage, and the overall economic viability of nuclear power production in light of other energy options.

The safety of nuclear reactors depends in large part on the efficiency of emergency core-cooling systems in the case of an accident. Barry Commoner describes these systems:

The core is surrounded by a heavy shield to protect workers from emitted radiation. The entire reactor is sealed into a massive containment vessel – a concrete hemisphere 150 feet across. In the vessel there are spray systems to drain off radioactive material if the core should rupture into it. A complex system is provided for cooling down the core if the normal water circulating system should fail. There are elaborate control and warning systems, often in multiples to reduce the risk of failure. Safety and environmental control measures account for a large part of the cost of a nuclear reactor. All this is to avoid the consequences of a failure that might cause the core to overheat. If it became hot enough to melt, after a day the molten core could burn a hole through the bottom of the container and then release massive amounts of radioactive material into the environment.[8]

Those who are in favour of nuclear energy argue that the reactors are safe. The Canadian Nuclear Association (CNA) has maintained from the outset that "with all the precautions in design, construction and operation, the likelihood of an accident serious enough to release a significant amount of radioactive material from a CANDU nuclear power station is estimated to be less than one in a million per year. Even if such an event did occur, the chance of anyone being actually harmed is quite small so the risk is really much lower."[9] The CNA also contended, on the basis of the WASH-1400 reactor Safety Study headed by Norman Rasmussen,[10] that "the likelihood of being killed in a reactor accident is about one in 300,000,000 for each 60 reactors in operation."[11] This low-probability, high-consequence risk,[12] it is pointed out, is far less than the risk of a fatal car accident or drowning. The CNA concluded that "the risk from nuclear power is very small, and society must eventually decide whether or not it is acceptable in view of the benefit of ample electrical power at reasonable cost."[13]

Those opposed to the construction of more nuclear power plants have argued that the likelihood of an accident is being underestimated by the nuclear establishment. One group organized by the Union of Concerned Scientists (UCS) maintained that an accident killing 50,000 people had a one in 100,000 chance of happening.[14] This was in line with the view of Robert Jungk, who contended that "the data that Rasmussen and his colleagues were called upon to review relied, as they would have to admit, almost totally on material supplied to them by companies that built and operated reactors. So right from the start, in this supposedly independent study they obviously served the interests of the nuclear industry."[15]

Whatever figures one accepts, however, one should still confront the question that Commoner asked in 1975: "Shall we build nuclear reactors which, with a very low probability, may suffer an accident resulting in, let us say, 5,000 to 50,000 deaths, and many more injuries and billions of dollars of damage?"[16] Commoner argued that no answer is possible if we make misleading comparisons. "In human moral terms it seems to me there is no valid comparison between the risks of personally tragic individual events like auto accidents and the risks of operating a device which has the acknowledged, designed capability – however improbable – of killing tens of thousands of people at once."[17] Commoner's conclusion was that the risk was too great.

A Canadian critic of the nuclear program, Fred H. Knelman, drew the same conclusion: "No matter how small the probability of an accident, the risk is still too large to be acceptable to present or future generations ... Only zero risk would be socially acceptable, given the fact that there are alternative options for securing society's genuine energy requirements."[18] Commoner's and Knelman's positions were more absolute than that of the UCS. Acknowledging that every energy option entails risks, the UCS maintained only that the risks were too great *at that time.* They urged a drastic reduction in the construction of new nuclear power plants until "major progress is achieved in the required research and in resolving present controversies about safety, waste disposal and plutonium safeguards."[19] The accident at Three Mile Island in 1979 actually led to this drastic reduction – for political and economic rather than ethical reasons – not only in the United States but everywhere except France and Japan.[20]

The word "safety" is not a technical term. It means "of acceptable risk." "Acceptable" is a political term meaning what the government will accept. "Risk" is a scientific term. But when nuclear power was proposed as a solution to our energy needs, scientists did not know what the risks were and governments did not know whether they were acceptable. The approach adopted was to begin slowly down the nuclear road, calculating theoretical risks by breaking the industrial process down into its component parts and drawing up a fault tree before further implementation. However, theoretical risk analyses may give results that vary greatly because the numbers that go into each of the components are multiplied by all the other numbers. A difference of a factor of ten on three different numbers can lead to a difference of a factor of a thousand on their product. One risk analysis may conclude that there is one chance in a thousand of an accident, while another will conclude that there is one chance in a million. The actual, as opposed to the theoretical, risks can only be determined by proceeding with the process and by assembling statistics of the *actual* accidents that have taken place historically. Now, after more than forty years, there is a (rather small) statistical base that can be compared with the theoretical estimations.

This is the approach accepted by Alvin Weinberg, the main nuclear advocate of the last forty years. He wrote in 1979:

Before the Three Mile Island Accident, all of us in the nuclear enterprise were fairly comfortable with the estimates made by Norman C. Rasmussen of MIT in his famous 1975 study on the probabilities and consequences of a reactor accident. He estimated that for a light-water reactor, the probability of a core meltdown that would release at least a few thousand curies of radioactivity was one in 20,000 per reactor per year. Most of these accidents would not cause physical damage to the public. A few would, and a very few, estimated at one in a billion reactor years, might be a major catastrophe – 3,300 immediate radiation deaths, 45,000 extra cancers, $17 billion in property damage.[21]

A similar risk analysis approach has been taken to the second main issue of the nuclear debate, the problem of the disposal of nuclear wastes. By the beginning of the new millennium, little practical progress had been made on it. (In Canada it took until 2002 for a Nuclear Fuel Waste Act to be passed by the federal government.)[22] Both sides in the debate have been in general agreement about the seriousness of the hazards presented by the wastes, and about the need to deal with them safely. These wastes are commonly divided into three types: those with short half-lives of one year or less, those with medium half-lives of a hundred years or less, and those with long half-lives.[23] Of the last, Commoner states, it is generally acknowledged that plutonium-239 is "the most dangerous radioactive material among the many that the Nuclear Age has bestowed on us. Plutonium emits a particular form of radiation, alpha particles, which consist of helium nuclei. An alpha particle is so massive that it is stopped by a living tissue after penetrating only a very short distance into it. Because the particle's energy is released in a short distance, its effect is intensely localized and is very damaging to the cellular material."[24] The problem is that "the actinides including plutonium take about 250,000 years to decay."[25] Thus it is also generally acknowledged that, as yet, no way to dispose of the wastes has proved itself to be safe.

In the early 1970s the nuclear establishment was confident that, in the near future, the radioactive wastes could be disposed of by being incorporated into highly stable solids, so that "it [would be] unlikely that they will be harmful to present or future generations."[26]

For some reason nuclear advocates have become even more confident since then, even though no permanent waste storage facility
has been built anywhere on the face of the earth. In 1979 Alvin
Weinberg argued in an article, "Salvaging the Atomic Age," that he
would put

disposal of toxic radioactive wastes in the category of lesser problems.
This is largely because potentially dangerous wastes occupy so little
space (two cubic meters per reactor per year), and because after about
1,000 years, the wastes are no more hazardous than the original uranium from which the wastes were formed. (This uranium is part of
nature and it seems unreasonable to require the sequestered wastes to
be less hazardous than the original uranium.) To sequester waste for
1000 years simply does not strike me as beyond reason.[27]

Gordon Sims, a Canadian nuclear power advocate, likewise argued in 1990 that "as a result of scientific research many of the
reservations expressed about deep geological disposal in the mid-
1970s are known to be inapplicable."[28] This scientific research
(done in Canada at the Whiteshell Nuclear Research Establishment in Manitoba) involves "assembling information on the longevity of the containers, the rate of dissolution of uranium oxide,
the transit time through the vault and the transit time through
the geosphere."[29] Sims' conclusion was remarkable because it assumed that scientists can *know* what will happen to materials that
have never been stored in the manner proposed: "*It is known* [my
italics] that there will be zero dose to the population for tens or
probably hundreds of thousands of years after the vault has been
closed."[30] He admitted that the fuel container used to store the
wastes underground "must last for five hundred years. By then all
the medium life radioactive material will have decayed away." But
Sims went on to assert that "even under the most adverse conditions plutonium-239 in a waste depository will move so slowly that
it will contribute only a negligible amount to the total radiation
dose at the surface."[31] The technical debate about how long the
wastes must be successfully stored remains unresolved among
advocates of nuclear power.[32]

Some opponents of nuclear proliferation have argued – ambiguously, we should note – that no new plants should be constructed

until the problems connected with radioactive waste disposal have been solved. The question about how one can know *with certainty* (or with what degree of certainty one can know) that the problem has been solved, short of performing an experiment that will last somewhere between 600 and a million years, is not addressed. One cannot prove that an accident (like an earthquake) will not happen, but, short of a proof, how can one say that the problem has been solved?

Both sides in the debate acknowledge that the waste fuel that is stored in pools of water at nuclear sites "is generating both heat and radioactivity and must be managed with great care."[33] Thus, failure of the disposal method could mean appreciable and irreversible damage to the entire life-cycle owing to the contamination of the groundwater over large areas of the earth's surface. Nevertheless, because the nature of the quasi-permanent storage method has not been definitively determined, neither side has calculated the likelihood of leakage or the harm that might result from it. If we follow the procedure of the nuclear establishment in their consideration of reactor accidents, such calculations might be performed using a fault-tree analysis; the risk of ecological disaster could be weighed against the benefits that will be received by society if the nuclear future is realized.

When such calculations are carried out even in a rough way, it becomes clear that the benefits of nuclear energy will accrue to three or four generations (assuming that fission technologies are transitional because we will run out of uranium and that solar technologies will eventually replace breeder or fusion reactors because they are much safer),[34] while the risks will be borne by somewhere between 17 and 8,000 generations of human beings into the far distant future. How such a risk/benefit calculation could lead to the conclusion that the nuclear option is a good one has not been made clear by the pro-nuclear forces. Perhaps this calculation has not been made because it would force nuclear advocates to acknowledge the possibility of failure. The original judgment of the CNA (and the nuclear industry) has merely been reaffirmed: "if radioactive wastes are incorporated into highly stable solids and excluded from the biosphere (perhaps by deep burial) it is unlikely that they will be harmful to present or future generations."[35]

The anti-nuclear forces have, from the outset, taken the risks associated with disposal much more seriously. Some find cost-risk-benefit calculations irrelevant. E.F. Schumacher spoke for them when he declared over thirty years ago:

No degree of prosperity could justify the accumulation of large amounts of highly toxic substances which nobody knows how to make "safe" and which remain an incalculable danger to the whole of creation for historical or even geological ages. To do such a thing is a transgression of life itself, a transgression infinitely more serious than any crime perpetrated by man. The idea that a civilization could sustain itself on the basis of such a transgression is an ethical, spiritual and metaphysical monstrosity. It means conducting the affairs of Man as if people did not matter at all.[36]

It is interesting to note that in considering reactor safety and waste disposal, both groups of *scientists* take a similar approach. They generally assume the validity of utilitarianism (that "the good" is the greatest good of the greatest number) and a cost-risk-benefit analysis can reveal where the greatest good is to be found. They argue that the ethics of a particular process can be determined by comparing the costs and the risks of the process with the benefits. "The 'harms' or destructions of good are listed on one side as 'costs' of the intervention; the 'goods' are listed on the other side as benefits; each column is added, and the costs are subtracted from the benefits. If the costs are greater than the benefits, so that the 'bottom line' is a negative number, the project is presumably not worth pursuing; but if the benefits outweigh the costs, so that the 'bottom line' is positive, then presumably it is reasonable to go ahead."[37]

Such an approach assumes the conventional distinction (which from a philosophical point of view is as questionable as the fact-value distinction upon which it is based)[38] between risk (which relies on scientific calculation of probabilities) and the acceptability of risk (which takes into account political and social factors). Within this context, then, scientific risk analysis is a necessary first step toward determining whether the risks of an industrial process are acceptable in light of the benefits,[39] whether the risk and the benefits are being distributed equitably, or whether some citizens are being subjected to unfair risks for the benefit of the whole society or of special interests. Risk analysis is also thought to be a necessary first step toward establishing the limits of risks to which individuals and communities may be ethically subjected. Risk analysis is concerned with hazards for which a probabilistic approach to evaluation is needed, either because there is uncertainty about the nature of the impacts or about the probability of occurrence, or both. Risks that have received the most attention in recent years include nuclear energy, toxic waste disposal, acid precipitation, genetic engineering, and the transportation of dangerous goods. The inadequacy of this procedure has already been hinted at, and will be considered in greater detail later.

In 1989 the Canadian government established a concept environmental assessment panel to consider the burial of nuclear waste (as proposed by Gordon Sims) in the Canadian Shield. Blair Seaborn was appointed as its chair. After ten years and a thirteen-month public hearing, the Seaborn Panel issued its report.[40] Its technical conclusion was vague: "On balance, we think that the models the proponent used are sufficiently well developed to demonstrate that its concept of deep geological disposal can be used as the basis for designing a site-specific facility that is likely to meet regulatory requirements. There is general agreement that a final conclusion would require site-specific data and performance analyses that are based on site-specific designs."[41] According to a 2001 report by the Sierra Club, "the Seaborn Panel report, released in March 1998, concluded that the AECL concept was not acceptable, and identified many technical problems with the burial concept as presented by AECL and Ontario Hydro."[42] In April 2001 the federal government introduced legislation that was eventually passed in 2003 as the Nuclear Waste Fuels Act (NWFA). This act in turn required electricity-generating companies that produce used nuclear fuel to establish a Nuclear Waste Management Organization (NWMO) to provide recommendations to the Government of Canada on the long-term management of used nuclear fuel and to establish segregated trust funds to finance that long-term management.[43] An advisory council (with David Crombie as its chair) was formed to propose approaches as well as recommend an approach to the minister of natural resources for the management of used nuclear fuel.

Northwatch, a public interest group in northeastern Ontario, was critical of the NWFA for failing to implement many important recommendations of the Seaborn Panel, particularly that an independent agency be "formed *at arms length* [my italics] from AECL and the nuclear utilities, in order to manage the programs related to long-term nuclear fuel waste management, including detailed comparison of waste management options."[44] Northwatch pointed out, for example, that Elizabeth Dowdeswell, the chair of NWMO, was in 2001 a member of the board of directors of ITER (International Thermonuclear Experimental Reactor) Canada and publicly expressed support for the development of fusion reactors.[45]

In November 2005 NWMO issued its final study report, which recommended the "Adaptive Phase Management" of nuclear waste.[46] In her speech to the National Press Gallery, Dowdeswell stated that this was

both a technical method and a management system … The technical method is isolation and containment of the waste deep underground in a central location. It is a method that allows the waste to be monitored continuously and to be retrieved if necessary for many years into the future – a key requirement of Canadians. The management system is phased in with explicit decision points along the way adapting to new social learning and technological innovation over the decades. Confidence is built in the technology and supporting systems before the final phase is actually implemented. It builds in contingencies. For example, there is an option to move the fuel earlier if necessary to shallow underground storage at the central location itself before the deep repository might be available.[47]

With a straight face, we presume, Dowdeswell went on to say that the Adaptive Phase plan "is rooted in values and ethics. This was not something that was designed by technical people, it actually came from the grass roots. It will engage citizens and allow for societal judgements as to whether there is sufficient certainty to proceed step by step."[48]

Ignoring its mandate, the NWMO report made no explicit recommendations with regard to the siting of future disposal of nuclear waste. It proposed that over the next thirty years, that is, until 2035, the storage and monitoring of radioactive waste continue at reactor sites. NWMO will select "a site for shallow underground storage, an underground characterization facility and a deep geological repository."[49] It will decide whether to construct a shallow depository and transport the radioactive waste to it. Sometime after 2035, when most of the members of committee will be dead, NWMO may begin to transport the waste, and it will conduct research and testing at the characterization facility to "demonstrate and confirm the suitability of the site" and "decide when to construct the deep repository at the central site for long term containment and isolation." After 2065, when most of the children of committee members will have departed the earth, the radioactive waste will be stored in long-lived containers, which will be placed "into the deep geological repository for final containment and isolation."[50]

At the end of her speech to the National Press Gallery, Dowdeswell made it clear that "the future of nuclear was not a focus of our study. We did not examine the question or make a judgement about the appropriate role of nuclear power in Canada." She then went on to state that "it would be sheer hubris to think that we could anticipate new knowledge and societal change over hundreds of thousands of years."[51] Some nuclear critics, like the Sierra Club of Canada, would argue that the entire nuclear experiment has been predicated on that type of hubris.

The third issue discussed in the nuclear debate concerns the danger to which the civilian population would be subjected if terrorists gained entry to a nuclear power plant, bombed or crashed into it by air, or stole the plutonium, which is a byproduct of the energy production and which can be used to make atomic bombs. (Obviously, this security concern has become more significant since the terrorist attacks in the US of 11 September 2001.) Concern about plutonium will become more significant if plans go ahead for the development of breeder reactors, which use it as fuel. Although both Canada and the United States seem to be moving away from breeder reactors for economic and safety reasons, the breeder has remained attractive because of projected shortages of uranium if the atomic age is salvaged and construction of nuclear power plants is taken up again as planned.[52]

Those who favour nuclear development acknowledge that there is some risk from terrorist activity. However, they have argued from the outset that

sabotage of the nuclear part of the station would be very difficult. It would require an intimate knowledge of the design and construction of the station, its operational controls and its safety systems. The fail-safe design and control interlocks would thwart all but the most expert attempts at sabotage. While a determined group of saboteurs might gain access to the station and do a considerable amount of damage to the reactor, it is very unlikely that it could produce an exact chain of events necessary to release large amounts of radioactive material to the environment.[53]

Needless to say, this argument has little relevance if we are concerned about suicidal airplane hijackers who might attack nuclear plants rather than more symbolic targets.

Although those opposed to the proliferation of nuclear power plants have been, until recently, more concerned with the sabotage of a plant, they fear more the theft of plutonium, "which can be made into a devastating bomb by one or a few people working with material available from a hardware store and an ordinary laboratory supply house."[54] Knelman pointed out many years ago that "the problem of the transfer and the transportation of special nuclear materials is global. With vast increase in the traffic, the probability of illicit trafficking becomes absolute. There have already been thefts, misplacements, accidents, and material unaccounted for in large quantities."[55] The only way to control such thefts is to establish a global security system that would account for every ounce of plutonium. But this brings with it its own danger. Commoner states, "The threat of terrorist attempts to steal plutonium – whether real or not – could be used to justify a system of military control over the entire nuclear power system."[56] Knelman went further and argued that a plutonium economy, based on breeder reactors (which must be developed if the nuclear power system is to survive well into the twenty-first century), "renders absolute the probability of accident, acts of madness or miscalculation, with their immeasurable social and environmental costs. To protect society against such events is neither technically feasible nor socially desirable, since it would involve massive social engineering and abrogation of civil liberties – in effect, the creation of a garrison state."[57] Regardless, after 11 September 2001, the US (and Canada) have moved in that direction.

Alvin Weinberg had argued that the problem of protecting nuclear plants from sabotage or theft was quite manageable. Greater security measures are required, he argued, and these measures are merely part of the Faustian bargain made with society.[58] But such security can be achieved by such methods as cluster-siting of reactors. "It is easier to guard ten reactors on a single site than 10 reactors on separate sites."[59] If the US continues, in the interests of security, to make the air space above nuclear power plants no-fly zones, future construction will have to heed Weinberg's proposal.

The fourth area of contention in the nuclear debate, the basic efficiency and economic viability of nuclear power, has become more important as our experience with nuclear energy has grown over the past thirty-five years.[60] At its inception, the nuclear power program promised much cheaper electrical energy than that generated by any of the fossil fuels, and until recently it seemed to fulfil that promise. We say *seemed*, because, due to the intertwining of military and civilian involvement in the early phases of nuclear research and development, it is difficult to say what the actual cost of the first reactors was.[61] The costs of construction, it can be assumed, were but a small portion of the total. At any rate, until 1985 the representative claim of the CNA that "nuclear power offers a reliable and relatively low-cost source of energy" was rarely disputed.[62] The rise in the price of oil after 1973 merely reinforced the apparent veracity of conventional wisdom.

A number of factors have placed this wisdom in doubt. The capital costs of the construction of nuclear power plants rose by 150 per cent in the United States between 1970 and 1976.[63] (During the same period the cost of construction for refineries increased by 10 per cent and for coal-fired power plants by 60 per cent.) The spiraling costs of construction at the Darlington plant in Ontario would indicate that the escalation of costs has been as prevalent in Canada as in the US. Darlington was begun (without an environmental assessment) in 1976 and was scheduled for completion by 1985 at a cost of $3.5 billion. It was actually completed in 1993 at a cost of more than $14 billion.[64] The main reason, of many, for this increase in costs was the delays caused by the introduction of more elaborate safety devices that were demanded by environmentalists and acknowledged as necessary by Atomic Energy of Canada. It is clear today that the cost of electricity now depends much more on capital investments than on the cost of uranium, although its cost is also rising precipitously.

Commoner argued some thirty years ago that this was the reason that the United States should abandon plans for the breeder reactor. Since the breeder is even more complex than conventional reactors, the capital costs of construction will be even higher, and the low cost of its fuel (plutonium) will become less significant. Commoner projected that "sometime before nineteen eighty-five the average price of electricity produced by nuclear power plants will probably catch up with and thereafter exceed the price charged by coal-fired plants."[65] Ontario Hydro's experience with its Bruce and Pickering plants has confirmed Commoner's prediction for another, unanticipated reason: the average lifespan of the Candu reactors has been substantially shorter than the thirty to forty years projected, and the cost of repairs has been much higher. (This, along with the Darlington debt, accounted for the substantial increase in the cost of electricity in Ontario through the nineties.) Until recently, the Canadian nuclear industry has been unable to convince the public (or the energy establishment) that more reactors should be built.[66] It has relied on contracts with Romania, Korea, and China to stay in business over the past fifteen years.

Commoner predicted the long-range economic unviability of nuclear power plants because they are inefficient in terms of the second law of thermodynamics:

Nuclear power is a kind of thermodynamic overkill ... In a power plant the basic task to which the energy source is applied is to boil water to produce the steam that drives the generator. If this task is to be accomplished with thermodynamic efficiency, it requires temperatures in the range of 1000–2000 degrees Fahrenheit. At such temperatures, fuels produce chemicals (such as sulfur dioxide and nitrogen oxides) that cause pollution problems. The pollutants and the cost of controlling them are the required price that is paid to achieve the necessary thermodynamic linkage between the energy source and the energy requiring task. In a nuclear reactor the price is much higher, for the extreme energy of the ionizing radiation of the nuclear radiation is well beyond the range appropriate for the task of generating steam. Expressed in terms that are equivalent to the temperature scale, the energy associated with the nuclear fission process is in the range of a million degrees. All the difficulties and dangers due to the radiation associated with the nuclear reactor are, in this thermodynamic sense, unnecessary since the task of generating steam can be achieved by the much lower energies of ordinary fuels.[67]

Using nuclear power to boil water, Commoner said, was like using a chainsaw to cut butter. He concluded in 1976 that capital investment in and research money for nuclear power generation should be cut back, and that the research money being used to "perfect" the nuclear generators should be reallocated in favour of research into solar technologies.

However, members of the nuclear establishment continue their fight. They have argued that without the Pickering and Bruce stations the cost of electricity would be much higher in Ontario. With further experience and research, the management of these plants will become even more efficient, and a breakthrough to nuclear fusion could solve the problem of waste disposal and uranium shortages. We would be one step closer to Alvin Weinberg's dream of energy so cheap that we would not need to meter it.[68]

In the nuclear debate as we have summarized it thus far, two positions have emerged. The pro-nuclear forces have asserted, first, that nuclear reactors are *relatively* safe and will become safer as experience with them becomes broader; second, although radioactive wastes from nuclear reactors are not at present disposable, a technical solution is available and can be implemented in the near future as the entire fuel cycle is transformed into a relatively benign process; third, the problems of sabotage or terrorist activity and the threat they pose to political stability can be managed by tighter security measures; and fourth, we should continue to construct nuclear power plants because they can produce electricity more cheaply than any other option. In addition, nuclear power is more environmentally friendly because it does not add to the greenhouse effect by emitting carbon dioxide.[69]

Against this, the anti-nuclear forces have argued, first, that nuclear reactors are in no sense fail-safe and although the risk of an accident may be relatively low, the effects of an accident are so horrifying as to preclude further nuclear plant construction *until* the plants can be demonstrated to be safe; second, no more radioactive wastes should be produced until it has been proved that they can be safely disposed of; third, the statistical risk of terrorist activity can only increase as more lethal plutonium is produced, and since such risks could only be minimized by moving toward an authoritarian state, which is politically and morally abhorrent, no more plutonium should be produced; and finally, nuclear energy will become more and more expensive as the capital cost of generating plants increases and uranium supplies are depleted. The nuclear option should, therefore, be abandoned because it will leave us even more dependent on fossil fuels in the future.

Both the pro- and the anti-nuclear positions have been defended on the basis of a quasi-ethical concern. Those in favour of nuclear expansion have expressed four moral purposes: the relief of poverty, the establishment of economic independence and political sovereignty, improvement of an environment already ravaged by pollution due to the profligate use of fossil fuels, and the maintenance of social stability. They argue that only by choosing the nuclear option can modern society guarantee the economic development required so that the poverty of our society and that of the third world can be eradicated and the disadvantaged can come to share in the good things of life. They maintain that only with the development of nuclear energy can countries like Canada and the United States become truly self-reliant. As countries become progressively more dependent on foreign oil, their political sovereignty will be eroded and they will lose their authority as independent nation states. Supporters also claim that since the radiation from nuclear reactors can be contained, energy produced from nuclear fission is environmentally more friendly than that produced by fossil fuels which add to the greenhouse effect. Although they may be ecologically less harmful, solar technologies simply cannot support the energy requirements of today, much less fuel the growth required and projected for tomorrow. Without nuclear energy we may find ourselves in danger of freezing to death in a cold climate and involved in a mad scramble for alternative sources of energy. Finally, they claim that, if we abandon nuclear energy, our economic system might collapse and the social chaos involved in a depression would be our lot. In the light of these considerations, the pro-nuclear forces conclude that nuclear energy is the only *ethical* option.

The ethical concern of members of the anti-nuclear forces is more patent (although not for that reason more authentic). They have argued that "fission power threatens the present and forecloses the future. It is unethical, and inferior to non-fission futures that enhance survival for humans, alive and yet to be born, and nature with all its living entities."[70] Nuclear energy is deemed unethical because it demands technical infallibility and political stability for an impossible length of time. It requires, as we have seen, "a Faustian bargain with society." Alvin Weinberg put it this way: "In a sense we have established a military priesthood which guards against inadvertent use of nuclear weapons ... Plans for nuclear energy probably will make demands of the same sort on our society."[71] For those opposed to nuclear power, such a Faustian bargain jeopardizes the future principally not from an environmental but from a political perspective. Nuclear energy is "an alienating technology. It invites and supports large power-concentrated political centres and a new priesthood of protectors and managers."[72] Nuclear power is also inevitably elitist. Because of the expertise required to understand the functioning of nuclear power plants, the public is practically excluded from making any decisions about it.[73] "Large, complex, centralized, high technologies are intrinsically inimical to the social evolution towards equity of energy and information."[74]

At first sight it would seem that the pro-nuclear belief in science and technology could be contrasted with the scientific skepticism and technological conservatism of the anti-nuclear forces. The nuclear establishment clearly shares the view of the dominant minority – and the silent majority – in our society that science and technology are the means of progress toward a better society. The anti-nuclear forces seem to question those claims because they advocate a conservationist approach to the problems we face. They appear to have lost faith in science and its technological application. But if the contrast between the two positions were indeed so obvious, the anti-nuclear forces would have been simply dismissed as obscurantist pessimists. They would have been suppressed like the Luddites of old. There would have been no nuclear debate.

The anti-nuclear faction is not outside the mainstream of the common faith. A few considerations should be sufficient to dispel that notion. First, it is in their position as *scientists* that the Union of Concerned Scientists, Barry Commoner, Fred Knelman, members of Greenpeace, and others get a hearing. Second, their rejection of the nuclear option is in no way a rejection of global technological expansion. This becomes clear if we note that the recommended alternative to nuclear energy is usually a mix of conservation; expanded uses of fossil fuels, especially coal; and intensive research into and rapid development of wind and solar energy. The purpose of conservation is twofold: it will give us time to perfect other forms of energy production, and allow the industrial system to adapt and develop in new directions.

It is not our intention here to dispute the wisdom of conservation measures, but it is clear that these measures do not have as their purpose a return to a simpler lifestyle or the establishment of

a more stable or conservative society. The development and implementation of new types of power will no doubt require tremendous
amounts of scientific research, technological innovation, industrial
production and social change. Contrary to popular rhetoric, these
are not the stuff of which conservative societies are made.

It should be evident by now that the two sides in the nuclear debate actually have much in common. They both support technological change that enables us to more effectively control nature in the
hope of providing an economy of plenty. Opponents insist that
technological development must remain subject to political and
moral direction, which in turn must be determined by a vision of
the *common* good. Knelman, for example, objects to nuclear energy
on the basis of an appeal to populism or democracy, which he
contrasts with the elitism of the nuclear establishment. And
Commoner recommends a form of socialism as a cure for what he
sees as the economic and ecological insanity of nuclear power proliferation: "the energy crisis and the web of interrelated problems
confront us with the need to explore the possibility of creating a
production system that is consciously intended to serve social needs
and that judges the value of its product by their use, and an
economic system that is committed to these purposes. At least in
principle such a system is socialism."[75] Obviously Commoner is appealing not to Russia or China or Cuba as models of such socialism
but to a new creation "consistent with both the economic democracy of socialism and the political democracy inherent in the US
tradition."[76] This new creation would not be authoritarian but
would democratically direct the technological expansion that is at
the heart of the modern vision of reality.

Both sides also appeal to the ideal of *sustainable sufficiency* to justify their positions. Pro-nuclear arguments focus on the problem of
sufficiency: we need nuclear energy to guarantee that we will have
enough energy to keep our advanced economies functioning. But
the important question is avoided: How much is enough? And the
prior question is ignored: Enough for what? On the other hand,
the anti-nuclear forces are much more concerned with *sustainability*: the generation of nuclear power cannot be sustained indefinitely because of its risks and its costs. But again the important
questions are avoided: How do we know that the risks and the costs
are unsustainable? Unsustainable until when? We have sustained
nuclear power for thirty-five years; why should we not be able to

sustain it for another twenty-five or fifty? We have accepted the risks (and the wastes) until now. Why not longer, particularly since fossil fuels seem to bring with them serious risks of another type? Anyway, the wastes already produced are not going to disappear.

In Ontario, the Liberal Party in 1985 and the New Democratic Party in 1990 were elected on anti-nuclear platforms that stated that the construction of the Darlington plant should be terminated. Once in power, both agreed to its continued construction and completion but accepted a moratorium on the construction of new nuclear power facilities. This political compromise demonstrates how useless the ideal of sustainable sufficiency is as a *practical* ethical guideline in the energy field. The utilitarian calculus that is at the root of the practical, bottom-line mentality of the business ethos of our society provides no answer to the basic questions: What are benefits, and when do they cease to be benefits? What are risks, and when do they cease to be acceptable? What costs are appropriate? After more than forty years of nuclear experience we are no closer to answering these questions. We are no closer to determining limits to the benefits we think are needed, the risks we think are acceptable, or the costs we think are appropriate.

The common rationale for the acceptance of nuclear power is that its risks are no greater than those of many other modern industrial hazards. This may well be true, but it is of little consolation. Other technologically produced hazards, like global warming, may also jeopardize human life on the planet, as may accidents in genetic engineering, nuclear warfare, or computer breakdown and global economic collapse. The link between global warming, and increased emissions of carbon dioxide invites an ethical approach that would set clear limits to these emissions so as to minimize their effects and prevent us from exceeding the "tolerance margins of nature." If this requires setting limits on the burning of fossil fuels to avoid the risk, then we should accept the requirement. Likewise, it seems to me that in principle the global community could begin to scale back and eventually eliminate those industrial processes whose effects exceed what has been called "a human scale."

Later we shall consider in greater detail what "a human scale" is. For now we can say that it has always been difficult for humans to care seriously about lives lived by the next generation – even when envisaged through the persons of their children. It is not easy for human beings to envisage or take responsibility for the context of the lives of their grandchildren. But before the industrial era, one's personal or collective actions had no known consequences beyond the next generation. This is no longer the case, as Zygmunt Bauman has pointed out: "The scale of possible consequences of human actions have [*sic*] long outgrown moral imagination of the actors. Knowingly or unknowingly, our actions affect territories or times much too distant for the natural moral impulses which struggle in vain to assimilate them, or abandon the struggle altogether."[77] But to abandon the struggle altogether is to succumb to nihilism, that is, to take the view that it does not matter what we do individually or collectively. The alternative is to eliminate or refuse to undertake those technological projects that have serious negative consequences or risks for which we cannot take responsibility. More and more of the industrial processes required by modern "progress" have consequences into the distant future, consequences that may be destructive of life of this planet.

It is often argued in reply to this concern that we don't know what will happen in the future: the earth may be struck by a huge asteroid or comet, the fading of the sun may bring about a new ice age, or background radioactivity may naturally increase and lead to mutations. However, the human race is not responsible for these possibilities, and in that sense we have no *absolute* responsibility for the future. We are finite beings. We are responsible for the future only when our actions threaten it and we could reasonably be expected to know the risks of a disastrous outcome in advance.

Human beings have generally understood this much. If you do not *know* the water is safe, do not drink it. Surely we can say: If you do not know whether dumping a toxic chemical into a stream will contaminate the drinking water, do not dump it. If you do not know whether the human community will be able to safely store nuclear wastes for 1000 years, do not produce the wastes. If you cannot know with certainty that the effects of an industrial process will not be disastrous, don't subject those who may be living in the distant future to the risk. Ethics involves setting limits to what human beings may do in the world. Such limits can be set on the basis of our ignorance; what we do not know can hurt us. A technological society that forgets the basic principle of Hippocratic ethics – first, do no harm – will inevitably be seduced by the charms of the limitless and the desire to live "beyond good and evil," even as it attempts to factor in its ethics after the fact.

Clearly, the setting of limits based on our inevitable (and expanding)[78] ignorance is not the path of reform that has been politically implemented in the technological society. We have, without any public debate, accepted all of the implications of what Ulrich Beck has called the "risk society."[79] The risk society makes the globe the laboratory for its experiments. As we have seen,

Theories of nuclear reactor safety are testable only after they are built, not beforehand. The expedient of testing partial systems [what we have called risk or fault-tree analysis] amplifies the contingencies of their interaction, and thus contains the sources of error which cannot themselves be controlled experimentally. If one compares this with the logic of research that was originally agreed upon, this amounts to its sheer reversal. We no longer find the progression, first laboratory, then application. Instead, testing comes after application and production precedes research. The dilemma into which the mega-hazards have plunged scientific logic applies across the board; that is for nuclear, chemical and genetic experiments science hovers blindly above the boundary of threats. Test-tube babies must first be produced, genetically engineered artificial creatures released and reactors built, in order that their properties and safety can be studied.[80]

Beck has explained that in a "reflexive modernity" the logic of wealth production is displaced by the logic of risk avoidance and risk management. This logic leads to a non-linear understanding of knowledge, where there is a multiple field of competitors acting on knowledge with dissent and conflict over rationality and principles, so that a compulsion to open oneself to outside knowledge results. "The implacable 'more' and 'faster' of primary modernity collides everywhere with the problems, erosions and obstructions it generates; destroyed nature, empty coffers, more demands and fewer jobs despite or perhaps because of the economic upswing and economic growth. This is how politics becomes unbound, while the established political institutions are becoming zombies – the living dead institutions."[81]

Somewhat paradoxically, in a pseudo-dialectical manner, Beck draws the conclusion that "there is a utopia built into risk society and risk society theory – the utopia of a responsible modernity, the utopia of another modernity, many modernities to be invented and experienced in different cultures and different parts of the globe."[82] Beck attempts to provide a new and optimistic model for understanding our times. We no longer ask ethical questions. We ask, rather, "How can the risks and hazards systematically produced as part of modernization be prevented, minimized, dramatized, or challenged?"

Zygmunt Bauman is less sanguine and more direct. He agrees with Beck that "the gravest of problems mankind confronts today and technology has to cope with are those 'resulting from techno-economic development itself.'"[83] But Bauman argues that reflexivity about these problems and their attendant risks "may well increase, rather than diminish, the suicidal tendency of technological rule."[84] He points out that the language of risk is associated with gambling rather than ethics. The gambler enjoys the play even if he loses his bet. What is at stake in a risk society, however, is not merely the loss of a wager but the loss of the planet as a human habitat. Modern science is engaged in an experiment with the human environment and even human nature; it is a game whose results cannot be known with any certainty. It appears, however, that as science piles risk upon risk and encourages us to gamble with the future of the earth, scientists, like those in the nuclear industry, claim to be indispensable in solving the problems that industry has produced. They act "according to the principle 'We have made this mess; we will clean it up'; and more pointedly yet, 'This is a kind of mess only we know how to clean.'"[85] Ethics has been reduced to risk management.

5

Modern Weapons:
The End of the Just War Theory

In the eighteenth century Francis Bacon observed that "knowledge is power," and that account of knowledge has more or less defined the project of modern science – and it also reflects a certain truism regarding the character of modern warfare. It should be remembered that before the modern era, men and women in the Western world did not conceive of knowledge, science, or warfare in the terms suggested by Bacon's maxim. The accounts of knowledge found in the pages of Plato, Aristotle, Augustine, and the Book of Wisdom assume that the desire for insight or understanding, must be somehow related to a desire for the good. The Baconian account of scientific inquiry, on the other hand, sees the pursuit of knowledge as morally neutral – or, rather, it defines the good in terms of the pursuit of knowledge instead of the other way around, which amounts to the same thing.

The moral vacuity of modern science is perhaps nowhere more chillingly evident than in the words of Robert Oppenheimer in a speech he delivered to the team of scientists he led in the development of the atomic bomb: "If you are a scientist, you believe ... that it is good to turn over to mankind at large the greatest possible power to control the world and to deal with it according to its lights."[1] At around the same time the US undersecretary of war observed: "We will make our plans to suit our weapons, rather than our weapons to suit our plans."[2] This raises a question: If the scientists presume that moral considerations are the exclusive domain of those political and bureaucratic elites who apply the science, and if those elites, for their part, openly declare that their "plans" will accord with the science and not the other way around, then who is doing the ethical reflection? And what principles are to guide it?

Throughout most of the common era, Western societies held to some version of a "just war" ethic as a guiding principle in evaluating the purposes and conduct of nations in situations of armed conflict. The tradition of just war teaching was at least officially upheld, in one version or another, by the Christian churches as well as by the liberal nation states of eighteenth- and nineteenth-century Europe. The just war doctrine allowed that certain circumstances could make armed conflict unavoidable, but those circumstances, in order to constitute a moral justification for violence, had to conform to a number of conditions. In addition, certain principles defining appropriate conduct on the part of combatants had to be observed. (It goes without saying that these principles were rarely applied with any consistency. Indeed, those most "Christian" of military adventures, the Crusades, already featured gross violations of the most basic just war principles. But there *was* fierce debate, even at the time, about the ethical conduct of Christian armies during those infamous campaigns. The relevance of an ethical principle is not determined so much by its immediate efficacy in practice but by its ability to animate genuine reflection and critical debate.)

The twentieth century, which in military terms began with the First World War, witnessed the demise of the just war tradition. This resulted not from any direct refutation or rejection of just war principles but simply because, as moderns, "we make our plans to suit our weapons." The capacities and possibilities opened up by the destructive power of our weapons arguably no longer allowed much scope for the consideration of appropriate ethical standards for the conduct of war. Weapons of mass destruction have rendered meaningless the old distinction between combatant and non-combatant, which had been a central principle in the just war tradition.

However, some would argue that the development of so-called precision-guided munitions represents a new phase in the history of war and its technology; we now possess the means to aim our destructive capacity in such a way that military campaigns can at last be both efficacious and humane. Because this moral optimism has, in our view, arisen within a context of widespread nihilism, we shall have to submit it to some scrutiny. Let us consider the tenets of the traditional just war doctrine and then ask ourselves if, and how, such an ethical framework might continue to apply in light of the twentieth century's two most remarkable developments in military technology: the A-bomb and the Smart Bomb.

When one views the near 2,000-year history of Christianity, a complex picture of religious attitudes toward war emerges.[3] From the New Testament period to the time of Constantine in the fourth century, it appears that a clear anti-violence, anti-war mentality dominated the ethical thinking of the disciples of Jesus of Nazareth and the members of the early Church.[4] Early Christianity opposed the military profession, and there is no evidence of military service by Christians before 170 AD. Justin Martyr, Clement of Alexandria, Irenaeus, Tertullian, and Cyprian, all important early Church fathers, were opposed to military service for Christians and suggested that pacifism was more consistent with the mind of Christ. Roland Bainton, in *Christian Attitudes towards War and Peace*, quotes a passage from Tertullian as representative of early Christian thought on violence. Referring to the arrest of Jesus in the garden and Peter's defence of Jesus with a sword, Tertullian said, "Christ in disarming Peter ungirt every soldier."[5]

However, by the end of the third century, a shift in attitude had evidently occurred among Christian believers, and increasing numbers of them were joining the Roman military. Under the emperor Diocletian, repeated purges of Christians in the army preceded the mass public persecutions (c. 303 AD) for which he was infamous. During this period, the martyrdom of Christian soldiers such as Marcellus was prompted more by their refusal to perform required pagan rites than by their unwillingness to bear and use arms. With Constantine's Edict of Milan in 313 AD, the legitimation of Christianity took place; indeed, it became the official religion of the Roman Empire. Constantine could only have risked this complete reversal of policy if he was assured of the loyalty of Christian soldiers. As early as the Council of Arles in 314 AD, the Church reversed its earlier position and declared: "Those who throw down their weapons in peace shall be excluded from communion." By the early fifth century, during the reign of Theodosius II, only Christians could be in the army.

Does this change in attitude toward military service represent a cynical abandonment of biblical principles, or is it the result of the maturation of the Church's self-understanding and sense of responsibility as it became institutionalized? Is it reasonable to compare the belief and practices of a committed and persecuted Christian minority to the policies of a universal, non-exclusive, institutional Church? After all, the Roman Empire, in decline and lethally menaced by pagan barbarians, was in danger of collapse. With a Christian emperor and within a secure, defended territory, the possibility of creating a Christian civilization emerged and a Christian ethic of war developed.

The just war teaching is not so much a single theory as a tradition of thought based on a common set of presuppositions and principles. Implicit in the theory is the notion that military action can only be justified by recourse to a higher principle. Rather than endorsing violence, the just war theory states that, in normal circumstances, violence is inconsistent with Christian belief and may only be resorted to when justice (goodness) is unavoidably threatened by evil. Thus it was argued, for example, by Ambrose, bishop of Milan, that in a fallen world, even one redeemed by Christ, it may be necessary for a society to use force to defend itself. But it cannot defend itself using any and every means at its disposal. It may resort to war, but war must be limited. War must remain a rule-governed activity, bound by the laws of a moral universe created by God. Justice may defend itself, but not by any and every means.

These two principles, that violence must be justified and that violence may not be indiscriminate, are found in all forms and expressions of the just war theory from the time of Constantine. However, the theory was developed and refined in three main stages after Ambrose's initial articulation.

Augustine, the bishop of Hippo in North Africa in the fifth century, was keenly aware of the strong early Church tradition (based on Jesus' command to love one's enemy)[6] against militarism and violence. But he lived during the final days of the Roman Empire, and he could see the need to protect the common good. He agreed with Ambrose that the end of the Empire put in jeopardy the existence of Christianity, and so he set out to harmonize and synthesize the tension between the demands of Christian love and the common good. He did so by making a distinction between public and private life.[7] Augustine condemned killing in self-defence by an individual but suggested that, in a sinful world, military force may be justified if it combats evil and protects the weak. Reason, he believed, could objectively determine which side, if any, was on the side of justice. Since Christians who were fighting for the Empire were protecting their faith from desecration by pagans, warfare in this instance was justifiable. In the waging of war, however, the Christian combatant must be governed by mercy.

In the thirteenth century, at the height of the Middle Ages, Thomas Aquinas accepted Augustine's general propositions and systematized them by outlining three specific conditions for a just war.[8] First, he maintained that war could be waged only for a just cause: to address an evil, to restore a right, or to defend oneself. Second, a war could be waged only by a legitimate authority, a sovereign nation directed by its leaders. Third, a war could be fought only with right intention; the purpose of the combatants must be to promote good and not merely to conquer or to avenge previous losses.

The third main contribution to the just war theory was made by a group of Spanish scholastics of the sixteenth and early seventeenth century. Vitoria (d. 1546) and Suarez (d. 1617) were the most notable. They wrote during the upheaval of the Reformation, when nation states were emerging in Western Europe. The political unity of Augustine's world was gone, the religious unity of Aquinas' world was a thing of the past, and new, more destructive methods for waging war were appearing. The Spanish scholastics' concern was no longer merely to identify the just reasons for going to war but to determine the just *means* that could be used in waging war. They realized that war legitimates violence, which tends to escalate and to lead to the destruction of the lives and property of many innocent parties who had no role in starting the war or in keeping it going. Reflecting on the chaos and violence of the day, the scholastics added the concepts of proportionality and non-combatant immunity to the theory. Vitoria argued that, although a nation or principality may have just cause to go to war, the war is not just if the violence and damage done is out of proportion to the good being defended. Similarly, if large numbers of non-combatants are killed in the strategy of waging the war, then that war cannot be just.

With the contribution of the scholastics, the final constitutive element of the just war theory was provided. The modern just war theory can thus be summarized in this way. It has as its purpose the limiting of war by hedging it in with restraints. War is considered necessary when it is used as a defensive measure: to defend the lives of innocent people, to preserve basic freedoms in the face of aggression, or to liberate people from situations of degrading poverty or political oppression. The theory provides strict criteria by which one might legitimize and evaluate these exceptions. The criteria can be placed in two broad categories, the *jus ad bellum* criteria (largely derived from Augustine and Aquinas), which specify the conditions necessary to go to war justly, and the *jus in bello* criteria (largely derived from the scholastics), which specify how war should be waged if it is to be just.

To summarize, the *jus ad bellum* criteria are that war must be declared by a competent and legitimate authority; there must be a just cause for the war, for example, defence against an unjust aggressor; war must be waged with a right intention, for example, defence of justice and a return to peace, not for purposes of vengeance; war must be a last resort and all other peaceful diplomatic alternatives must have been exhausted; there must be a reasonable hope of success, so that the state of one's country after the war will not be worse than its state before – in other words, one cannot fight a just war if there is little chance of winning it and a good chance that one's army will be decimated in the process; the values of justice to be defended must be in appropriate proportion to the evils that attend the use of force, which include the brutalization and barbarization of civil society by war; and there must be a formal declaration of war.

If the war is to be conducted in a just way, *jus in bello* conditions must be adhered to: those engaged in battles or manoeuvres must discriminate between combatants and non-combatants (whether civilians or those who have laid down their arms), who are kept immune from *direct* attack; and the total harm caused by a particular military manoeuvre must be proportionate to the good that the manoeuvre is meant to accomplish.

This framework of ethical principles continues to be invoked by ethicists, politicians, and even military analysts.[9] What seems odd is that, for the last half-century, the world's dominant powers have possessed, and have consistently made it known that they are prepared to use, a military technique that by its very nature cannot be reconciled with the just war principles. The atomic bomb, as was made perfectly clear at Hiroshima and Nagasaki, is indiscriminately destructive. Further, a nuclear exchange cannot be expected to accomplish any military or political objectives because it would almost certainly result in destruction on such a vast scale that there would be few, if any, goods of a material or political nature to be salvaged in its aftermath. At any rate, the good to be achieved could never be weighed against the horrors to be undergone by all of the world's peoples if such an exchange should occur between any two powers. The intention to use such weapons when necessary, an intention that is implicit in the policy of nuclear deterrence, is in essence an intention to disregard, if it is deemed necessary, the principles of the just war doctrine. Any strategy that involves the use, or threatened use, of the atomic bomb already departs from the teaching. So how did a civilization that had for centuries, at least in the public rhetoric of its churches, legislatures, and academies, held to a set of ethical principles that demanded a reasonable, moderate, and humane approach to matters of war find itself in the twentieth century totally committed to a technology of indiscriminate destruction?

First, it should be noted that the willingness to use terrible weapons of war that are both disproportionate and indiscriminate emerged long before the development of thermonuclear weapons. The First World War saw the first use of chemical weapons like chlorine, tear gas, and mustard gas, which of their very nature could not be targeted accurately. The use of planes to deliver explosives led to the perfecting of carpet bombing and firebombing techniques in World War II, when thousands of homes were destroyed and civilians killed in cities like Tokyo, Coventry, and Dresden. The dropping of nuclear weapons was consistent with the systematic destruction of civilian populations that had been undertaken using "conventional weapons" in the years leading up to Hiroshima and Nagasaki.[10]

However, few analysts anticipated that the development and use of atomic weapons to end the war with Japan would lead to the proliferation of indiscriminate and disproportional weapons as deterrence became the basis of defence for the superpowers after World War II ended. Throughout the four decades of the Cold War, the United States and the Soviet Union funnelled vast amounts of wealth into the endless project of keeping pace with the other in nuclear capability. Each acquired the power to completely destroy the other and almost certainly the rest of the planet in the aftermath of a nuclear exchange.

The Cold War has ended, but that destructive capacity remains, as a number of other nations have now joined the nuclear club – including China, India, Pakistan, Israel, South Korea, South Africa, and, most recently, North Korea. Much like the old Soviet–U.S.

arms race, the expansion of the nuclear arsenals of countries like India and Pakistan is driven by paranoia and mutual antagonism. In fact, the end of the Cold War has changed little. Although the axes of potential conflict have realigned, the reality of a global arms race remains. And perhaps its most tragic consequence, aside from the ever-present risk that nuclear weapons might again be used either accidentally or intentionally, is the unconscionable mis-allocation of resources in a world of poverty.

Ian Barbour pointed out in *Ethics in an Age of Technology* that by the end of the 1980s, global military expenditures amounted to close to $1000 thousand million, or $1 trillion ($1,000,000,000,000), annually.[11] For fifteen years thereafter, thanks to the end of the Cold War, expenditures declined, but by 2005 they had increased again, to more than $1.1 trillion.[12] In economic terms, the destructive power of nuclear weapons was evident without a shot having been fired.

But how did the arms race begin, and what fueled its expansion? One possible answer, the shortest answer, is found in political history. During the Second World War many believed that Nazi Germany was far along in nuclear weapons research. The Americans began their program in response; then, after the war, when the Soviet Union developed its own program, nuclear weapons development spiralled into an arms race, with each superpower driven to produce greater and greater stockpiles. Part of this short answer includes a description of the Manhattan Project (which was directed by the enigmatic American physicist Robert Oppenheimer, employed over 150,000 people, and produced the first atomic bombs at Los Alamos, New Mexico, in 1945). But the long answer – and the more profound one – will require an examination of the development of contemporary physics in the twentieth century and the destruction of any ethical framework that might have guided science and technology and thereby limited the invention (not merely the deployment) of weapons of mass destruction in the twentieth century.

Robert Oppenheimer described the early years of the development of the quantum theory of atomic systems as a heroic time: "It involved the collaboration of scores of scientists from many different lands, though from the first to the last the deeply creative and subtle and critical spirit of Niels Bohr guided, restrained, deepened and finally transmuted the enterprise. It was a period of patient work in the laboratory, of crucial experiments and daring action, of many false starts and many untenable conjectures ... For those who participated it was a time of creation. There was a terror as well as exaltation in their new insight."[13]

Although it was a time of creation, it seems that there was, right from the beginning, a premonition of global destruction associated with the explorations and experiments of subatomic physics. This was not initially linked to the possibility of a nuclear disaster. In 1903, long before the discoveries of modern physics made possible the splitting of the atom, Ernest Rutherford "made the playful suggestion, that 'could a proper detonator be found, it was just possible that a wave of atomic disintegration would make this world vanish in smoke.'"[14] This same anxiety was expressed in the 1930s, when "Leo Szilard and George Gamow began serious analysis of whether a nuclear chain reaction could accidentally set off an endless sequence."[15] The scientific question emerged: "Would conditions be created in the interior of a nuclear explosion which might fuse under great heat and pressure, hydrogen, helium and nitrogen, and thereby ignite the world's atmosphere?"[16]

Ironically, once serious research and development began in the Manhattan Project, this was the only ethical concern that was allowed to surface and to slow down the scientific work. F.P. Szasz describes the crisis in this way:

In July of 1942, a group of scientists began discussion of the issue in Le Conte Hall on the campus of the University of California. Edward Teller made some of the initial calculations and his figures indicated that the bombs would indeed create enough heat to ignite the earth's atmosphere. Oppenheimer immediately called a halt to the meetings and sought out Arthur Compton, head of the metallurgical laboratory of the University of Chicago ... The scientists met frequently to analyze the issue. In a 1959 interview with author Pearl Buck, Compton recalled that he took the initiative in the early days of the discussion. If the calculations showed that the chances of igniting the atmosphere were more than approximately three in one million, he said he would not proceed with the Manhattan project. Nothing, not even the horrifying possibility of a Nazi victory, justified taking this risk. Revised calculations showed figures slightly under that and so the project continued.[17]

No indication is given as to what "approximately three" might mean, or where the figure "approximately three in one million" came from – nor why three in one million was deemed an "acceptable" risk. Did this mean that four in one million would have been an unacceptable risk? We can be confident that such a judgment was not based on a cost-risk-benefit analysis, where the cost represented the expense of mounting the Manhattan Project, the benefit would be winning the race to develop and deploy an atomic bomb and thereby defeating the Nazis, and the risk was that, in deploying it, one might make the earth uninhabitable. We do know that, as part of the Manhattan Project, further risk calculations were done by Edward Teller and Hans Bethe. They later told the American public: "We were sure on theoretical grounds that we would not set the atmosphere on fire."[18]

Again it is not clear what the basis for or the meaning of this statement was. Did the two scientists mean that the risk of a runaway explosion was much lower than previous calculations had indicated, and therefore the risk was clearly worth taking (given the benefits of victory), or did they mean that it was theoretically impossible for such a horrendous accident to take place? That is, were they arguing from necessity or were they arguing from probability? Like most statements by scientists or politicians about the safety of scientific experiments, this one was ambiguous. One fears that it was intentionally so. How small would the risk of the destruction of the earth have to be before the benefits made such a risk acceptable?

By the time the actual plans were being made to test the atomic bomb in the Nevada desert, American intelligence had learned that German physicists had taken a wrong turn in their atomic research.[19] The Americans were no longer under immediate *military* pressure to proceed. In other words, they took the risk of a chain reaction, however low it may have been, in the awareness that the war could be won without it. We know that anxiety remained about the possibility of a runaway fire in the atmosphere. When the first atomic explosion lit up the New Mexico desert on 16 July 1945, a senior military officer in the Manhattan Project was heard to shout: "Good God! I believe that the long-haired boys have lost control."[20] As it turned out, they hadn't, at least not in the way that was feared. Oppenheimer's reported utterance, a quotation from the Bhaghavad Gita ("I am become death, destroyer of worlds") summed the situation up more dramatically, albeit more enigmatically.

The early premonition of global disaster associated with the development of subatomic physics was countered by a classic expression of the Enlightenment belief in the inherent goodness of knowledge – any knowledge. After the first atomic explosion, Oppenheimer remarked that his "faith in the human mind had been somewhat restored"[21] by the success of the blast.

This passion for knowing everything served later to justify the Manhattan Project and atomic research, even when they were no longer needed to guarantee the Allied victory. After the atomic bombs had been dropped on the (predominantly) civilian populations of Hiroshima and Nagasaki, Oppenheimer gave one last speech to the scientists at Los Alamos. He stated: "When you come right down to it, the reason we did this job was because it was an organic necessity. If you are a scientist, you cannot stop such a thing."[22]

Later, Oppenheimer was more ambivalent about the Manhattan Project and his role in it. After the war, he told President Truman that he felt he had blood on his hands.[23] In a 1946 speech to the National Academy of Sciences, he questioned the "goodness" of science, but then went on to reaffirm it: "We have raised again the question of whether science is good for man or whether it is good to learn about the world, to try to understand it, to try to control it, to help give to the world of men increased insight, increased power ... Because we are scientists we must say an unalterable yes to these questions ... Knowledge is a good in itself, knowledge and such power as must come with it."[24]

This affirmation of the goodness of physics was repeated in 1952, when Oppenheimer was pressed by Edward Teller to support the development of the hydrogen bomb, which he had initially opposed. During the security hearings of 1954, Oppenheimer accounted for his original opposition on purely technical rather than ethical grounds: "The program we had in 1949," he said, "was a tortured thing that you could well argue did not make a great deal of technical sense. It was therefore possible to argue that you didn't want it even if you could have it. The program in 1951 was technically so sweet you could not argue about that."[25]

The goodness of scientific knowledge and the sweetness of technology are the beliefs that Enlightenment philosophers like Voltaire or Comte proposed would replace the obscurantism, authoritarianism, and corruption of the Christian Church. In his masterful study of the eighteenth-century philosophers, Carl Becker maintained that two facts formed the basis of the Enlightenment: "One of these contained the sum of those negations which we understand so well – the fact that the supposed revelation of God's purposes through Holy Writ and Holy Church was a fraud, or at least an illusion born of ignorance ... The other fact contained the sum of those affirmations which we understand less easily – that God had revealed his purpose to men in a far less mysterious way through his work ... It was not in Holy Writ but in the great book of nature, open for all mankind to read, that the law of God had been recorded. This is the new revelation and thus at last we enter the secret door of knowledge."[26] Becker does not refer to modern science as a form of gnosticism, but the implication seems clear.

Modern physics, then, on the Enlightenment account, must be understood as part of the new revelation. To limit the scope of its experimentation on any other but purely scientific grounds would be to revert to the obscurantism, authoritarianism and superstition of the Dark Ages. As Oppenheimer himself said in 1958: "The idea of scientific progress seems to me to have become indissolubly linked with the notion of human destiny. To me, this conception appears to be alien to religion."[27] But Oppenheimer gradually came to realize that although religion should not be allowed to interfere with science, physics itself offered no criteria for limiting the scope of its own experimentation.

Somewhat ironically, it was Oppenheimer himself who, in 1959, related the arms race and the threat of nuclear annihilation to the abandonment of a Christian moral framework:

It is incontrovertible that we are living on our inheritance from the Christian tradition. Many of us are believers, none of us is indifferent to the Christian order, to the injunctions and hopes of Christianity. This is why I am profoundly disturbed to note that no moral discussion of any quality or significance has been started on the problem of the new weapons, the atomic weapons. There have been discussions in terms of security, strategy, force relationships. But what can we think, what are we to expect of a civilization which has always looked on moral values as an essential element in human life but which is incapable of envisaging the prospect of an almost universal holocaust except in terms of strategy?[28]

In that same speech Oppenheimer went on to condemn the United States for its bomb threats and its policy of deterrence: "Every time the West, and more particularly my own country, has expressed the opinion that it is legitimate to employ weapons of mass destruction provided that they are employed against an adversary who has done something evil, we have been wrong."[29] Oppenheimer was as categoric in his opposition to the United States' threat to use nuclear weapons as he had been in his support of his government's duty to develop them in the first place. His circumspection with regard to his country's nuclear deterrence policy was evidently motivated by some kind of ethical concern regarding the use or threatened use of weapons of mass destruction, but it does not seem to have led to any fundamental critique of the role of science in developing and perfecting such technology.

If Oppenheimer was appealing to the principles of just war when he declared that it was unjust to use weapons of mass destruction, it is unclear from his own words to which principles he was referring. One can only assume that he had identified the same issues that we have noted above: the lack of proportion between the destruction atomic weapons would cause and the good they might achieve, as well as their inherent inability to discriminate between combatants and non-combatants. Clearly Oppenheimer's stance had changed from 1941, when, on his advice, the decision was taken by the U.S. military and the defence department to develop nuclear weapons of mass destruction, and from 1945, when he went along with the bombing of civilian centres in Japan. (We know that one of the reasons for the choice of Hiroshima and Nagasaki was "scientific." Since they had not been previously attacked, the effects of the new bombs could be easily studied after the Japanese surrendered.)[30]

Oppenheimer seems to have sensed the conflict arising from science's claim of ethical neutrality. He nevertheless reaffirmed that claim, as indeed most modern scientists have. Within the modern context, science is understood to be morally autonomous; that is, research and free inquiry must be allowed to proceed without regard to moral considerations. In the security hearings of 1954, Oppenheimer stated: "When you see something that is technically sweet, you go ahead and do it, and you argue about what to do about it only after you have had your technical success. That is the way it was with the atomic bomb. I don't think anybody opposed making it; there were some debates as to what to do with it after it was made."[31] But from the point of view of the scientists, these debates could not have been more than academic discussions.

In the official policies of the Cold War superpowers we see reflected both the autonomy of modern science and the implicit nihilism of technocrats who "make their plans to suit their weapons." It is hard to imagine how any civilization whose ethics and politics had not already been subverted by the technological imperative could ever have accepted "mutually assured destruction" as a reasonable way to ensure peace between powerful enemies. It is unthinkable that a civilization that seriously adhered to the just war tradition could ever have conceived of such a notion. But, again, the scrapping of the just war doctrine in favour of an official policy of constant nuclear threat was not a political decision; the conditions that made it inevitable arose simply because they were "technically sweet."

Not everyone agrees that the policy of nuclear deterrence directly undermines the authority of the just war tradition. The doctrine of deterrence has in fact been defended by many ethicists. Among these was the Roman Catholic philosopher Michael Novak, who in *Moral Clarity in the Nuclear Age*[32] claimed to be applying the just war theory. One would assume that Novak would agree that the actual use of nuclear weapons, because they lack proportionality and discrimination, has to be unjust. It does not take great perspicacity to see that, as we have argued, the good that might be achieved by the use of nuclear weapons, even in a just cause, could never be worth the destruction they would cause. Civilians, naturally, would not be immune to this destruction or the fallout. But for Novak, writing in the eighties, this did not mean that one cannot *threaten* to use nuclear weapons. It did not mean that one cannot *intend* to use them, even though it would be immoral to use them.[33] Novak argued that "the complexities of nuclear deterrence change the meaning of *intention* and *threat* as these words are usually used in moral discourse."[34]

In his review of Novak's book, James Cameron pointed out that the author gives no explanation as to what new meaning the words have.[35] What Novak did was outline a moral conundrum, one that is insoluble within the context of Roman Catholic moral theology. According to Cameron, Novak tried to solve it by confusing the issue, stating: "Those who intend to prevent the use of nuclear weapons by maintaining a system of deterrence in readiness for use do intend to use such weapons, but only in order not to use them, and do threaten to use them, but only in order to deter their use."[36] Novak went on to explain:

The fundamental moral intention in nuclear deterrence is never to
have to use the deterrent force ... Besides this fundamental intention,
however, deterrence requires by its nature a secondary intention. For
the physical material weapon by itself is no deterrent without the engagement of intellect and will on the part of the entire public which
called it into being ... A people which would be judged incapable of
willing to use the deterrent would tempt an adversary to call its bluff.
Thus a secondary intention cannot be separated from deterrence.
Without that secondary intention, distinct from the fundamental intention, a deterrent is no longer a deterrent but only an inert weapon
backed up by a public lie.[37]

   The doctrine of deterrence relies, no doubt, on the pragmatic
paradox outlined by Novak: "In order to make sure that a nuclear
war doesn't break out we have to be prepared to fight one, and this
entails, for example, that the commanders of submarines with nuclear weapons targeted on Russian cities must faithfully enter into a
prior engagement to send the missiles on their way if ordered to do
so."[38] Cameron pointed out, however, that for a Catholic philosopher, the pragmatic paradox cannot be legitimated by the just war
theory. If, according to Roman Catholic moral teaching, one cannot kill the innocent as a means to no matter what good end, one
cannot intend or threaten to bomb civilians either, even in the
defence of democracy or the American way of life, no matter how
superior these are to totalitarian government.[39] Boyle, Grisez, and
Finnis drew this conclusion in their discussion of the morality
of deterrence.[40]
   The American Catholic bishops arrived at the same position in
1982 but went on to legitimate deterrence as an *interim* measure,
provided that disarmament was being worked at by the American
government.[41] They feared the destabilization that unilateral disarmament might entail. But they also laid down clear, empirical political conditions under which American Catholics might accept
deterrence.[42] The Reagan government, with Caspar Weinberger as
secretary of defense, virtually ignored the bishops' conditions, expanded the defence budget, and accelerated the arms race. The
bishops, who received a great deal of attention when they drafted
The Challenge of Peace, did little to explain and propagate its teaching among their people. This suited the Reagan government. Some
might argue that the end of (just war) ethics in the age of nuclear
weapons was evidenced in the failure of those who were in the best

position to articulate its requirements to make a clear moral condemnation of nuclear sabre-rattling. Be that as it may, there is no doubt that if the future of war continues to involve deterrence using nuclear weapons, then this ethical framework becomes little more than a kind of moral anachronism.

Ironically, it was not the actions of American religious leaders but the daring initiative of the "godless" communist Gorbachev in 1989 that finally let the US to reconsider on the issue of disarmament. The American reasons for doing so had little to do with moral principle and much to do with national interest and public relations. The Soviet reasons had little to do with moral principle and much to do with economics. Gorbachev could afford to be bold because it was his own people who were suffering from the misguided (and rapidly failing) attempts of the USSR to keep up with American defence spending. In the US, on the other hand, the economic well-being of the major corporations was linked to the defence establishment and to defence spending. The American government, therefore, had no idea what to do or say as peace broke out in Eastern Europe in the fall of 1989. It was, it seemed, relieved when the Gulf crisis of 1991 demanded both its attention and military spending.

It appears that the just war theory had as little to do with the end of the arms race between the Soviet Union and the US as it did with its beginning forty years earlier. A theory that could have no role in controlling the scientific research and technological development of horrendous weapons of mass destruction could have nothing to say about limiting their use. However, no other theory that might limit war has emerged.

Today, some would argue that, even if the reduction of the threat of nuclear annihilation since the end of the Cold War was not the result of moral considerations, we find ourselves in a situation wherein the just war theory can have a renewed relevance. For reasons quite unlike those of Michael Novak, whose moral reflections on nuclear deterrence are perhaps a leading modern example of casuistry in the service of *realpolitik*, they would suggest that our obituary for the just war theory is premature. Their reasons for saying so are based on a rather different account of the recent history of military technology and of technology in general than we have been offering. They would point out that the most recent military campaigns involving major world powers (e.g., the US and its allies versus Iraq in 1991 and 2003, as well as the conflicts in the former Yugoslavia and in Afghanistan) have not involved any nuclear threat and have, on the contrary, demonstrated the capacities of precision-guided munitions to enable a more humane, effective, and less generally destructive war.[43]

For example, Jean Bethke Elshtain, professor of social and political ethics at the University of Chicago Divinity School observes, regarding the 2001 invasion of Afghanistan: "The improved accuracy of the US air war, conducted with weaponry that is more precise and does less damage to the surroundings than was possible only a few years ago, serves the ends of discrimination."[44] Writers like Elshtain would implicitly reject the thesis that the technological imperative trumps any and all ethical concerns; on the contrary, they see in this technology an expression of Western liberal values. Elshtain's observation directly links the capabilities of precision-guided munitions to the first of the *jus in bello* conditions: the obligation to discriminate between combatants and non-combatants and to protect the latter from all deliberate harm. In a similar spirit, George and Meredith Friedman observe that "the image of a tomahawk missile slamming precisely into its target when contrasted with the strategic bombardments of World War II does in fact contain a deep moral message and meaning."[45] There may be some truth in this claim, but we need to consider just what the meaning of this truth could be.

The public first got a glimpse of the new "shock and awe" way of war and its spectacular technology during the 1991 conflict in the Persian Gulf. Throughout the weeks of the US-led coalition's bombing campaign, incredible videogame-like images were fed to the media: bombs zeroing in on bridges and flying down smokestacks, Patriot missiles intercepting Iraqi Scuds in the skies over Saudi Arabia and Israel. Oddly, as Chris Hables Gray points out, television viewers did not see many bodies. The human body, whether alive or dead, was largely absent in the imagery and rhetoric around the Gulf War. "The number of Iraqi tanks and planes destroyed was always available; the count of dead bodies was not."[46] In fact, General Schwarzkopf, the coalition commander, could remark: "We are not in the business of killing."[47] On one level, this statement is self-evidently absurd. It is generally accepted that at least 100,000 Iraqi military personnel (mostly untrained conscripts) and several thousand civilians were killed as a direct result of the bombing.[48] The US Census Bureau reports that within the

first year after the war approximately 70,000 Iraqis died as an indirect consequence of the war and a Harvard University study determined that another 100,000 people, mostly children, died in the
following year.[49] Although not all of these deaths can be attributed
directly to the "business" of warriors like General Schwarzkopf – the
economic blockade was responsible for much of this misery –
the meaning of his remark is nevertheless hard to fathom. It does,
however, reflect an important characteristic of late twentieth-
century warfare and its technology. The distribution of casualties
between the two sides was so disproportionate, thanks largely to dis-
parities in technology, that death became, from the point of view of
the Western media consumer, something of an abstraction. Part of
Schwarzkopf's job, and the task of his media relations people and
his many thousands of techno-warriors, was to keep it that way.

If Schwarzkopf's dissimulation of the lethality of modern war
seems absurd, the remark of General Tommy Franks, the US commander of the 2003 invasion of Iraq, is at least more honest. When
questioned about civilian casualties, he replied, "We don't do body
counts."[50] The unwillingness of the Western military powers to
provide any statistics concerning civilian casualties (information of
which few seriously believe they could have been unaware) has
been a matter of some frustration for human rights groups,
journalists, and policy analysts. In a 1991 report, Human Rights
Watch noted the remark of General Robert B. Johnston, General
Schwarzkopf's chief of staff during the aerial campaign against
Iraq: "I quite truthfully cannot tell you of any reports that I know of
that would show inaccurate bombing, particularly north of the
Saudi–Kuwaiti border … I cannot tell you of any that I know of that
grossly missed the target." The Human Rights Watch report goes
on to list a number of confirmed incidents of "collateral damage,"
including hits on 400 homes, 19 apartment buildings, two hospi-
tals, two schools, and a mosque, as well as a number of restaurants,
commercial buildings, and market areas in Basra, Falluja, Samawa,
and al-Kut. Their report notes a *Washington Post* story claiming that
the Pentagon was in possession of extensive footage documenting
the effects of these "errors" but was not prepared to release any of
it to the media. Dick Cheney, then US secretary of defense,
dismissed calls to release this material, saying it was "pretty dull,
boring stuff."[51] Apparently it was felt that the endless hours of
videogame-style footage, faithfully replayed on CNN, depicting missiles homing in on their targets, had greater entertainment value.

The controversy concerning the number of casualties, the human reality behind the Orwellian euphemism "collateral damage," was perhaps most dramatically illustrated in the case of Beth Osborne Daponte, the researcher who carried out the 1992 US Census Bureau study mentioned earlier. Her study claimed that 13,000 civilians were killed during the initial phase of the campaign, 70,000 civilians died subsequently, and 40,000 Iraqi soldiers were killed during the conflict. However, after the contents of her report were picked up by the media, the report disappeared from her desk and she was dismissed from her position on the grounds of having released "false information." A number of social scientists subsequently examined her research. Her methodology was vindicated in a statement from the American Statistical Association, and the American Civil Liberties Union took up her case. She was eventually reinstated in her position.[52] But the episode made it quite clear that the department of defense was not willing to have its policy of official silence on the matter of civilian casualties undermined by other branches of the federal government bureaucracy.

The tightly managed media spectacle that was the 1991 Gulf War involved a kind of fetishism of the machine that changed many people's conception of war. Herein lies a serious ethical danger. Robert E. Lee once observed, "It's good that war is so horrible, lest we grow too fond of it."[53] Whether or not we are ever likely to grow fond of it, there is no question that the public's tolerance for military solutions to global disputes increases as risk-free warfare becomes more and more possible. George Bush repeatedly referred to the Gulf conflict as a "just war," but Michael Ignatieff, who has generally supported a policy of judicious interventionism, still finds it necessary to ask whether "a war ceases to be just when it becomes a turkey shoot."[54] Ignatieff voices the concern that a society shielded from the consequences of war might lack compelling reasons to practice restraint in the exercise of military force.[55]

Precision-guided munitions give rise to a peculiarly attractive illusion: that of a low-risk, casual war. Elliot Cohen argues that this new generation of weapons, weapons that home in on laser reflections or infrared signatures or are guided by global positioning system navigation, are, for the first time in modern military history, more likely than not to actually hit their target, but they also offer the possibility of striking with impunity.[56] Nevertheless, despite their accuracy, Cohen points out that their military effectiveness has actually proven itself to be quite limited. The range of objectives that one can reasonably hope to achieve by waging a war from thousands of feet up or from miles out to sea is narrow. Cohen points out that the Gulf War achieved only one of its three explicit objectives: it did not re-establish legitimate governance in the region, it did not bring stability to the Persian Gulf, and while it did forcibly remove Iraq from Kuwait, it accomplished this limited objective at the price of great misery and hardship for the Iraqi people.[57]

One could make similar claims about the 1999 war in Kosovo. If the Gulf War evinced the possibility of a casual war, Kosovo was the first example of one in practice. To be sure, it was not quite as casual as NATO military officials had initially hoped. It was believed that an intense, well-directed air campaign involving missiles and guided bombs would force the Serbians to capitulate within two weeks. The architects of the NATO campaign also felt that they could achieve their objectives by bombing only Serbian military targets. In the end, the bombing campaign took six weeks and targeted key sites in the Serbian economic and social infrastructure, including bridges and a television station. Albert Coll observed: "Reliance on air power alone meant that for NATO to compel Milosovic to accept its terms it had to attack targets of value to the general civilian population, and it had to conduct these attacks in a way that put civilians at risk."[58] Coll, who examined the war in Kosovo on the basis of the just war doctrine, did not question the legitimacy of the motives for going to war with Serbia. There was, in his view, and in the view of many, no question that the threat of an explosion of ethnic violence against Kosovar Albanians was growing and that another Bosnian war was quite possibly in the making. What Coll did question, perhaps surprisingly, was NATO's strategic reliance on precision-guided munitions that could be launched from great altitudes or from great distances. And he questioned this reliance not only on the basis of tactical efficacy but on the basis of the just war doctrine.

Coll argued that the new technologies create an expectation that war can be waged by a powerful country or coalition without the loss of any of its soldiers. It also creates the expectation that such a war can be waged without loss of civilian life. Ultimately, however, the longer a war drags on, the more the former concern trumps the latter. This is precisely what occurred in Kosovo. "Morally, one of the great contradictions involved in NATO's conduct of the war was its tacit decision to value the lives of its soldiers above those of the

enemy's non-combatants, including those ethnic Albanians on behalf of whom NATO launched its humanitarian intervention."[59]
(This same logic allowed President Truman to drop atomic bombs
on the largely civilian populations of Hiroshima and Nagasaki
in 1945.)

NATO was astoundingly successful in keeping its soldiers out of
harm's way: no NATO soldier was killed in active combat. However,
as Anthony Cordesman pointed out, NATO bombing also did very
little damage to the *Serbian* military. It was the crippling of Serbia
economically that established the conditions for a NATO victory. As
was clear in the case of Iraq, it is difficult to assess the long-term effects on a population of the destruction of its infrastructure. But
Human Rights Watch, who conducted an extensive and thorough
post-conflict investigation, documented over 500 civilian casualties
in 90 separate incidents of "collateral damage." In particular, their
report cited 90 to 150 deaths involving cluster bombs.[60] In several
cases, convoys of refugees were hit when NATO pilots believed they
were seeing Serbian troop movements. Although some of these
"collateral damage" incidents came to light at the time (in particular, the dropping of five 2,000-pound bombs on the Chinese em-
bassy after NATO tacticians mistook it for the Yugoslav Directorate
for Supply and Procurement), Cordesman pointed out that official
NATO information consistently obscured and sometimes completely
ignored the realities of "collateral damage."

It would seem that the aspect of precision-guided munitions
technology that Western governments are most eager to capitalize
on is their promise of risk-free warfare, which, of course, is not risk-
free for enemy soldiers or civilians. Understood in terms of the just
war tradition's *jus in bello* criteria, it must be argued that precision-
guided munitions create the kind of moral distance between
ourselves and an enemy that leads to casual disregard for the consequences of our destructive actions. This exposes, as in the case of
Kosovo perhaps, a certain moral hypocrisy with respect to motives.
Michael Ignatieff observes: "The concept of human rights assumes
that all human life is of equal value. Risk-free warfare presumes
that our lives matter more than those we are intervening to save."[61]
It is true that the loss of civilian life in the Kosovo war was not great
compared with that of other twentieth-century wars. But neither
were the aims and objectives of that conflict particularly ambitious.
For example, NATO's actions to secure peace and respect for

human rights in the region were not sufficiently serious and robust to prevent the retaliatory violence of the Kosovo Liberation Army and of ethnic Albanians against their fleeing Serb neighbours. The just war tradition requires us to measure the harm inevitably caused by military action against a reasonable expectation of the good to be accomplished. In the case of Iraq, we may note that many Americans under the Clinton administration were not even aware that, long after the Gulf War was behind them, their government was continuing to drop thousands of bombs on Iraqi targets, causing prolonged suffering in the name of objectives that were increasingly obscure and, given the nature of the tactics and technology, probably quite unrealizable.

The ongoing "virtual war" (to use Ignatieff's phrase) against Iraq exposed a more sinister dimension to the new technology of war. Bacevich and Cohen point out that President Clinton, who once appeared to embody post-Vietnam baby-boomer ambivalence about American militarism, and who was "the first post-cold war president, [also] employed American military power more often, in more places, and for more varied purposes than any of his predecessors."[62] We can now think of war in terms of gadgets rather than real human bodies; we see footage involving only machines; we no longer seem to risk losing friends and loved ones. We have entered an age when war has become so distanced from our moral domain that, paradoxically, it has silently become harmless and ubiquitous. As Coll observed, "the notion of 'war without casualties' has chipped away at the firewall laboriously built up throughout the twentieth century against the casual use of military force. To the extent that they view Kosovo as a 'success,' political leaders may come to view the use of force through air power as a sanitized instrument of statecraft requiring few moral scruples and no international sanctions."[63]

Fundamentally, we have not moved past the principle of tactical and moral decision-making reflected in the statement "we make our plans to suit our weapons." The new technology of war has changed not only the way we fight but also our reasons for fighting. The Kosovo war represented a fundamental shift in the NATO mandate, away from a territory-specific defensive alliance to an active extra-territorial offensive military force. James Kurth pointed out that, in the post-Cold War era, the American military has been called upon to act as a kind of global constabulary, able to discipline and punish states like Afghanistan, Iraq, Iran, Libya, and

North Korea, states that "represent the antithesis of the American ideology of liberal globalism."[64] In other words, the technology of war is now sufficiently flexible (in both tactical and moral terms) to form an effective means by which to establish the hegemony of the Western technological system – a system that, as we have repeatedly seen, requires open markets, global institutional homogeneity, and a political culture in which states function as kind of managerial bodies with powers no more extensive than is required to efficiently serve the interests of their client-consumers.

Michel Foucault reversed von Clausewitz's famous dictum that "war is the continuation of politics by other means." Politics, Foucault wrote, is war by other means. This may in fact reflect a reality of our age. The technology of war has become an integral part of the modern technology of politics. In the case of Kosovo, it may be that ostensibly humanitarian reasons for going to war concealed a deeper political logic. Western powers initiated the bombing campaign because of the failure of the Rambouillet negotiations of February and March 1999. US diplomats were involved in the negotiations until those negotiations were broken off, presumably because no deal could be worked out that would guarantee the security and human rights of the Albanian population in Kosovo. That may well be true. But Kurth pointed out that an examination of the documents from those negotiations "strongly indicate that the United States wanted Serbia to reject a political solution to the problem posed by Kosovo. This rejection would then be used to justify a NATO war against Serbia." His main evidence for this claim was an appendix to the document that Serbian officials were being asked to sign. Appendix B, entitled "Status of Multi-national Military Implementation Force," required that Serbia allow international peacekeepers to have access to all of its territory. The last time Serbia was offered such an ultimatum was by the Austro-Hungarian empire in 1914. Serbia rejected the demand in 1914, and many Serbs consider that rejection a heroic moment in their history. It is not surprising, then, that they rejected a similar ultimatum in 1999. In the end, the point was of so little significance to the NATO officials that it was not even included in the document that Serbia was forced to sign after being bombed into submission. And yet it is difficult to believe that US diplomats were unaware that this stipulation would make the document unacceptable to the Serbs and would inevitably lead to war.[65]

Kurth suggested that in the era of globalization, the US needs NATO to serve a different, broader role. Kosovo provided an opportunity for NATO to expand its mandate, not only in terms of geography but also in terms of its criteria for determining when it is appropriate to go to war. After the long deadlock of the Cold War, and with a new range of technical military capabilities at the ready, armed force could now be used more flexibly and to achieve a broader range of goals. At the time of the campaign in the former Yugoslavia, no one could have anticipated, however, that two years later an event would occur that would significantly alter the geopolitical terrain and, with it, the condition of modern warfare.

It has become a commonplace that the tragic events of 11 September 2001 changed the world. There certainly have been some significant changes, but the meaning of these changes is open to discussion. The two conflicts considered thus far were somewhat limited in their strategic objectives and, tactically, were prosecuted largely by means of aerial bombardment. The two (so far) main post-9/11 conflicts, in Afghanistan and Iraq, on the other hand, have been framed within the context of a "war on terror"; they have involved a new set of justifications and new strategies and tactics. The "war on terror," as it has been played out in these two conflicts, is something of an amalgam of a large-scale police operation and an effort at nation-building. So far at least, one can discern little meaningful success on either front, but, six years into it, we continue to be told that this war will take time and that its successful prosecution calls for much patience.

The "war on terror" has also, apparently, breathed new life into the tradition of just war theory. The "deep moral message and meaning" that George and Meredith Friedman saw in "the image of a tomahawk missile slamming precisely into its target" is no doubt heightened by contrast with the images of commercial airliners, loaded with fuel and passengers, slamming equally precisely into office towers teeming with doomed civilians going about their workaday business. A terrorist enemy is by definition unconcerned with the distinction between combatant and non-combatant; he is unconcerned with the question of proportionality, and any claim to just *cause* that he may have is effectively nullified by the manifest injustice of his means. George Weigel, in a 2003 article defending the applicability of just war theory to the "war on terror," claims that "terrorist organizations provide a less ambiguous example of a legitimate military target, because, unlike conventional states (which are always admixtures of good and evil, against whom military action sometimes threatens the good as well as the evil), the 'parasite states' that are international terrorist organizations are unmitigated evils whose only purpose is wickedness – the slaughter of innocents for ignoble political ends."[66] (Weigel seems to overlook the fact that military actions against terrorists do not occur in a vacuum but have in fact been carried on against *states* that are claimed to be guilty of harbouring terrorists.)

Similarly, Jean Bethke Elshtain has insisted on the moral asymmetry between the parties in the current conflict. She views the careful use of precision-guided munitions as reflecting the Western powers' deep concern with discrimination, whereas "the terrorist commits himself to violence *without limits.*"[67] The horror of the events of September 11, the sheer malevolent destructiveness of the terrorists, the realization that failed or "rogue" states are liable to wind up as "havens" for such terrorists, all combined with the capacity of the Western powers to wage a putatively more humane high-tech war with precisely guided weaponry, have perhaps made it inevitable that the concept of the just war would come back into circulation.[68]

But are we really witnessing a revival of the just war tradition in the post-9/11 period? The question here is not whether or not there are theologians, ethicists, and moral philosophers still pondering the just war theory and the wisdom of employing its guidelines for real-world decision-making. After all, just war theorists were, as we have seen, working away throughout the Cold War while the realities around them manifested a general disregard for their scruples. The purpose of the question here is to determine whether or not the just war theory has played a role, or can reasonably be *expected* to play a role, in political decision-making about war. The fact that the US and its allies are no longer involved in a geo-political game of which a very conceivable outcome is the destruction of hundreds of cities, combined with the fact that the enemies in the current "war" are evidently morally odious fellows for whom the *jus in bello* criteria mean less than nothing, arguably allows us to conceive of our military policies in terms of the just war tradition.

But if this just war renaissance comes down to a certain set of propitious, although largely contingent, historical and technological factors, then a resurgence can perhaps only give us the illusion that the unfolding of our technological capacities can be guided by

such ethical principles. Again, it may turn out that, as in the Cold
War period, we continue to make our plans, and possibly also devise the ethics by which we "guide" our plans, to suit our weapons.
And even this possibly evanescent grace period for just war discourse may be based in part on illusion. As we have suggested, the
"image" of the Tomahawk missile slamming precisely into its target
may be no more than that, a carefully crafted "image." If the claim
we are making is correct, then it will be the case that the putative
relevance of just war thinking to the current "age of terror" depends in part on the selection, and interpretation, of certain salient
facts concerning the prosecution of the war, and the nature of the
means at our disposal.

One subject of debate is the matter of civilian casualties. The
number of casualties directly resulting from bombardment or shell-
ing is a crucial index of the seriousness of the US and its allies
about the principle of discrimination; the number of "casualties"
resulting from blockades or from the destruction of civil infrastructure could possibly impugn their seriousness about the principle of
proportionality. Elshtain's *Just War against Terror* contains a number
of jibes aimed at "opponents of the war in the academy and in religious communities [who] knowingly exaggerate the number of civilian casualties in order to discredit the war effort."[69] Among the
targets of her scorn are Amnesty International, the op-ed writers at a
number of US newspapers, and newspapers like the UK's *Independent*
and the *Guardian*, which she dismisses as "anti-American."

Elshtain takes aim at Edward Said, for example, for his claim that
in Iraq in the 1990s "hundreds of thousands" were killed as a result
of the "U.S.-maintained sanctions against the innocent civilian population of Iraq." "Where," Elshtain asks, "is the evidence for these
figures?" In fact, Said's claim accords with the results of a study carried out by UNICEF, with technical assistance from the World Health
Organization, which investigated child and maternal mortality during the period of the sanctions. Researchers randomly selected
24,000 households in the south and central region of the country
and 16,000 households in the north. They compared, on the basis
of their sample, infant and maternal mortality in the period 1994–
99 with data from 1984–89. Although they worked with local Iraqi
authorities in conducting the study, they claim to have had full control of every aspect of the research, "from design to data analysis."
The study concluded that "if the substantial reduction in child

mortality throughout Iraq during the 1980s had continued through the 1990s, there would have been half a million fewer deaths of children under five in the country as a whole during the eight year period from 1991 to 1998."[70]

Elshtain is aware of this study but claims that "the figure, most credible analysts agree, is wildly inflated."[71] There is little doubt that the credibility of the United Nations and its branches is at an all-time low among the intellectuals of the American right. Nevertheless, although it is one thing to reject a source from a writer making a controversial empirical claim, it is another thing to simply dismiss a readily available and reputable source on the basis of the uncited counter-claims of *unnamed*, putatively "credible analysts" Elshtain's real disagreement, it seems, is with the idea that the US is somehow responsible for deaths resulting from the sanctions. To this one can only say that, however odious it may otherwise have been, Saddam Hussein's Ba'athist regime ruled Iraq at a time when infant mortality was dropping (in the 1980s), and that same regime was in power during the period when infant mortality spiked (during the late 1990s); the relevant difference, then, between the two periods was a program of UN sanctions that were largely pushed for, and enforced, by the US, coupled with a continuous series of US aerial bombardments.

The UNICEF study may have suffered somewhat from certain constraints imposed on researchers. However, even if we allow for a significant margin of error – given the chaotic situation in post-war Iraq – the picture of human suffering it attests to is so massive that the UN sanctions, which never did bring down the regime of Saddam Hussein, must be seen as a cruel and catastrophic mistake. But there can be no doubt that the sanctions furthered military objectives during that interwar period that could not have been accomplished by air power alone. Indeed, much of the optimism concerning the prospects for the 2003 invasion derived from the knowledge that the erosion of Iraqi infrastructure and morale had made its once formidable military a shadow of its former self.

Within a month of al Qaeda's September 11 attacks, bombs were falling on Afghanistan. The US-led war combined relentless aerial bombardment with material and tactical support for a rather shady and loose affiliation of warlords and tribal militias calling themselves the Northern Alliance. Once again it was made to appear, particularly in the US media, that a war was being carried out with surgical precision. In fact, the circumstances of the war made it difficult to get an accurate picture of how many civilians were dying – and, once again, the Pentagon was not eager to share what information it may have had. The standard US government response when reports of "collateral damage" were brought forward was that "these reports cannot be independently confirmed." The media was also not pressing the point. At the end of October, the *Washington Post* printed this remark made by Walter Isaacson, chair of CNN: "It seems perverse to focus too much on the casualties or hardship in Afghanistan."[72] What, we might ask, could possibly be "perverse" about accurate coverage of the cost to civilians of the war in Afghanistan? It seems that anything that might have tended to obscure the stark moral contrast between "terror" and the war *on* terror was somehow itself morally suspect. A front-page headline in the *Guardian Weekly* of 14 February 2002 declared: "Afghans still dying as air strikes go on. But no one is counting." The *Guardian*'s Seumus Milne had his own hypothesis concerning the reasons for the growing number of civilian dead: "The decision to rely heavily on high-altitude air power, target urban infrastructure and repeatedly attack heavily populated towns and villages has reflected a deliberate trade-off of the lives of American pilots and soldiers, not with those of their declared Taliban enemies, but with Afghan civilians."[73] This, the reader will note, is the same critical evaluation that was made by commentators with respect to the NATO campaign in the former Yugoslavia.

As Elshtain points out, the US government subsequently investigated these concerns and admitted that there had been some problems. Perhaps not surprisingly, they attributed the problems to faulty information: "The investigation concluded that too many men had been given cell phones to call in intelligence; not all of them shared the interest of the coalition fighting terrorism in trying to uproot the last of the Al Qaeda–Taliban nexus."[74] These findings suggest that the high number of civilian casualties resulted from technical problems having to do with intelligence-gathering procedures. Presumably a technical problem admits of a technical fix. The moral contrast between the conduct of the coalition forces and that of its terrorist enemies is thus apparently maintained. But the destructiveness of high-tech aerial bombardment, including its consequences for civilians, is quite predictable. Nowhere is the technological asymmetry between the Western powers and its recent "rogue state" enemies more evident than in the air, and that advantage has been, and will likely continue to be, fully exploited in spite of the scruples of just war theorists about discrimination and proportionality.

It should also be kept in mind that technical improvements in the accuracy of the guidance systems in our weapons have in many cases been matched by an increase in their destructiveness. In an April 2003 report entitled "Iraq: Civilians Under Fire," Amnesty International urgently called for the cessation of the use of cluster bombs which were being used by both US and British forces. Film footage from a hospital at al-Hilla, in Iraq, showed the devastating consequences, for combatants and non-combatants alike, of the use of these weapons. Reuters and Associated Press decided that the images were too awful to be released for television coverage. When these bombs explode, they spray smaller bomblets over an area the size of two football fields, distributing shrapnel and shredding human bodies. Even when used against military targets, says the report, the effects must be considered "disproportionate." The report then makes the obvious point that "the devastating consequences of using cluster bombs in civilian areas are utterly predictable."[75] Predictable indeed. On 20 July 2003, the *New York Times* reported on the air strikes on Iraq: "Air war commanders were required to obtain the approval of Defense Secretary Donald L. Rumsfeld if any planned air strike was thought likely to result in deaths of more than 30 civilians. More than 50 such strikes were proposed, and all of them were approved."[76] As Elshtain and the other just war defenders of the "war on terror" will hasten to point out, there is a moral distinction to be made between *intended* and *unintended* civilian casualties; there is, however, also a third category, which can be termed unintended but readily *foreseeable* civilian casualties. In the spirit of the just war tradition, it is to this category in particular that we must pay attention when attempting to discern whether the achievable goals of a military action are worth the price that must be paid.

The debate over the number of civilian casualties continues. A British organization called Iraq Body Count puts the number of civilian deaths, as of 2 June 2007, at between 64,776 and 70,934.[77] Iraq Body Count uses a survey of online news reports, which they cross-reference for credibility and accuracy. Some have criticized Iraq

Body Count because its dependence on media reporting makes the number of casualties appear smaller than it likely really is. On 25 October 2004, the well-respected British medical journal the *Lancet* published the results of a cluster study that put civilian casualties during and after the period of so-called "major combat" at around 100,000. They compared the increase in the risk of death, before and after the war, by comparing rates of death within their sample clusters for the two periods.[78] One of the problems with these kinds of statistical studies is that it is difficult to determine whether the casualties were the direct result of military action or the indirect result of, say, economic hardship, or a climate of anarchic violence and lawlessness, etc. But from the point of view of the just war theory this distinction is perhaps not so relevant. Part of the task of decision-makers, if they are to take the just war tradition seriously at all, is to factor in the *anticipated* destructive consequences of military action, and then to discern the value of their anticipated outcomes in that light. The good to be hoped for (within reason) cannot be outweighed by the harm that can reasonably be expected to occur.

With respect to what we might reasonably hope for in the "war on terror," the picture is far from clear. And the trope that 9/11 "changed everything" has dangerously distorted perceptions of the history of US relations to the states and peoples of the Middle East. The bright moral contrast of images between our Tomahawk missiles slamming precisely into our targets and passenger jets slamming precisely into theirs, may have blinded us to a number of other salient facts.

Elshtain says that one of the values of the just war tradition is that it does not tend to indulge utopian illusions, but rather enjoins a "tough-minded moral and political realism."[79] She is fond of quoting Hannah Arendt's remark that "politics is not the nursery." But to what extent does the picture of a world in which sometimes overcautious, sometimes blundering, but most often benevolent torchbearers for democracy and human rights square off against inexplicably malevolent, nihilist villains actually reflect such a "tough-minded" realism? One of the most striking, immediate, and lasting effects of the September 11 attacks is a pervasive sense that to ask what might have formed the context and background for such acts of violent hatred is not only in bad taste but somehow implies an unwitting complicity, on the part of the questioner, with the terrorists and their aims.

For the defenders of the "war on the terror" (which, in the interest of clarity, has included a war on Afghanistan and Iraq as well as the detainment of thousands of individuals outside the scope of local or international law), the question "Why?" is irrelevant. As Elshtain puts it: "I argue that such persons hate us for *what we are and what we represent and not for anything in particular that we have done.*" She dismisses the arguments of those who point to a disastrous history of US involvement in the region, for example, its uncritical support for Israel and for the occupation of Palestinian land: "It is reasonable to argue that certain changes in US foreign policy *might* reduce the attraction of radical Islamism to many young men. It is unreasonable to assume that changes in US foreign policy would disarm radical Islamism."[80]

Given the fact that the real danger in this "age of terror" is the evident capacity of violent extremist organizations like al Qaeda to form a large and lethally effective international network, it seems a little hasty to separate the issue of "the attraction of radical Islamism to many young men" from the aspiration to "disarm radical Islamism." There may well always be radical Islamists in the world, just as there may well always be Nazis, but the conditions that enable them to attract widespread support in the streets, and to mobilize an effective force, must be seen to have something to do with those decisions of governments that have touched directly on the lives of ordinary people.

Few would deny that the decisions of the parties to the Treaty of Versailles might have had something to do with the creation of conditions for Hitler's rise to power in pre-war Germany. Likewise, many would claim that those same decision-makers, the British, French, and (to a somewhat lesser extent at the time) American architects of the post-Ottoman Middle East, created an untenable situation there. Robert Fisk, a foreign correspondent for the *Independent* who has covered every major conflict in the region since the Soviet invasion of Afghanistan, and who has won more international awards for his work than any other correspondent, is alarmed by the unwillingness in the US media and governing elites to even engage the question of the background and context for the rise of militant Islamism.

The "why" question was quickly disposed of by the US administration – and left unvisited by American journalists – with a one-liner: "they hate our democracy." You were with us or against us ... the idea that the United States somehow "deserved" such an assault – that more than three thousand innocents should pay some kind of death-price for America's sins abroad – was immoral. But without any serious examination of what caused these acts of mass murder – political, historical reasons – then the United States and the world might set themselves on a warpath without end, a "war on terror" which, by its very nature, had no finite aim, no foreseeable conclusion, no direction except further war and fire and blood.

Fisk points out that, from the point of view of the Middle East, the claim that September 11 "changed everything" could not be credited: "Countless massacres of far greater dimensions had occurred in the Middle East over the previous decades without anyone suggesting that the world would never be the same again. The million and a half dead of the Iran–Iraq war – a bloodbath set in train by Saddam, with our active military support – elicited no such Manichean observation."

At the moment that the attacks in New York City began, Fisk was on a plane over the Atlantic expecting the next morning's *Independent* to carry his extensively researched story about a few days in September 1982 when "Israel's Phalangist militia allies started their three-day orgy of rape and knifing and murder in the Palestinian refugee camps of Sabra and Chatila."[81] This infamous massacre, for which many, including many Israelis, have held the Israeli Defence Forces directly responsible, was merely the darkest episode in a US-sanctioned Israeli invasion of southern Lebanon that cost 17,500 Lebanese and Palestinian lives.

It is difficult to imagine how any intellectual could maintain that a "tough-minded moral and political realism" can avoid reckoning with the facts of the history of constant humiliation suffered by the very people from whom the rank and file of al Qaeda must inevitably be drawn. No one has taken the trouble to compel Israel to comply with UN Security Council resolutions 242 and 338, which call for a withdrawal from the occupied territories. In fact, the current US government has consummated this betrayal of the Palestinians by now referring to their land as the "so-called" occupied territories. Few trouble to remember that long before the recent hapless US attempts to bring democracy to a devastated Iraq, there was in fact already a democracy in the Middle East – in the early 1950s, Mohamed Mossadeq governed Iran as its first and only democratically elected prime minister – and that it was toppled thanks to an Anglo-American plot because it was believed that Mossadeq was planning to interfere with a scandalously exploitative oil deal. Few trouble themselves to remember that the poisonous gases that President George W. Bush would later condemn Saddam Hussein for having possessed were in fact used extensively during the Iran–Iraq war with American knowledge and complicity – they had, after all, been supplied by the West. There are many who, like Elshtain, would say that these are not particularly relevant facts with respect to the attacks in New York – and that may well be a legitimate observation if we were conducting a war crimes trial – but the task of those who would, in a spirit of "tough-minded moral and political realism," bring the just war theory to bear in formulating a morally appropriate and effective response to terrorism is precisely to consider the whole context within which we must act. They must ask themselves whether the powers that overthrew the Middle East's first democracy in the name of oil interests, or whether the British, who mired themselves in a hopeless colonial occupation of Iraq less than a century ago, can now presume a *tabula rasa* upon which to write the latest chapter in the history of their meddling in the region. Our "tough mindedness," if we are to be serious about just war ethics, should first of all be directed toward our own most cherished illusions about our virtues. We must, after all, if we are planning to act, be in a position to seriously believe that the good we expect to accomplish will outweigh the harm that we will do.

Realism, in the tough-minded moral and political sense that Elshtain invokes, must be contrasted with the seductive and illusory power of the "image." The carefully crafted image of President George W. Bush, in 2003, standing on the deck of an aircraft carrier and declaring the "end of major combat" has become, in light of the cold fact that many more have died, and will continue to die *after* that declaration of victory, an ironic reminder of our hubris and our impotence. We are involved in what can only be an endless "war on terror" in part because we make our plans to suit our weapons; the power of our technology, and the images it projects, continue to delude us. Eventually, the Anglo-American occupiers will withdraw from Iraq, whatever the condition of the society they leave behind. High-tech aerial warfare does not build nations, and it does not rid the world of terror. One might hope that, rather than simply engaging in casuistry that would legitimate what our leaders, bureaucrats, and military planners would do in the future with the high-tech powers put at their disposal, just war theorists might seek to emphasize the limits of human moral action. But as the rhetoric heats up on the question of Iran's nuclear program, we can be assured that, even if it is never carried out, a plan for "surgical strikes" is being formulated, computer simulations are being run, and just war theorists will have to figure out how much flexibility they can find in their doctrine.

The new technology of war has by no means rendered the older nuclear technology innocuous. Whenever India and Pakistan rattle their nuclear sabres over the barbed wire of Kashmir, the world drifts perhaps once again to the brink of a catastrophe. Nevertheless, we are, for the time being, out from under the stranglehold of mutually assured destruction. Precision-guided munitions, being more accurate than older weapons, may enable armies to target strategic objectives without having to engage in indiscriminate bombings. But they also enable us to make war without heed for the consequences. They put the consequences of our violence at a greater remove, and they thereby enable us to casually incorporate such violence into the business of international diplomacy and police work.

The modern technology of war, like all modern technology, is its own engine. We did not develop precision-guided munitions to uphold the just war doctrine, any more than we developed nuclear weapons to subvert it. In both cases, what came to pass did so because it was "technically sweet." That motive force has, quite simply, become indifferent to our scruples.

6

Reproductive Technologies:
The End of Sexual Ethics

From time immemorial, as they say, human beings, like every other animal species, have perpetuated themselves by what might be called the essentially natural processes of sexual intercourse between males and females. Insofar as there was a specifically human control over this process, it was provided by human culture, which assigned specific roles to men and women in society. Culture, which transformed animal breeding with its rutting seasons into human sexual relations based on social relationships, determined the nature of kinship and gender, the roles of males and females, and the appropriate context for sexual relationships and procreation. Although methods of contraception have been used since ancient times,[1] until the nineteenth century little was known about the process by which ovum and sperm combined to form a human conceptus, and less was known about the process by which the genetic inheritance of the fetus was determined. It was inconceivable, therefore, that either conception or genetic transmission could be controlled.

In the twentieth century all this changed as our knowledge of biology and genetics increased immensely. As well, we learned to apply the knowledge and techniques developed in animal husbandry to human procreation. With our expansion of knowledge has come the "technologization of reproduction." This has taken a number of specific forms in the twentieth century. Reproductive technologies generally function within these contexts: positive eugenics, negative eugenics, a cure for infertility, and DNA research. Each of these has raised serious ethical issues for the human community and in the process has revealed the confusion and, at times, the nihilism at the heart of the modern scientific project.

Positive eugenics, which involves identifying a specific genotype and breeding for it, lost much of its allure for scientists after it was undertaken by the Nazis for specifically racist purposes. In its simplest form, it entails the storing of the sperm and the ova of particularly valued human beings (Nobel prize-winners has been one group suggested), and then the use of artificial insemination from a donor for selective conception. Artificial insemination is routine now, but, given the terrible consequences of German experimentation that were revealed during the Nuremberg trials,[2] neither scientists nor politicians have seriously proposed using reproductive technologies to improve the race in this way. However, as the cloning of human beings becomes more feasible, one can only assume that there will be specific genotypes recommended for artificial reproduction, undiluted by sexual generation. For the present, positive (or progressive) eugenics is likely to remain on hold. We will not be overly concerned with this kind of eugenics in this chapter or the next.

Here we are concerned, although only indirectly, with medical or therapeutic genetic manipulation – a particular form of negative eugenics – which may equally have as its purpose to improve the genetic pool or, at least, to prevent it from deteriorating. In this case, it is argued that although the effects of genetically transmitted diseases (for example, diabetes) have been controlled thanks to new medical treatment (for example, the development of insulin), this means that, from generation to generation, more people with diabetes (who, before the discovery of insulin, might have died before reaching child-bearing age) are having children. One way of limiting the deterioration of the genetic pool is by the voluntary sterilization of those carrying genetic diseases. Gene-line therapy, whereby the basic human genetic code is mapped and manipulated, and "sperm and/or egg cells are changed to permanently alter the reproductive line for all generations to come," is being proposed.[3] In other cases genetic surgery may be used to engender a child without defective genes. Scientists, it is said, "can identify genetic sequences that are defective, and soon scientists will be able to replace these defects with properly functioning genes."[4] Either artificial insemination or innovulation might be used to provide a healthy substitute for the sperm or the ovum of the parent who carries the defective gene.

All these procedures entail extensive genetic screening, which often is combined with selective abortion or pre-implantation genetic diagnosis to minimize the number of children born with specific genetic defects. The medical profession in most developed countries has encouraged genetic screening, has legitimated abortion in such cases, and is sometimes arguing for the acceptability of infant euthanasia on similar grounds. This combination of genetic screening and selective abortion is arguably a form of negative eugenics. If so, then it is the most widely accepted and practised form of eugenics since the fall of Nazi Germany. Those who would argue that this practice does not constitute a form of negative eugenics claim that screening and selective abortion are matters of individual choice (i.e., the mother's choice), while positive eugenics, such as that practised by the Nazis (to "purify" the race), was a matter of coercion and state power. Whether or not this distinction is decisive is a matter of some ethical import. We shall briefly consider this problem in chapter 8.

Regardless, the most widespread, and perhaps still the most dramatic, applications of reproductive technology over the past fifty years do not attempt to improve the human race but to provide a solution to infertility. In doing so they open up the possibility of improving the quality of our offspring. Test-tube babies,[5] surrogate mothers, and frozen embryos have become commonplace, as have the legal problems that have emerged with reproductive procedures. The absence of a clear ethical framework within which we can think personally and legislate politically about these new methods of procreation has become obvious.

Let us first outline some of the intricacies of such procedures. In its simplest form, the infertility of a woman may be caused by some type of mechanical blockage that prevents a partner's sperm from uniting with her ovum. In this case, artificial insemination using the husband's or partner's sperm may solve the problem. If, however, the infertility is the result of the partner's inability to produce sufficient or adequately healthy sperm to fertilize the woman's ovum, artificial insemination from an unrelated or anonymous donor may be employed. In both of these cases, the conception takes place in the woman's womb and the embryo is biologically the mother's child. Obviously, in the second instance, the child is legally but not biologically the partner's.

If the fertility problem is due to the woman's inability to produce healthy ova, artificial innovulation from an (ordinarily) anonymous donor may allow her to bear a child who is biologically her partner's but not her own. But this requires *in vitro* fertilization (IVF), the combining of sperm and ova in a petri dish, the development of the embryo to a certain stage, and then the transplanting of the embryo into the woman's womb, where it can develop normally. IVF may be used as a cure for infertility using the sperm and the ovum of a couple (homologous *in vitro* fertilization) when for medical reasons the couple is unable to conceive through sexual intercourse. Ova are extracted by laparoscopy and fertilized by the partner's sperm. Laboratory culture is performed to the blastocyst stage, when the embryo is transferred to the woman's uterus.[6] In this case the child is biologically the man's and the woman's, even though it was not conceived by them. When a woman is unable to produce her own ova, heterologous IVF, using another woman's ova, may be used, and she can carry her partner's child to term. Surrogate motherhood may be used when a woman is unwilling or unable to carry the child to term. It allows a couple to have a child who is biologically theirs if another woman will agree to carry the embryo conceived in a petri dish.

All of these procedures do not so much cure infertility as bypass it; that is, they do not medically solve the physical problem preventing a couple from conceiving. They have been widely accepted in developed societies in the last thirty years. Just as men and women have, thanks to contraceptives, been freed to have sexual relations with minimal risk of having babies, they have, when necessary, sought to have babies conceived without sexual relations but with reproductive technologies. These procedures leave us with a broad range of ethical and legal questions that can be (over) simplified in this way: what are the limits to our rights to conceive, bear, abandon, or kill human offspring? The medical profession has not waited for an answer. The quest for technical solutions to perennial human problems has spurred doctors and biologists onward, and they have generally been guided by the technological imperative "What can be done should be done."

The question of the ethical (as opposed to the technical) limits to the biological experiments designed to solve the infertility problems of married couples, or to eliminate defects from the gene pool, was raised most explicitly by Paul Ramsey over thirty-five years ago. In 1970, he wrote:

We need to raise the ethical questions with a serious and not a frivolous conscience. A man of frivolous conscience announces that there are ethical quandaries ahead that we must urgently consider before the future catches up with us. By this he often means that we need to devise a new ethics that will provide the rationalization for doing in the future what men are bound to do because of new actions and interventions science will have made possible. In contrast a man of serious conscience means to say in raising urgent ethical questions that there may be some things that men should never do. Good things that men do can be made complete only by the things that they refuse to do.[7]

Ramsey went on to outline three contexts within which the acceptability of biological experimentation should be considered: the ethics of abortion and respect for human life, the ethics of experimentation on human subjects, and the ethics of human parenthood. The ethics of abortion is not relevant to the discussion of artificial insemination from either the woman's partner or an anonymous donor because no fetal life is destroyed or put at risk in these procedures. We will therefore focus our discussion on IVF.

This procedure has required the destruction of human embryos at a very early stage of their development in order to perfect the technique. Even now, IVF ordinarily involves the fertilization of two or three ova and the destruction of those embryos that appear less perfect in order to guarantee that the one transferred into the mother's womb is as healthy as possible. The routine destruction of embryonic life has been and is ordinarily required for the creation of test-tube babies. The attitude of many doctors and ethicists considering this experimentation has followed the transformation of societies' attitude to abortion; the legalization of therapeutic abortion has meant that "in law" the "humanity" of fetal life is denied. The human fetus is not a "person"; it does not deserve legal protection while in its mother's womb. It would seem to follow that a human embryo does not deserve legal protection in the lab.

A similar approach has often been used to eliminate any concern that might arise from the "ethics of experimentation on human subjects," or what has been called "the Nuremberg tradition."[8] If embryonic or fetal life is not human, then all of the legal provisions put in place by the Nuremberg code as a response to the atrocities perpetrated by Nazi medical practitioners like Dr Mengele do not apply. The medical researcher is then liberated to "create" human life in the laboratory, experiment on it in the interests of science, and destroy it at the appropriate time because it is not deemed human.

In 1970, before such experimentation became commonplace, Paul Ramsey explained why he viewed it as unethical:

Because we ought not to choose for a child – whose procreation we are contemplating – the injury he may bear, there is no way that we can morally get to know whether many things now planned are technically feasible or not. We need not ask whether we should clone a man or not, or what use is to be made of frozen semen or ovum banks, or what sort of life we ought to create in hatcheries, etc., since we can only begin to perfect these techniques in no other way than by subjecting another human being to risks to which he cannot consent as our coadventurer in promoting medical or scientific "progress." The putative volition of the child we are trying to learn how to manufacture, must, anyway, be said to be negative, since researchers who work with human beings do not claim that they are ever allowed to ask volunteers to face possibly suicidal risks or to place themselves at risk of grave deformity.[9]

In the late 1970s Leon Kass, who has become the most prominent bioethicist of our era and who recently chaired the President's Council on Bioethics in the US,[10] began to articulate Ramsey's ethical concern about medical experimentation on human subjects. He pointed out that the problem of infertility due to tubal obstruction could be cured by "surgical reconstruction of the oviduct, which, if successful, permanently removes the cause of infertility (i.e., it treats the underlying disease, not merely the desire to have a child)."[11] Because IVF constitutes an experiment on the prospective child "beyond any loose sense in which we might call the generation of any child experimental,"[12] we should prefer oviduct repair.[13]

The third context within which Ramsey considered the new reproductive technologies was the ethics of marriage and human parenthood. Needless to say, as Western societies have been secularized, there is as little consensus about the norms that should govern this aspect of human life as there is regarding abortion and human experimentation on embryonic life. Traditional Christian morality understands marriage to have two main purposes: the mutual love and sanctification of the partners, and the procreation of children. Sexual relations were to be limited to the context of marriage because they were considered symbolic or sacramental, that is, they expressed the committed love of the partners, and they opened the couple to the possibility of pregnancy, which could be handled responsibly only in the context of that committed love. Modern liberal societies have moved toward the dissociation of the two goods of marriage; people have begun to view sexual expression as a free, personal end that has no necessary relation to procreation or to interpersonal love, and they have begun to view procreation as a technical procedure that can be dissociated from what theologians like Ramsey have called the "act of love" and the "sphere of love."[14]

Ramsey took the view that, ideally, conception should take place through an act of love, that is, through sexual intercourse that is an expression of mutual caring and self-giving, and in a sphere of love, that is, in a committed relationship between the man who contributes the sperm (and thereby his genetic inheritance) and the woman whose ovum is fertilized by it. If there is committed love between the contributor of the sperm and the ovum, conception need not take place through an act of love (sexual intercourse), provided that the ethics of abortion and the ethics of human experimentation are respected. For this reason, Ramsey judged artificial insemination from a husband donor morally acceptable but rejected artificial insemination from an anonymous donor since there is no committed love between the donor and the prospective mother. Even though in homologous IVF the child is conceived within a sphere of love, he opposed it on two grounds. At least in its experimental phase, it required the destruction of fetal life and it involved an illicit experiment on the unborn. Needless to say, Ramsey's arguments have been deemed irrelevant to a post-Christian world, where liberalism makes a distinction between what is human and what is a person.

A position consistent with political liberalism (which defends the right to choose not to have a child if it is already conceived and to produce a child artificially if a couple is unable to conceive) has been developed.[15] Many of its implications were spelled out by Mary Warnock. A former fellow of St Hugh's College, Oxford, and subsequently a Cambridge philosopher, Warnock was asked in 1984 to chair a national committee of inquiry into the ethics of embryo use and assisted human fertilization in Great Britain. The committee, made up of doctors, lawyers, theologians, social scientists, and ordinary citizens, considered IVF as well as other reproductive technologies. It issued what came to be known

as the Warnock report. *A Question of Life* offered public policy advice and recommendations to government ministers.[16]

After looking at some of the British statistics for IVF treatment
between October 1980 and May 1984, Warnock concluded that the
technique had passed the research stage and was now an established procedure.[17] She seemed to be saying that what had
transpired without ethical discussion should now be legitimated
ethically and controlled professionally. She recommended, therefore, that IVF should continue to be available "subject to the same
type of licensing and inspection recommended with regard to the
regulations of AID [artificial insemination from a donor]."[18] One
aspect of this regulation was that any third party donating sperm or
ova for an infertility treatment should remain anonymous to the
couple being helped.[19] Any IVF treatment must be administered by
a registered medical practitioner, and subject to licensing arrangements.[20] The consent in writing of both partners should be obtained before treatment wherever possible as a matter of good
practice.[21] Furthermore, when the donation of gametes – the specialized germ cells that come together during fertilization (conception) in organisms that reproduce sexually – is involved, the IVF
child should be treated in law as the legitimate offspring of the
woman who carries the child and her husband unless it can be
shown that the husband has not consented to the procedure.[22]

Warnock recommended that the number of children who can be
fathered by donations from any one donor be limited to ten. In addition, there should be a gradual move toward a system where semen donors are paid only their expenses. On reaching the age of
eighteen, the child should have access to the basic information
about the donor's ethnic origin. But the donor must have no parental rights or duties in relation to the child.[23]

Warnock expressed much concern about the embryos produced
by IVF, although this concern did not include a discussion of the legitimacy of the experimentation undertaken in bringing them into
being or their right to continued life once they have been brought
into being. She recommended regulating storage and ownership of
and experimentation on embryos. Warnock stated that embryos
should be stored for a maximum of ten years, after which time the
right to use or dispose of them should pass to the storage authority.[24] She recommended that there should be no right to own a human embryo, but that the couple should have the rights, subject to

limitation, to the use or disposal of an embryo. Where there is disagreement between the couple, the right to determine the use or disposal of an embryo should pass to the storage authority. Warnock also made it clear that for the purposes of establishing progeniture, the time of birth, not the time of fertilization, should be the determining factor.[25]

With respect to research, Warnock felt that human embryos should not be used if the same purposes could be achieved by the use of other animals or in some other way.[26] Research on human IVF embryos should be permitted only under licence.[27] The same should apply to human gametes or embryos.[28] Furthermore, no human embryo that is derived from IVF and not transferred to a woman should be kept alive or used as a research subject beyond fourteen days after fertilization, not including any time during which the embryo may have been frozen.[29] Research might be carried out on an embryo, regardless of whether it was a spare embryo or one created for the purposes of research. However, the consent of the couple for whom the spare embryo was generated would be necessary.[30]

Warnock omitted any lengthy discussion of Paul Ramsey's third concern, the ethics of human parenthood, which bears directly on the question of who should have access to IVF. She mentioned that "as a general rule" it is better for children to have both a mother and a father, but she did not recommend that this be dealt with in restrictive legislation. She approached the issue from a "situation ethics" approach, and maintained that "this question of eligibility for treatment is a very difficult one … The committee decided it was not possible to draw up comprehensive criteria that would be sensitive to the circumstances of every case."[31] Warnock assumed, therefore, that IVF would be available to married or single women on the grounds that "normal" conception happens to both married and single women and that children may be raised without fathers. But she assumed also that IVF could be made available to people for whom "normal" conception was not possible (for example, post-menopausal women). No absolute principles deriving from the ethics of parenthood could be applied in the case of IVF.

And yet Warnock remained unequivocally opposed to surrogate motherhood on the grounds that the relationship between the surrogate and the couple becomes exploitative when financial interests are involved.[32] (Did she really think that financial considerations would not be involved in the establishment and utilization of IVF clinics?) Her opposition to the commodification of reproduction led her to accept an absolute principle in this case. On the other hand, she argued that principles cannot exist to regulate procedures that have only been possible for less than twenty years. Utilitarian considerations, a concern for the common good, and existential individualism are all combined into a situation ethic that has the flexibility to manage IVF without restricting it in the name of any of the ethical criteria proposed by Ramsey.

The Warnock Report was issued in June 1984. It became the basis of a subsequent bill responding to the recommendation that had been at the top of the Committee's list, "that 'a new statutory licencing authority be established to regulate both research and those infertility services which [they had] recommended be subject to control.' [It] had been implemented ... by the establishment of an 'interim' body to undertake licencing and inspection of fertility services and research establishments."[33] The other recommendations were put on hold until a White Paper was published in the fall of 1987. It formed the basis of a series of debates at the committee stage. As a result of these debates, "the crucial clause permitting research using human embryos up to fourteen days from fertilization was passed by a substantial majority."[34] The Human Fertilization and Embryology Bill was passed in the British House of Commons in 1990.

About the same time, feminists expressed a vital concern to manage the use of reproductive technologies in general (and IVF in particular) in the interests of women. For liberal feminists this did not mean restricting access to IVF. A good example of their approach was provided by Christine Overall in *Ethics and Human Reproduction: A Feminist Analysis*, which highlighted "women's experience, needs and behaviour in connection with reproduction."[35] Overall's approach assumed that women have been and are the victims of oppression and patriarchy. She opposed a socially sanctioned biological determinism in which sexual and reproductive differences between the genders are fundamental to their different roles. The Marxist roots of her feminism were apparent in her concerns about the commodification of reproduction,[36] whereby economic relations are introduced into the social patterns of human reproduction so that the embryo/fetus is considered a type of consumer good that can be made to order and purchased on the open market. As such it is treated as a product that can be planned and improved upon. The actual cost of an embryo can be seen clearly in the prices charged for such services as IVF.[37]

Overall maintained that the embryo/fetus has become a new type of property to be owned. Obsession with ownership, in turn, increased the potential for the manipulation and exploitation of women. For example, poor women may be induced to supply embryos for profit. This creates a new opportunity for "using the bodies of women and exerting control over their reproductive capacities."[38] Overall argued that the designers, promoters, and deliverers of fetal treatments such as IVF would profit from them, while scientists and physicians would decide who was eligible for them and which embryos would be transferred. But women, particularly poor women, would be left out of the decision-making process.

Although artificial reproduction may enable an infertile woman to have her own child, it is a doctor or a scientist, usually male, who "gives" this child to her. Hence Overall stated that the "use of technology represents a powerful version of the male appropriation of women's reproductive power."[39] She quoted Germaine Greer, who referred to the successful fertility specialist as the "technological version of the polygamous patriarch,"[40] and argued that IVF may reinforce passive, uninvolved acquiescence, especially on the part of female patients.[41] Overall pointed out that the desire for children is at least in part manufactured, as is the need to have a child that is genetically one's own.[42] But she argued that the importance of this genetic link does not, by itself, justify the use of IVF. On the other hand, the availability of technologies such as IVF contributes to the desire for one's own genetic offspring.

Overall characterized her approach to reproductive technologies as "a sort of *via negativa*,"[43] which says more about what should *not* be done than about what should be done in the treatment of the embryo/fetus. First, she proposed the stringent restrictions of all programs, institutions, research projects, and contracts that serve to promote the commodification of reproduction. We should cease to treat the embryo/fetus as an ongoing work of art or a scientific experiment.[44] She argued that less emphasis should be placed on providing apparent benefit for this embryo/fetus and more emphasis on the Hippocratic injunction "*primum non nocere*" ("first do no harm"), that is, the moral obligation of non-maleficence. Thus the burden of proof would be on those who might cause harm rather than on those who wish to avoid it.[45] Third, Overall insisted that the embryo should not be discussed in a way that divorces it from the woman within whom it flourishes. She blamed techniques like IVF for encouraging the acceptance of the idea that the embryo/fetus is a separate being with no relation to the woman who gestates it.[46]

In spite of all these concerns, Overall's liberalism prevailed against all ethical considerations (even those that would appear to be enjoined by her feminism), and she refused to recommend any legal restriction to the development or implementation of IVF on the basis of any moral principle. Her concern for the embryo/fetus did not lead her to limit abortion or IVF in any way. Her principle of non-maleficence lead her, in a brilliant circumlocution, to recommend that we use the "least mutilating means of abortion which ... [take] all reasonable measures to preserve the life of the fetus insofar as these are consistent with carrying out the abortion."[47] Nor did the principle of non-maleficence lead her to restrict the experiments in the production of embryos. Presumably, the desire to have a child of one's own was enough to legitimate such experimentation to start with. As for the ethics of human parenthood, it provides no hard and fast rules. "Fitness to parent cannot ... be evaluated on an a priori basis; ... it can be assessed only from an individual case."[48] Whether single or married, homosexual or heterosexual, all women should have equal access to IVF. Although reproductive technologies like IVF may have negative consequences for women, Overall's liberal feminist ethics did not want to close any doors.

The radical feminism of Janice Raymond, on the other hand, presented a challenge to reproductive liberalism. All of the feminist concerns that failed to move Overall to restrict IVF led Raymond in the opposite direction. She began *Women as Wombs* by questioning the idea that infertility is a disease.[49] She argued that "as traumatic as the absence of children may be for some people, infertility is no more a disease than is the absence of other capabilities."[50] Her concern was that the medical profession was "hyping infertility to market technological reproduction."[51] To this end it had created an image of infertility as a feminine disease and arbitrarily defined it as the failure to conceive after one year of intercourse without contraception. Yet it is known that male-factor infertility is as common as

women's could
choose to
work with "patriarchal"
notions, etc.

female-factor infertility, and as many as half of the couples considered infertile will conceive within two years without treatment.[52]

Like Overall, Raymond believed that women's preoccupation
with fertility was rooted in a spermatic economy, in which women
exist for sex and reproduction. Reproductive freedom must, therefore, include a resistance to motherhood as the primary social institution by encouraging the option not to marry and not to have
children. Doctors' preoccupation with reproductive techniques
like IVF is motivated more by the desire to test their techniques
than to treat women. Raymond asked the question, "Do these technologies benefit women – not only individual women but women as
a social group?"[53] Her answer was no. She urged feminists to move
away from the liberal view that if reproductive technologies were
regulated and imbued with woman-caring principles (as Warnock
and Overall proposed), they might serve women better.[54] Regulation was intended only to promote reproductive technologies and
manage the risks to women, not to eliminate those risks. Hence,
according to Raymond, we must abolish IVF. The vendors and pur-
veyors of technological reproduction must be penalized. Any interventions at the national level must also be enforced internationally,
and any laws enacted must not limit women's rights in other areas.[55]

Raymond was aware that one could permit any reproductive
technology, no matter how unethical, in the name of the rights of
choice, privacy, and procreative liberty, since any new technology
would increase women's choices. She wanted, therefore, to ground
rights in power, justice, self-determination, and international relations. Yet she applied these concepts to women alone and did not
consider the fetus as having any status or rights independent of the
mother. As a pro-choice feminist she seemed to assume that the fetus has only the status that the mother gives it. Although Raymond
opposed the harvesting of fetal tissue from abortion clinics, she did
so not because she rejected abortion but because she feared that
women might be pressured into becoming pregnant, for example,
with the intention of aborting for a family member who had
Parkinson's disease and needed such tissue.[56]

Raymond condemned IVF because she judged that the consequences of the procedure were collectively negative for women,
even though the procedure might be considered positive in the view
of individual women. (In this respect, then, women should *not* have
the right to choose.) But her condemnation had no relationship to

Ramsey's principles derived from an ethics of parenthood, namely that a child should be born as a result of an act of love between father and mother, or in their sphere of love, ordinarily marriage. Raymond was in favour of "debiologizing" – which we take to mean de-procreatizing – sex. This led her to favour the unlimited extension of women's reproductive rights to birth control and abortion, which allow women to have sex without having babies. Yet she argued against reproductive technologies like IVF, which allow people to have babies without having sex.

Raymond's rather confused argument (which relies on the ambiguity of the verb "biologize") goes like this:

The biologizing of sexual relationships reduces physical capabilities, feelings and experiences, such as orgasms and breast feeding, to instincts or drives. Physical elements and biological capacities, such as the mother's ability to feel the fetus moving in the womb, become statements about maternal instincts and bonds. It has taken centuries to begin the debiologizing of sexuality. It is time that we debiologized motherhood as well, not by technologizing or making it into a contractual issue, not by denying its location in female bodies, but by refusing its identification as female nature.[57]

One might point out in passing that the postmodern, largely Nietzschean, critique of all forms of essentializing, and the rejection of (normative) doctrines of human nature, generally serve to legitimate the technological project. Human beings do not have a nature; they have a history; history describes the past; it can never either predict the future or give us criteria about how it should be ordered; it is up to human will and imagination to direct the refashioning of all of nature, including human nature. The postmodern critique of essentializing (since it involves a sustained attack on the doctrine of natural law) is not able to provide us with any conception of degradation or degeneration by which we might ethically evaluate processes like the "debiologizing" of sex (via the techniques of birth control or abortion) or parenthood (via reproductive technologies like IVF or asexual reproduction like cloning). If motherhood – or parenthood – has no essential nature, then no mutation of motherhood (including that involved in the technologization of reproduction) can be considered "dehumanizing."

Feminists like Overall and Raymond come to different conclusions about reproductive technologies because their notion of what women's fulfillment entails is different. But there is nothing absolute or permanent about that notion. For a liberal feminist like Overall, women's freedom of choice is good in itself, regardless of what women's choices are. She thinks that if positive life choices are promoted for women and reproductive technologies are shown for what they really are, women will not opt for procedures such as IVF. On the other hand, a radical feminist like Raymond argues that although freedom of choice is necessary for women, it is not sufficient grounds for permitting procedures that, in her view, are clearly harmful to women. One must look past the issue of freedom of choice and introduce restrictions based on the judgment that it is harmful for women to view (their own) children as essential to their fulfillment.

Neither Overall nor Raymond offers us any *clear and consistent* feminist principles that might guide the development and restriction of IVF. They simply provide an analysis of consequences. But consequences can only be known after the fact, and they leave the feminist with only one question: How are women affected by the procedure? In the light of the evaluation of the social and personal consequences for women, one can then either restrict the implementation of IVF by determining public policy and legal practice, as Raymond wishes, or one can rely on persuasion (which in a capitalist society means advertising and education) to guide the free choice of women. Since we live in a liberal capitalist society, is it any surprise that liberal feminism (with its refusal to establish restrictions or set limits on IVF) has triumphed?

Perhaps the ethical reflections of Leon Kass[58] (who is considered by many of his critics to be extremely conservative in his approach to bioethics) demonstrate the reasons why. Unlike Warnock, Overall, or Raymond, Kass is aware of the philosophical and ethical dilemma that is at the heart of the debate about reproductive technologies. These procedures, he argues, must be placed within the context of genetic engineering and behaviour control "with which men deliberately exercise power over future generations." Kass sees the import of the point C.S. Lewis made over sixty years ago:

If any one age really attains, by eugenics and scientific education, the power to make its descendants what it pleases, all men who live after it are patients of that power. They are weaker, not stronger: for though we may have put wonderful machines in their hands, we have pre-ordained how they are to use them ... The real picture is that of one dominant age ... which resists all previous ages most irresistibly, and thus is the master of the human species. But even within this master generation (itself an infinitesimal minority of the species) the power will be exercised by a minority smaller still. Man's conquest of Nature, if the dreams of some scientific planners are realized, means the rule of a few hundred of men over billions and billions of men. There nei-ther is nor can be any simple increase of power on man's side. Each new power won *by* man is a power *over* man as well.[60]

Kass, interestingly, does not see the greatest danger as being the use of the newly achieved scientific knowledge or control by the state, the medical profession, or research scientists in an Orwellian way. Technical control will not likely be used in a totalitarian way against the will of the individual patient or the public. Rather, the greatest danger is voluntary self-degradation or willing dehuman-ization "as the unintended yet often inescapable consequences of relentlessly and successfully pursuing our humanitarian goals."[61] Kass sees the cautionary dystopic vision of Aldous Huxley's *Brave New World* as more likely than Orwell's vision in *1984*, although we need not contrast the two. They can go hand in hand: Nihilists and last men will both abound, according to Nietzsche's prediction. Kass contends: "The use of technology, uninformed by the wisdom of proper human ends, and untempered by an appropriate humil-ity and awe, can unwittingly render us all less than human. Unlike the man reduced by disease or slavery, the people dehumanized à la *Brave New World* are not miserable, don't know they are dehu-manized, and what is worse, would not care if they knew. They are, indeed, happy slaves with a slavish happiness."[62]

Kass fears the depersonalization (and the consequent dehu-manization) that will result from increasing our control over pro-creation by transferring it from the home to the laboratory; he fears the degradation of human parenthood and the dissolution of the family. And so, in considering IVF, he returns to the basic questions raised by Ramsey. He does so with an awareness that the language of (individual) rights is inadequate to the discussion, even though in liberal societies it may be the only language available. "Ultimately, to consider infertility (or procreation) solely from the perspective of individual rights can only undermine – in thought and practice – the meaning of childbearing and its bond to the covenant of marriage. And in a technological age, to view infertility as a disease, one demanding treatment by physicians, automatically fosters the development and encourages the use of all the new technologies above."[63]

In an early essay, written in 1971, Kass, linking his concerns about abuses of power with those about the voluntary degradation of human beings, appeared to agree with Ramsey about the immorality and the illegitimacy of experimentation that generates human beings in the laboratory. He asked: "Can anyone ethically consent for non-therapeutic interventions in which parents or scientists work their wills or their eugenic visions on the child-to-be? Would not such manipulation represent in itself an abuse of power, independent of consequences?"[64]

In a later discussion of IVF, after it had become fairly common practice, Kass put the question in different terms: "Does the parents' desire for a child (or the obstetrician's desire to help them get one) entitle them to have it by methods which carry for the child an untested risk of deformity or malformation?"[65] He pointed out that, before the IVF of Louise Brown by Steptoe and Edwards in 1978, the risks were very much unknown, even in higher animal species like monkeys. He also explained that there was still no way of finding out whether the product of IV conception would be deformed. But Kass, relieved by 1985 that the IVF experience had been "so encouraging," then disagreed with Ramsey's judgment that we can only get to know how to perform the procedure by conducting unethical experiments. He concluded that

if having children is regarded primarily as the satisfaction of parental desires, to attain our own fulfillment and happiness, then Ramsey's argument seems to me decisive. But if we have children not primarily for ourselves but for our children, if procreation means to pass on the gift of life to the next generation, if the gift of life can be held to be morally at least the equal of therapy, then this clear benefit to a child-to-be – even to a child-at-risk as all of our children are – could justify the risks taken because they are taken in the child's behalf – provided, of course that the risks are not excessive. This is now my view.[66]

Kass went on to suggest that the risks should be approximately equivalent to the risks to the child from normal procreation. He did not attend to the fact that one could only determine the risks, much less their acceptability, by skating down the slippery slope that he had just flooded and frozen. If the benefit of existence was the reason for undertaking the risks, only one who would argue for the superiority of non-existence could oppose IVF in an a priori fashion.

Having already disposed of Ramsey's objection to IVF (that it is an illicit experiment on a human subject), Kass proceeded to a discussion of the status of the *in vitro* fertilized embryo and the disposal of surplus embryos. He pointed out that "while the egg and sperm are alive as cells, something new and alive *in a different sense* comes into being with fertilization. The truth of this is unaffected by the fact that fertilization takes time and is not an instantaneous event. For after fertilization is *complete*, there exists a new individual with its unique genetic identity, fully potent for the self-initiated development into a mature human being, if circumstance are cooperative."[67] This did not mean to Kass that a blastocyst was "in a *full* sense" a human being, but "even the human blastocyst *in vitro* is not humanly nothing; it possesses a power to become what everyone will agree is a human being."[68] Nor did this mean to Kass that the blastocyst was endowed with a right to life or that failure to implant it amounted to negligent homicide. But, he claimed, the blastocyst deserves our respect. "The human embryo is not mere meat; it is not just stuff; it is not a thing. Because of its origin and because of its capacity, it commands a higher respect."[69]

The question Kass was left with is: How much respect? And here he began to equivocate:

As much as for a fully developed human being? My own inclination is to say probably not, but who can be certain? Indeed there might be prudential and reasonable grounds for an affirmative answer, partly because the presumption of ignorance ought to err in the direction of never underestimating the basis for respect of human life (not least, for our own self-respect), partly because so many people feel strongly that even the blastocyst is protectably human. As a first approximation, I would analogize the early embryo *in vitro* to the early embryo *in utero* (because both are potentially viable and human). On this ground alone, the most sensible policy is to treat *the early embryo as a previable fetus, with constraints imposed on early embryo research at least as great as those on fetal research.*[70]

This analysis of the status of the embryo led Kass to accept implantation and thus to conclude that the IVF and transfer procedure "is perfectly compatible with a respect and reverence for human life, including potential human life."[71] Kass believed this to be the case even when several eggs were removed and fertilized to improve the chances of success. "Assuming nothing further is done with the unimplanted embryos, there is nothing disrespectful going on."[72] This was an odd statement since Kass knew that something further had to be done to the embryo: it would be killed or allowed to die either before or after being frozen as a possible backup to the procedure; it would be used in manipulative experimentation; or it could be used in experiments that attempt perpetuation *in vitro* beyond the blastocyst stage, ultimately perhaps to viability.

It was disingenuous for Kass to say that nothing disrespectful is going on because in the same article he rejected a simplistic naturalism. He asserted that "the natural occurrence of embryo and fetal loss and wastage does not justify all deliberate humanly caused destruction of fetal life. For example, the natural loss of embryos in early pregnancy cannot in itself be a warrant for deliberately aborting them or for invasively experimenting on them *in vitro*, any more than stillbirths could be a justification of newborn infanticide. There are many things that happen naturally that we ought not to do deliberately."[73]

The question, then, was not "may we destroy surplus embryos that have proven useless to the IVF procedure?" The question was, rather, "may we produce more than one embryo in the full awareness that one (or more) of the embryos must be disposed of or allowed to die?" Kass used the naturalist argument that he himself had just refuted to propose that we may. "The closeness to natural procreation – the goal is the same, the embryonic loss is unavoidable and not desired, and the amount of loss is similar – leads me to believe that we do no more intentional or unjustified harm in one case than in the other."[74]

This is a convenient belief, but it is not true. A couple who have accepted the legitimacy of homologous IVF but oppose the destruction of an embryo may decide to produce only one embryo for transfer and to accept all the risks that this entails.[75] The production of more than one means that the embryonic loss (the destruction of the embryo that Kass has argued deserves respect, or its

McCormia,
Hao Brown's word?

transfer for adoption into another infertile woman or its use for investigative purposes) becomes inevitable, intentional, and willed. This is not true of "natural" embryonic loss through miscarriage. In his earlier article Kass himself had been more accurate. He pointed out that

here, nascent lives are being deliberately created despite certain knowledge that many of them will be destroyed or discarded. (Several eggs are taken for fertilization from each woman, the extra ones being available for experimentation.) Unlike the unwanted fetuses killed in abortion, the embryos discarded here are wanted, at least for a while; they are deliberately created, used for a time, and then deliberately destroyed. Even if there is no wrong done by discarding at the blastocyst stage – and I am undecided on this question – there certainly would be at later stages.[76]

Kass concluded his later discussion of experimentation on human subjects and the treatment of surplus embryos by arguing against experimentation (and ectogenesis) on unimplanted embryos. For reasons to do with lineage, he opposed the use of surplus embryos by other couples. Kass drew an apparently "paradoxical conclusion about the treatment of the unimplanted embryos: leave them alone and do not create embryos for experimentation only."[77]

It is under the rubric of lineage, parenthood, embodiment, and gender that Kass dealt with what we have called the ethics of human parenthood. In the case of homologous IVF, like that of Louise Brown, he argued that these concerns are met:

The desire to have a child of one's own is a couple's desire to embody out of the conjugal union of their separate bodies, a child who is flesh of their separate flesh made one. This archaic language may seem quaint, but I would argue that this is precisely what is being celebrated by most people who rejoice at the birth of Louise Brown whether they would articulate it this way or not. Mr and Mrs Brown by the birth of their daughter, embody themselves in another, and thus fulfil this aspect of their separate sexual natures and of their married life together. They also acquire descendants and a new branch of their family tree. Correlatively, the child, Louise, is given solid and unambiguous roots from which she has sprung and by which she shall be nourished.[78]

But what of other uses of IVF and extramarital embryo transfers, including egg donation (using an egg from a donor and a husband's sperm), embryo donation (using egg and sperm from outside the marriage), and surrogate motherhood (using a host surrogate for the gestation of an embryo)? In most of these instances, according to Kass, "the new cases will serve not to ensure and preserve lineage, but rather to confound and complicate it. The principle truly at work in bringing life into the laboratory is not to provide married couples with a child of their own – or to provide a home of their own for children – but to provide anyone who wants one with a child, by whatever possible or convenient means."[79] He goes on to point out that many trends in our society serve to confound and complicate lineage: high rates of divorce and remarriage, adoption, artificial insemination, rising rates of illegitimacy and fatherless children, and surrogate motherhood. "Our age in its enlightenment is no longer so certain about the virtues of family, lineage and heterosexuality, or even about the taboos against adultery and incest. Against this background it will be asked, Why all this fuss about embryos that stray from their nest?"[80]

Kass has offered no simple answer to this question. In his sentiments, however, he veered very close to asserting the importance of family values expressed in the largely universal taboo against incest and the prohibitions against adultery that "defend the integrity of marriage, kinship and especially the lines of origin and descent. These time-honoured restraints implicitly teach that clarity about who your parents are, clarity in the lines of generation, clarity about who is whose, are the indispensable foundations of a sound family life, itself the sound foundation of civilized community."[81]

So what is to be done about IVF in a liberal society? According to Kass, little. We should give no encouragement to the implementation of embryo adoption or surrogate pregnancy; the federal government in the US should not fund research into IVF, even when such research will give us very useful knowledge about, for example, cell cleavage, gene action, fertilization, or implantation. Still, "it would perhaps be foolish to try to proscribe or outlaw such practices."[82] Kass thus retains his liberal credentials even as he engages in further hand-wringing about the possibilities for our voluntary self-degradation when we separate procreation and sexual love in the absence of the wisdom to guide and restrain our newly discovered power.

Over the last ten years, Leon Kass has decided that, however liberal our society's position is on IVF, a line should be drawn with regard to cloning. He has articulated his objections to asexual reproduction in a series of articles and books,[83] and has championed his arguments for a ban as the chair of the President's Council on Bioethics.[84] Arguments for reproductive cloning represent for Kass the inevitable result of the liberal slippery slope: "The principle of reproductive freedom currently enunciated by the proponents of cloning logically embraces the ethical acceptability of sliding all the way down: to producing children wholly in the laboratory from sperm to term (should it become feasible), and to producing children whose entire genetic makeup will be the product of parental eugenic planning and choice. If reproductive freedom means the right to have a child of one's own choosing by whatever means, then reproductive freedom knows and accepts no limits."[85] What began as compassionate concern for the infertile will end with eugenics, which Kass is certain will entail voluntary self-degradation.

Cloning for research purposes – embryonic stem-cell research, for example – seemed at first more acceptable to Kass. He "advocated a legislative 'third way,' one that firmly banned only reproductive cloning but did not legitimate creating cloned embryos for research."[86] But on reflection he drew back from this apparently neutral position, which would lead to cloning for research, which in turn would be "creating new human life solely to be exploited" and then destroyed. "Whatever one thinks of the moral status or the ontological status of the human embryo, moral sense and practical wisdom recoil from having the government of the United States on record as requiring the destruction of nascent life and, what is worse, demanding the punishment of those who would act to preserve it by (feloniously!) giving it birth."[87] He goes on to argue that a ban on reproductive cloning that allowed cloning for research purposes would be unenforceable. He concludes that "the only practically effective and legally sound approach is to block human cloning at the start, at the production of the embryo clone. Such a ban can be rightly characterized not as interference with reproductive freedom, nor as even interference with scientific inquiry, but as an attempt to prevent the unhealthy, unsavory, and unwelcome manufacture of and traffic in human clones."[88]

In Canada the elaboration of a legal policy with regard to reproductive technologies has taken a long time in coming, but in the end the position arrived at bears remarkable similarities to that proposed by Kass. In October 1989, the Canadian government established a Royal Commission on New Reproductive Technologies, whose mandate was to "inquire into and report upon current and potential medical and scientific developments related to new reproductive technologies, considering in particular their social, ethical, health, research, legal and economic implications and the public interest, and recommend what policies and safeguards should be applied."[89] Dr Patricia Baird, a geneticist from British Columbia, was appointed as chair. The commission had a very troubled history which included resignations and postponements of deadlines. "After having received a second extension, and after two research directors had resigned their posts, the commission submitted its report in November 1993. It consisted of two volumes, *Proceed with Care*, and made 293 recommendations."[90] Many of these elaborated on recommendations made in the Warnock Report.

Over ten years later, in February 2004, Patricia Baird pointed out in frustration that the Canadian government had not yet acted on her report, which "strongly recommended that certain practices (human cloning, selling eggs, commercial surrogacy) should be prohibited, and that a national regulatory body should be set up to oversee and set standards in this rapidly growing field."[91] Most of these recommendations were finally implemented when the Parliament of Canada passed an Act Respecting Human Reproduction and Related Research in March 2004, which was to a large extent patterned on the UK's Human Fertilization and Embryo Act 1990. Among other things, it forbids human cloning for both reproductive and research purposes, sex selection of an embryo for a reason other than medical, germ-line alteration, creating human/non-human combinations for reproductive purposes, and commercial surrogacy arrangements.[92]

When Mary Warnock updated her views on reproductive technologies in a 2003 book entitled *Making Babies*, her slippery slope had became even greasier; her pragmatism led her to even more liberal conclusions with regard to reproductive technologies. She came to accept, as Ronan Mullen pointed out in the *Irish Examiner* in February 2003, "reproductive cloning in extreme cases, surrogacy, IVF for homosexual couples, the storage of embryos to postpone childbirth (until career objectives are met), and even the design of a child to donate spare parts to a sibling."[93] Her rationale for embracing the slippery slope seems to have been motivated by the gung-ho approach to germ-line therapy proposed by Gregory Stock, director of Medicine and Technology at UCLA. Stock had pointed out that "two assumptions are implicit in the idea that one day we will be able to purposefully manipulate our genes. First, genes matter and are responsible for important aspects of who we are. Second, many of the influences our genes exert are straightforward enough to identify and select or rework."[94] He argued that people "will simply demand germ-line intervention, either on egg or sperm or on newly conceived embryos. The market will dictate what happens."[95] After expressing reservations about Stock's economic determinism, Warnock embraced it wholeheartedly in its most current ideological guise: "The more international and industry-driven research becomes, the less sensible it seems to try to lay down restrictions which, if they can be effective at all, can be so only in one country and within the compass of one legislature. In the face of the facts of globalization, and the powerful incentive of capturing world markets, efforts to regulate and control advances in technology, may seem not just futile but pitiful."[96] There is no reason why this logic would not apply to cloning, whether for research or reproductive purposes.

Over the past thirty-five years, none of the ethics of abortion (or respect for embryonic or fetal life), the ethics of experimentation on human subjects, nor the ethics of marriage and human parenthood have slowed down the technologization of human reproduction. Medical practitioners and scientists are returning to the original agenda of the eugenics movement: the improvement of the human race. DNA research into the means by which genetic traits are passed on, fetal research into the requirements of artificial maintenance of life outside the womb, and biological research into cloning or asexual reproduction of human life are proceeding. While there are ethical and (more commonly) legal objections to some dimensions of this research (for example, to the use of fetal tissue in the treatment of Parkinson's disease), quality of life considerations, in themselves, do not seem to offer any consistent framework within which they can be evaluated, much less resisted. Without such a framework, no principle of limitation can be proposed. In the absence of any clear-cut directives from governments, or unequivocal protest from the public, multinational pharmaceutical companies, as Mary Warnock has suggested, will determine the future.

Our society has placed the right of an individual or a couple to have a child above the right of humans not to be brought into being by an experiment in a petri dish. It could hardly be otherwise in a society that has already denied the relevance of any legal or ethical claim on behalf of an embryo or fetus. George Grant argued that in the decision of Roe *v* Wade, Justice Blackmun spoke "modern liberalism in its pure contractual form: right prior to good; a foundational contract protecting individual rights; the neutrality of the state concerning moral 'values'; social pluralism supported by and supporting this neutrality."[97]

In the US and Canada, as in most other liberal societies that lack the historical experience of fascism, the legal debate about the status of fetal life has been bypassed with regard to artificial insemination and IVF, which have become routine medical procedures. Having rejected the (ethical or legal) criteria drawn from their Christian past, these societies have replaced them with little.[98] The technologization of reproduction has thus far been free to proceed at the pace set by the medical and scientific community. Whether liberal societies can find within contractual liberalism coherent reasons to introduce or withhold a ban against cloning will tell us whether Roe *v* Wade has, as Grant argued, irrevocably raised "a cup of poison to the lips of liberalism."[99] The 1988 decision of the Supreme Court of Canada to strike down the law against abortion, and the failure of subsequent Canadian governments to pass any legislation that articulates principles concerning embryonic or fetal life, had a similar result in Canada. From 1988 to 2004, sperm, ova, and embryos could have been treated as raw material subject to medical manipulation for experimental reasons.

Canada, as we have seen, finally passed an Act Respecting Human Reproduction and Related Research in 2004. It prohibits creating embryos for research purposes and forbids cloning for either reproductive or research purposes.[100] Whether it can maintain its prohibition if other Western countries (particularly Great Britain and the US)[101] fail to legally impose one will tell us much about the relationship between technology, capitalism, and liberalism.[102] We will learn whether liberal societies can impose any specific moral restraints on research into reproductive technologies in the face of the drive to a eugenic future funded by the pharmaceutical industry.

7

Excursus on Genetic Testing, Selective Abortion, and the New Eugenics

The problem I raise here is not what ought to succeed mankind in the sequence of species (– the human being is a conclusion –): But what type of human being one ought to breed, ought to will, as more valuable, more worthy of life, more certain of the future.
— Friedrich Nietzsche, *Twilight of the Idols/The Anti-Christ*

The technologization of reproduction described in the last chapter was not in the first instance undertaken or legitimized for specifically eugenic purposes. After World War II, the Nazis' eugenic project was the source of so much revulsion that the very idea of either identifying or creating a superior genotype and then breeding for it was rejected out of hand. The Nazi war crime trials led to the formulation of the Nuremberg Code, which proscribed any experimentation on human subjects that was not clearly understood and consented to by a medical patient. Autonomy became the paramount value, and informed consent became the crucial factor in determining what could ethically be done to a human being by the medical profession. Somewhat paradoxically, autonomy is now being used to legitimate negative eugenics, the improvement of the gene pool by systematically eliminating those who are thought to have "defective" genes, that is, those who might be disabled.

The technique that initially made this possible was prenatal diagnosis.[1] (More recently, pre-implantation genetic diagnosis of embryos produced by IVF has been implemented for couples who are thought to be at greater risk of having a child with birth defects.[2] The procedure is much more complicated and expensive, but the eugenic consequences of both prenatal genetic testing and pre-implantation genetic diagnosis are the same; they were anticipated in the early 1990s.) In a 1991 article in the *American Journal of Law and Medicine*, Abby Lippman wrote, "prenatal diagnosis, already designated as a ritual of pregnancy, at least for white, middle-class women in North America, is the most widespread application of genetic technology to humans today."[3] Since the corresponding technology is not available to treat most diagnosable fetal disorders, it is clear that, at least for the time being, the practical aim of testing is usually to provide the criteria for the "systematic and systemic selection of fetuses, most frequently on genetic grounds."[4] This was confirmed by a 1990 study that found that 88 per cent of 22,000 women who had received positive results on fetal tests for Down syndrome subsequently terminated the pregnancy.[5]

The two most common testing procedures are amniocentesis and chorionic villus sampling (cvs). Amniocentesis involves inserting a needle into the abdomen of the pregnant woman to extract amniotic fluid, which contains cells from the developing embryo. The test can determine the number of chromosomes and allow for biochemical and genetic analysis. It is performed at between sixteen and twenty weeks into the pregnancy and takes three to four weeks to yield results. A woman is usually in a position to consider abortion by around the twentieth week. cvs involves extracting through the pregnant woman's cervix a small sample of tissue from the placenta and allows for a quicker fetal diagnosis of Down syndrome or neural tube defect.[6]

Other procedures may include the use of ultrasonography, amniography, fetoscopy, and the screening of alpha-foetoprotein levels. Among the variety of conditions that can now be diagnosed with prenatal testing are Down syndrome, spina bifida, sickle-cell anemia, Tay-Sachs disease, Huntington's chorea, hemophilia, cystic fibrosis, and a variety of dispositions for later-onset disorders. What future developments will add to this list is anyone's guess, but no doubt these will have as much to do with changing cultural definitions of abnormality as with breakthroughs in the world of science.

Jeremy Rifkin does not hesitate to identify genetic abortion as a form of eugenics, but he makes this distinction: "the old eugenics was steeped in political ideology and motivated by fear and hate, the new eugenics is being spurred by market forces and consumer desire."[7] Abby Lippman is equally clear: "though the word 'eugenics' is scrupulously avoided in most biomedical reports about prenatal diagnosis, except when it is strongly disclaimed as a motive for intervention, this is disingenuous."[8] There is little agreement, however, between critics and proponents, as to the meaning of the term eugenics.

"Eugenics" – a neologism combining the Greek words for *good* and *birth* – was coined by Charles Darwin's first cousin, Francis Galton. The ideology that made this idea seem so attractive in the early days of genetic science probably had its origins in Enlightenment progressivism. In 1792 a French aristocrat, the Marquis de Condorcet, epitomized the spirit of the age when he wrote that "the perfectibility of man is absolutely indefinite ... the progress of this perfectibility, henceforth above the control of every power that would impede it, has no outer limit than the duration of the globe upon which nature has placed us."[9] It would take another two centuries for this naive idea to move from the realm of philosophical anthropology to that of the biological and medical sciences.

After the discovery in 1900 of an obscure Austrian monk's writings on the principles of inheritance, people throughout the Western world began to speculate about genetic links for a whole host of human characteristics, from criminality and chronic unemployment to alcoholism and what was ambiguously termed "feeble-mindedness." A bizarre "science" quickly emerged, leading to the establishment of laboratories and think-tanks at reputable institutions throughout the Western world: the Galton Laboratory for National Eugenics was established at University College in London; the Eugenics Record Office was established at Cold Spring Harbour on Long Island with a massive grant from the Carnegie Institute of Washington; a chair for "racial hygiene" was established at Munich in 1923 (a full ten years before the Nazi eugenics program).[10] By the 1920s two dozen American states had eugenics laws on the books,[11] and in 1928 the legislature of Alberta passed the Sexual Sterilization Act; five years later British Columbia had a similar law.

These laws had widespread popular support. In fact, perhaps surprisingly, some of the most strident supporters were political "progressives." As Martin Pernick points out in *The Black Stork*, "the first American Eugenics advocates were radical utopian socialist communitarians like John Henry Noyes ... [who] drew upon the same faith in scientific expertise, modernism, and state activism that characterized many progressive reformers."[12] Where those who strenuously opposed eugenic measures early on included the Roman Catholic Church and a few somewhat conservative intellectuals like G.K. Chesterton, those who supported it "portrayed eugenics and euthanasia as progressive modern measures that questioned the authority of tradition."[13] Mocking the position of the Catholic Church, Anita Block, women's page editor for New York's famous socialist newspaper, *The Call,* suggested that the church was "eager to have millions of idiots and imbeciles born, so long as it [could] get them baptized."[14]

Canadian Commonwealth Federation founder Tommy Douglas, a man widely credited with having established socialized medicine in Canada, was among the many early supporters of eugenics. In 1933, while still a young Baptist minister, he submitted an MA thesis to McMaster University entitled "Social Hygiene and Public Health."[15] Famous suffragists Nellie McClung and Emily Murphy were also numbered among the early converts. In 1930 the Eugenics Society of Canada was established in Ontario and drew many members from throughout the political and economic elite of the province.[16] It is important for us to understand that the eugenics movement was not simply the creation of right-wing authoritarian demagogues.

What Rifkin calls the "old eugenics" was not perceived by its left-wing exponents as an aberration of the liberal principles of autonomy and progress for which they had been fighting. However, in the 1920s, when eugenics language began to be appropriated, at least in the United States, by those with social Darwinist and neo-Malthusian conceptions of poverty and population, the idea started to fall out of favour with the left.

The rise of the National Socialist movement in Germany, with its open commitment to what was then called "racial hygiene" (*Rassenhygiene*), began the first full-scale application of eugenics principles. News of widespread forced sterilization and involuntary euthanasia was greeted with popular disapproval in the West, putting the concept of state-sponsored eugenics decisively out of favour. However, it should be noted that, as was the case in North America, eugenics talk was not at first limited to extreme-right circles. For example, Alfred Grotjahn, widely considered the father of socialized medicine in Germany during the days of the Weimar Republic, felt that some form of eugenics could be an appropriate complement to other forms of curative medical care and initiatives in public health (although he preferred the term eugenics to *Rassenhygiene* because he did not approve of the latter's racist implications[17]).

In *Racial Hygiene: Medicine under the Nazis,* Robert Proctor points out that most of the medical journals in Germany were publishing on the subject of eugenics and that the medical faculties in most German universities offered courses in racial hygiene long before the rise of the Nazis. Many top German scientists were preoccupied with the search for genetic links behind a variety of diseases. In fact, there was a widespread commitment to a "hereditarian" paradigm in German medical science, which formed the rationale behind the Nazi eugenics program. In the early 1930s, Fritz Lenz, who first investigated the genetic link behind Down syndrome, wrote that "the only way to eliminate genetic illness is through the negative selection of afflicted families."[18] As Proctor argues, there is little evidence that scientists and physicians were coerced into offering their support to the Nazi eugenics program, and in fact many showed great enthusiasm for the idea well before the Nazis were in a position to exercise such coercion. Furthermore, when a two-volume manual on genetics and racial hygiene, co-authored by Lenz, was published in English in 1931 it was glowingly reviewed in such journals as *The New Statesman, The Nation,* the *American Sociological Review,* and the *Quarterly Review of Biology.*[19] The biological determinism that eventually issued in the horrors of the Nazi eugenics and euthanasia program was, in the Kuhnian sense, normal science throughout the West. As Proctor concludes, "the experience of science and medicine under the Nazis represents an extreme case of the dangers of such a philosophy, but it is by no means the first, and certainly not the last, time intellectuals have hoisted a banner proclaiming that biology is destiny. It is a history, one might say, we have yet to conquer."[20]

Hugh Gallagher, in *By Trust Betrayed,* details the horrifying realities of the Nazi eugenics program. It is estimated that over 200,000 people with various disabilities were systematically killed by physicians. Gallagher observes that "behind the bestialities of the Nazi extermination ... lingers a still more gruesome dimension: the mechanistic belief that the pursuit of 'progress' can serve as a justification for mass killings."[21] Supporters of eugenics in the West had generally advocated sterilization rather than euthanasia as a means to achieve their "progressive" goals. The mass killings undertaken in the name of eugenics in Germany were greeted around the world, at least publicly, with shock and horror. The word eugenics came to be associated with the unspeakable atrocities of the Nazi regime.

The Nuremberg trials clearly marked the end of the old eugenics. However, James D. Watson and Francis Crick discovered the secret of the molecular structure of deoxyribonucleic acid (DNA) in 1953 and thus grasped the ordering principle of the genetic code. Six years later the chromosomal anomaly linked to Down syndrome was identified in a laboratory. Suddenly the possibility of developing means to identify genetic "disorders" of various kinds seemed a realizable technical possibility. By 1969 the post-war air had cleared sufficiently that Dr Robert Sinsheimer – who would later be instrumental in founding the Human Genome Project – could say, "For the first time in all time, a living creature understands its origin and can undertake to design its future."[22]

In 1983, the Genbank was established as a database for DNA sequence information at Los Alamos, New Mexico. (It is one of the strange ironies of our civilization that the work of mapping the "building blocks of life" was first undertaken at the very site where the most prodigious of our instruments of death was first developed and tested. Perhaps stranger still is the statement made by the scientist Walter Gilbert at a gathering at Los Alamos in 1986, that the mapping of the human genome was humanity's ultimate response to the Delphic bidding: "know thyself.")[23] The Human Genome Project grew, in part, out of this first initiative and since the 1980s has led to a whole variety of new discoveries in the field of genetics. It continues to make possible a growing number of identifiable links between DNA structure and inherited traits. This, in turn, ever-widens the possible range of applications of genetics technologies like fetal testing and selective abortion.

In this connection, we should remember that much of our current genetics research has its origins in the eugenics movement. In the late 1980s, James D. Watson was becoming the most prominent figure involved with human genome research while heading up the biological laboratory at Cold Spring Harbour, which, as noted earlier, had a long association with eugenics research. In fact, a host of institutions at one time connected with eugenics have become, since the war, genetics research centres. A historical view of the scientific development does not, in itself, permit us to make a sharp distinction between the old eugenics and the new genetics research and technology. The historical background of genetics research has for obvious reasons become an issue in Europe, but it is often overlooked in the North American debate.

In 1989 Benedikt Härlin, on behalf of the Committee on Energy, Research and Technology for the governing body of the European Economic Community, submitted a policy report on genome research to the European Parliament. The report warned that the stated intention of protecting people from genetic diseases clearly suggested "eugenic tendencies and goals." It cautioned that such applications of genetic research would involve eugenic decisions about what are "normal and abnormal, acceptable and unacceptable, viable and non-viable forms of genetic make-up of human beings before and after birth." It pointed to the threat of a "modern test tube eugenics ... an even more radical ... form of 'biopolitics.'"[24] The Härlin report slowed down and informed the legislative process by which the European Community committed itself to genome research, but it by no means stopped it. In fact, genetic research and technology development has taken the entire world by storm. The governments of countries throughout the developed world, along with hundreds of large corporations in the biotech industry, have committed huge financial resources.

In the United States, the Congressional Office of Technology Assessment reported that "new technologies for identifying traits and altering genes make it possible for eugenic goals to be achieved through technological as opposed to social control." Its report describes the new technology as making possible a kind of "eugenics of normalcy" on the basis of what the congressional office obviously perceived as the laudable principle that "individuals have a paramount right to be born with a normal, adequate hereditary endowment."[25]

In this regard, Canada seems to be going with the global flow. In January 1996, the Canadian government declared an interim moratorium on practices that legislators, acting on the advice of the Royal Commission on New Reproductive Technologies, deemed to represent potential threats to human dignity. A bill was drafted in 1997, based in part on the findings of the royal commission, but it missed final reading. In a 1996 document outlining the framework for legislation, Health Canada identified the following four areas of ethical principles: i) *balancing individual and collective interests*;

ii) *equality*; iii) *protecting the vulnerable*; iv) *non-commercialization of re-production and reproductive materials.*[26] It is interesting to note that in a similar 1999 document, a fifth principle was added. Evidently the principle calling for a "balancing of individual and collective inter-ests" was not considered sufficient, and a separate one affirming the right of "individual choice" was added.[27] Notwithstanding the commitment to individual choice, all of the government literature on the proposed legislation suggested that selective abortion on the basis of sex ought to be prohibited. In 2004, as we have noted in the preceding chapter, the Canadian Parliament passed the Assisted Human Reproduction Act. Alhough it prohibits the creation of em-bryos specifically for use in research, the act "sanctions the use of donated human embryos for research, under strict conditions, and bans unacceptable practices, including sex selection except to pre-vent, diagnose or treat a sex-linked disorder or disease."[28]

Groups representing the disabled argue that the scrupulous in-clusion of this prohibition serves only to highlight the correspond-ing lack of concern for the implications of selective abortion on the disability community. In much of the literature on the subject, dis-ability rights activists emphasize the social and moral importance of their perspective on these technologies.[29] Some argue that people with disabilities should be included not just in strategizing about guidelines and legislation but in providing educational material for use in genetic counselling. They argue that our society's ideal of "normalcy" and its fear of difference and disability prejudice the choices people are expected to make about testing and selective abortion. They suggest that the voices of people with disabilities speaking of the real richness of their lives, along with the concrete challenges they have faced and overcome, would provide a useful corrective to the discriminatory attitudes that often form the back-ground to individual decision-making.

Some of the particularly alarming developments, to which dis-ability rights groups refer, are in the field of ethics. It is a notewor-thy and somewhat peculiar fact that a number of prominent ethicists have expressed fewer misgivings about genetic technology and its eugenic implications than the biotech industry itself. Eike Kluge, a professor of bioethics at the University of Victoria and a member of the British Columbia government's special advisory committee on ethical issues, is quoted as having said, "it can be so-cially responsible not to bring a child into the world who is fated to suffer from a genetic disease."[30] Another renowned ethicist, Peter Singer, argues, in his *Practical Ethics,* that infants with disabilities (he uses the example of an infant with hemophilia) ought to be allowed to die if this would enable the mother to try to conceive a second child. Employing a utilitarian calculus, Singer argues that "the loss of happy life for the first infant is outweighed by the gain of a happier life for the second."[31] According to many activists and critics, it is precisely because these kinds of crude calculations and distortions are so often allowed to go unchallenged that pregnant women and their families often experience little actual free choice. They argue that we must begin to establish the conditions for genuinely free reproductive choice by redressing discrimination and exclusion.

There is something to be said for this position. However, one can't help feeling that the long history of the human endeavour to perfect itself and the recurrent difficulties that human communities face in dealing with those who are labelled "other" will push us in a particular direction. The longstanding belief that pain, hardship, limitation, and suffering can and should be overcome through any available technique, if not on our own behalf then at least on behalf of our offspring, will continue to influence the decisions that people make when the means are made available.

The power of the rhetoric of perfection that was evident in the 1792 writing of Condorcet is also evident in recent public comments made by James D. Watson, the co-founder of modern, DNA-based genetics. Watson, who has often tried to distance himself from the explicit language of eugenics, has acknowledged that some people are undoubtedly concerned that scientists will try and use genetic research "to produce pretty babies or perfect people." But, he counters, "What's wrong with that? It's as if there's something wrong with enhancements." He suggests that women and their right to make reproductive choices would move us toward an ideal future free of disability or disease.[32] One is, it seems, forced to concede to the inevitability of all this: if we develop eugenics technology we will have eugenics.

So the question is, can we give priority to those moral arguments by which we condemn eugenics and the technology that enables it when those arguments come into conflict with the claim of autonomy? The answer appears to be no. For example, Adrienne Asch and Gail Geller, speaking to the issue from the perspective of feminist ethics, raise a number of important and insightful questions only to arrive at the following conclusion: "If feminism has one response above all others to make to these technologies, it is that women must be free and enabled to make fully informed decisions: to be tested or not, to reveal test results or not, to undergo or forgo proposed interventions, to bear or not to bear children for whatever reasons they believe are appropriate for them."[33]

But does this position not ultimately close down a whole realm of moral discourse? If the affirmation of autonomy is seen to be a "response *above all others,*" then is that not the last word? Ruth Schwartz Cowan in an essay entitled "Genetic Technology and Reproductive Choice: An Ethics for Autonomy" argues that it is, and that it should be. "The only way ... to prevent a future in which mothers will be able to choose the characteristics of the fetuses they will bring to term will be to violate the norms of the scientific community, return the medical community to paternalism, and restrict women's access to abortion."[34] She goes on to ask, "Why fear a future in which ever more children will be ever more wanted by their mothers? ... What we have to fear, I believe, is government interference with any part of prenatal diagnosis – from controls on scientific research, to controls on access to information, to controls on abortion."[35] There is nothing in Cowan's reasoning that would allow for the possibility of any kind of collectively determined limit to the development of technological means in this area. The old Western equation, dating back to Francis Bacon, of *knowledge* and *power* goes unquestioned in this kind of thinking. A very different perspective is suggested by R. Alta Charo, a professor of law and medical ethics at the University of Wisconsin. In a 1999 article in the *New York Times Magazine* she argues that "reproductive technologies cumulatively reduce the range of events that happen by serendipity and increase the range of events that happen by active planning. This changes the texture of life. One of the rights we have is the right not to have to make choices."[36] With autonomy understood as the right not to have to make choices, we may have come full circle.

This deep ambivalence about the language of autonomy is also reflected in an article by Bryan Appleyard. He shared the story of a severely disabled niece whose short life was, although filled with many hardships, an incomparable gift to those around her. He suggests that we are tragically incapable of recognizing such gifts when we consider disability in the abstract. He writes: "Normality in babies is reassuring, it promises a low-risk life. Oddity is alarming and threatens all kinds of pitfalls. When we are offered choices, we will choose normality." However, he goes on to observe that

the idea of a free market in moral choice is a dangerous illusion. The argument is that you give people the information and they make up their own minds. But what is this information and who is giving it? ... What is missing from this debate is any ethical concept of what constitutes a human self. For the truth is that a moral free market is meaningless. If the only value is that everybody makes up their own mind about everything, then plainly, there is no value. There is only the persuasive power of the dominant forces of the age. And there can be no doubt that the dominant force of our age is the medical-industrial complex that is now selling eugenics as a privatized industry.[37]

We are forced to reconsider Watson's observation that women exercising their reproductive choices would bring us an ideal future. This is more than just triumphalist gloating on behalf of science. It highlights the dreadful irony of our situation; that at the very moment in which we have never been more enslaved by the technological imperative, we can only see that technology as an expression of our freedom.

8

Technology and the End of Politics

In the opening chapters of this book we described how the technological society emerged as the history-making spirit replaced the
doctrine of providence and its acceptance of natural law. By the end
of the eighteenth century, the Enlightenment faith that the evils of
scarcity, labour, disease, and war could be gradually eliminated from
the world if ignorance and superstition were dispelled was dominant. This Enlightenment faith entailed a trust in reason, but reason was gradually reduced to positivist, experimental science; this
positivism showed its efficacy in the accomplishments of the new
physical sciences and the industrial revolution.[1] It is not always appreciated, however, that the new physical science – the marriage of
experiment (empiricism) and reasoning (rationalism) – was motivated by, and found its meaning within, a new political science. This
new political science was contractual liberalism.

As Christopher Lasch has shown,[2] the Enlightenment faith was
not universally espoused even in the nineteenth century, nor were
the principles of liberalism totally accepted either in Europe or
America. But those principles did carry the day over against various
types of regional populism and communitarianism, as well as against
fascism and national socialism. Of course, throughout much of the
twentieth century, liberalism, in its democratic capitalist form, saw
its main adversary as Marxist communism. With the collapse of the
Eastern bloc, many of the ideologues of the West believed their version of liberalism to have been vindicated by history. (This, not surprisingly, was also hailed as a victory for the progressivist account of
history in terms of which military and economic hegemony can be
conveniently viewed as an indication of moral superiority. Perhaps

the most notable example of this triumphalism was Francis Fukuyama's *The End of History and the Last Man.* Fukuyama's idiosyncratic reading of Hegel in support of his apologetics for American capitalism is perhaps most instructive as an example of the perversion of political philosophy into propagandistic sophistry.)

What is often overlooked in this account of the Cold War ideological divide between communism and capitalism is that they each reflect different aspects of the same liberal vision of the self and society. They have different conceptions of liberty (derived, in the one case, from Hobbes, Locke, and Mill, and, in the other, from Rousseau and Marx), but both capitalism and socialism were committed from the outset to the expansion of collective human freedom through progressive mastery over nature and the creation of an economy of plenty through scientific research and technological expansion. Both were moved by the prospect that human fulfillment would be achieved through the emancipation of the passions from external constraints.

Historically, for liberalism, those external constraints were thought of as having to do with nature (primarily scarcity and exhausting manual labour) and with a *social* order that was putatively established on the basis of the *natural* order – or, to be more precise, a social order in which each individual was, in terms of opportunity and social mobility, restricted to what was thought of as his or her *natural* position. Liberal theorists proposed a new vision of a society wherein men and women could win their freedom from nature's tyranny by consenting to new institutional forms. A degree of personal submission to the collectivity would, of course, be necessary, but liberal theorists were able to think of this submission, paradoxically, as an expression of human autonomy because it was based on a relation that was essentially contractual rather than natural. This de-naturalized conception of society and justice is the very essence of liberalism. It culminates in a politics that is really a kind of technology. In fact, it is our argument here that technology and liberalism are not only philosophically related and historically coeval, but that a technological society is *necessarily* a liberal society (using "liberal" in the broad sense for which we shall argue below) even if, in the end, the imperatives of technology must trump ethical concerns arising from liberalism's commitment to equality and human rights.

If we grasp, in this de-naturalized vision of society and justice, the very essence of liberalism, and of the fatefully fecund marriage of liberalism and technology, it will then be possible to see how Western capitalism and Soviet communism are both simply variations on a common theme. Whether the individual is forced to submit to the labour regime of General Motors or of the collective farm, the propaganda of CNN or of Pravda, the original bargain, although it may seem only a distant echo, is basically the same: the individual must submit to the regime of society (whose institutions are to be viewed as an expression of the common will) in order to achieve emancipation from nature, from scarcity, and from human institutions conceived of as naturally ordained. In each case, this emancipation was thought of as the long-term promise of history, where history is understood as the progressive realization of the potentialities of reason and human will.

At the end of the nineteenth century this new quasi-religion of progress had its critics, but few were to be found in the mainstream of European or American culture. The achievements of the industrial revolution (fueled by coal and the steam engine) were plain to see. After all, the productivity of agriculture, the speed of transportation and communications, and the efficiency of industry were greatly improved. The negative aspects of industrialization, all too evident in the slums of London and Manchester, would be eliminated over time as science was applied to more and more spheres of life and standards of living rose. The only question left at the end of the nineteenth century was which was the superior form of liberalism, capitalism or socialism? This quickly was translated into the question, which form of liberalism could better deliver the goods that went with technological expansion?

George Grant has argued that the answer could have been given on purely theoretical grounds. Liberal capitalism was more progressive than Marxist socialism because it was committed to the emancipation of *all* the passions, including the passion of greed. Socialism was theoretically committed to the restraint of greed in the interests of economic equality and some conception of the common good. Marxism was therefore a less progressive form of liberalism. "Even if socialists maintain that their policies would lead in the long run to a society of unrestricted freedom," Grant wrote, "in the short run they have always been advocates of greater control over freedom. This confusion in their thought is the chief reason why socialism has not succeeded in large technological societies since 1945. Western civilization was committed in its heart to the religion of progress and the emancipated passions."[3] It was also committed to the vehicle of that progress: scientific research and technological development. By 1989, the dismantling of the Berlin Wall and the collapse of communism apparently confirmed this judgment.

Marxist socialism is an openly atheistic and anti-Christian doctrine. For this reason it is correctly understood as an attack on the pre-modern (generally Christian) conception of politics and ethics. But the same might be said of democratic capitalism because, as an expression of liberalism, it also represented a rejection of the classical Christian view of human nature and social relations. We have seen how the classical Christian view was informed by the doctrine of natural law, with its clear sense of human limitations and an Augustinian belief in the fallen state of human nature. It did not see evil as rooted simply in ignorance, and therefore eradicable. It held that human fulfillment could be achieved only through the cultivation of virtue and with the grace of God. The passions of the individual were to be ordered by reference to the common good and the eternal good. For classical political philosophers, whether ancient or Christian, the goodness or justice of any society reflected the virtue (or vice) in the souls of those who governed it. For this reason, ancient and Christian philosophers were genuinely conservative; they entertained only modest expectations that improvement would be realized through political reforms. They had no utopian or progressivist hopes. "Since the conditions necessary for the actualization of the best regime depend on chance and are seldom if ever present, prudent men, the classical philosopher taught, will be content to establish or improve regimes, which, though best under existing circumstances and therefore just and legitimate, are nonetheless inferior to what is best simply."[4] For Christian theologians the kingdom of God would come as a thief in the night; it could not be coerced or constructed by human will.

Machiavelli was the first of modern political philosophers to challenge the classical view. Alhough one could never completely eliminate fortune or chance, he considered it possible to gain more control over society and politics. Machiavelli contended that "one can make probable if not certain, the right or desirable social order; one can conquer chance,"[5] although one cannot conquer it completely.[6] Modern political philosophy after Machiavelli can be contrasted with its classical counterpart in its assertion that the establishment of the just society does not require justice in the minds and hearts of those who establish it. Order in society need not be based on order in the souls of those who rule society.

The liberal individualist political philosophers who followed Machiavelli (Hobbes, Locke, Smith) hoped to ensure the progressive actualization of the good social order by lowering the standards of social action, that is, by defining the best regime with reference to the way human beings actually do live and to the objectives that all societies actually pursue. Put simply, all human beings seek to expand their property and power, to impose their will on others as a means of aggrandizing themselves. To this end, the dissimulation of virtue and the practice of vice are sometimes required. The actual practice of virtue, however, is a mug's game, because virtue requires moderation, self-restraint, and the willingness to acknowledge one's weakness. In short, those committed to virtue are naive about the way of the world that was best articulated by the Athenian envoys who said to the representatives of Melos, an island wishing to remain neutral in the Peloponnesian War: "For of the Gods we believe, and of men we know, that by a law of their nature whenever they can rule they will."[7] The strong do what they will, and the weak suffer what they must. No ruler can afford to forget this if he wishes to prosper.

In the modern view, then, the best regime does not require the rule of the virtuous; it is not an aristocracy in the classical sense. Modern political science begins with the acknowledgment that we are all, even the strongest of us, vulnerable to the violence of others. It sets out to limit that violence not by an appeal to the goodness of others but by the establishment of a social contract that acknowledges our mutual vulnerability. And so, "it depends for its success more on the operation of its institutions than on the virtue of its rulers."[8] Political problems, in this view, are technical problems, and good government requires efficient implementation of a social contract rather than a virtuous leader or a philosopher king.

Leo Strauss explained the principle that underlies this modern perspective: "There is no evil which cannot be controlled: What is required is not divine grace, morality, nor formation of character but institutions with teeth in them. Or to quote Kant, the establishment of the right social order does not require, as people are in the habit of saying, a nation of angels; hard as it may sound, the problem of establishing the just state is soluble even for a nation of devils, provided they have sense, that is, provided their selfishness is enlightened."9 When a nation of devils is selfishly enlightened, it will see the wisdom of accepting and institutionalizing the social contract.

Contractual liberalism is therefore dogmatically agnostic about what the good or the virtuous is. It simply brackets the question about the nature of the absolute good or the common good or the hierarchy of relative goods and puts it to one side. One may ask about the nature of goodness privately, but one's private answer can have no public significance in a liberal society. A liberal regime must protect the freedom of its constituents to pursue their own ends; it has nothing to say about what those ends should be. It is committed to procedural rather than substantive justice. Hobbes established this principle in the *Leviathan*. Since then contractual liberalism has asserted that although there is no way of determining (and no general agreement possible about) what the *summum bonum* is, we can all agree that violent death is the *summum malum*. Fear of death impels men to leave the state of nature and to enter the social contract. Modern justice then is thought to be conventional rather than natural, rooted in a contract that guarantees the right to self-preservation. Society must be ordered in the light of this right. Justice requires simply the enlightenment of people's self-interest so they will accept this contract. It does not require the ordering of their desires in the light of some conception of the good.

The emergence of liberalism in Europe has paralleled the Reformation and the wars of religion, as well as the secularization of Western society. It has culminated in the separation of church and state. But Christian belief and practice did not go out the back door when the contractualism of Hobbes and Locke came in the front. This meant that the pre-modern and Reformation Christian conception of virtue continued to provide, although in a more and more attenuated form, a conception of goodness and virtue that would order private and public life. The Enlightenment project set out to eliminate that notion of virtue as the key to ethical analysis. It attempted, as Alasdair MacIntyre has shown, to dismantle the classical teleological scheme, according to which "there is a fundamental contrast between man-as-he-happens-to-be and man-as-he-could-be-if-he-realized-his-essential-nature." Within the classical scheme

ethics is the science which is to enable men to understand how they make the transition from the former state to the latter. Ethics therefore on this view presupposes some account of potentiality and act, some account of the essence of man as a rational animal and above all some account of the human *telos*. The precepts which enjoin the various virtues and prohibit the vices which are their counterparts instruct us how to move from potentiality to act, how to realize our true nature and to reach our true end ... The desires and emotions that we possess are to be put in order and educated by the use of such precepts and by the cultivation of those habits of action which the study of ethics prescribes; reason instructs us both as to what our true end is and as to how to reach it.[10]

Contractual liberalism asserts that reason cannot tell us what our true end is or how to reach it. Religion may do so, but it can make no claim to be reasonable.

MacIntyre goes on to explain that, in the seventeenth and eighteenth century, the teleological scheme was rejected even by Protestant (as well as Jansenist) theologians and sceptics who were enamoured of the new science and its inductive methods. Knowledge was reduced to that which could be discovered by scientific experimentation or calculation. As Hume argued, human nature described humans as they are; it could say nothing about them as they could be if they realized themselves. It could not say anything about their telos or their essential nature, if indeed they had one. This is what occasioned the quest for a new rational basis for moral beliefs.

What ensued was the Enlightenment project, but MacIntyre has argued that it had to fail. Moral philosophers attempted "to find a rational basis for their moral beliefs in a particular understanding of human nature, while inheriting a set of moral injunctions on the one hand and a conception of human nature on the other which had been expressly designed to be discrepant with each other."[11]

MacIntyre traced this failure in the utilitarianism of Bentham and Mill, the intuitionism of Sedgwick, and the pragmatism of James and Dewey, all of which have culminated in emotivism. For the emotivist, science involves facts. Values are subjective or emotional responses to reality, and as such are irrational. Emotivism makes the basis of all moral choice the subjective feelings of the individual,[12] and thereby denies that there is any objectively rational basis for one choice rather than another. It informs the sociology of Max Weber in the form of the fact-value distinction that reduces sociology to statistical analysis and political science to polling.[13] It is systematized in the existentialism of Jean-Paul Sartre, with his emphasis on authenticity as the only basis for an ethics of freedom. All philosophy is epistemology and all history is biography. We have seen it in the despair of the liberal economist Heilbroner, who asserted that there can be no *rational* basis for a concern for future generations or for the survival of human life on planet earth.

The failure of the Enlightenment project has had important consequences for contractual liberalism. Liberalism has been driven into a corner and finds itself going in circles. This is manifested in irresolvable controversies. There is the interminable debate about what the principles of shared rationality are that would allow us to define the limits of freedom in a liberal society, and about what protection against the greatest evil, a violent death, should be guaranteed by law. At a practical or legal level, this is demonstrated in our inability as a society to deal with such issues as abortion or euthanasia, respect owed to embryonic or fetal life, or the defence of the civil liberties of alleged terrorists. These have become, in some sense, intractable problems.

The failure of liberalism has been revealed as it has become a tradition itself that subverts other traditions. "Liberalism, which began as an appeal to alleged principles of shared rationality against what was felt to be the tyranny of tradition, has itself been transformed into a tradition whose continuities are partly defined by the interminability of the debate over such principles."[14] As a tradition, liberalism eliminates other conceptions of rationality from the public realm. MacIntyre describes the dilemma this creates:

Every individual is to be equally free to propose and to live by whatever conception of the good he or she pleases, derived from whatever theory or tradition he or she may adhere to, unless that conception of the good involves reshaping the rest of the community in accordance with it. Any conception of the human good according to which, for example, it is the duty of the government to educate the members of the community morally, so that they come to live out that conception of good, may up to a point be held as a private theory by individuals or groups, but any serious attempt to embody it in public life will be proscribed.[15]

As such, liberalism is committed to what MacIntyre has called the privatization of the good: "Allegiance to any particular conception

of human good ought ... to be a matter of private individual preference and choice, and it is contrary to rationality to require of anyone that he or she should agree with anyone else in giving his or
her allegiance to some particular view."[16] The failure of the Enlightenment project and the privatization of the good have had important consequences for liberalism.

One of these consequences, MacIntyre has argued, is that, in
fact, liberalism does not defend pluralism but dissolves the traditions of the (religious, ethnic, or cultural) communities it theoretically protects.[17] But he does not advert to the link between
liberalism and technology that was spelled out by George Grant a
generation ago. "Pluralism," Grant wrote,

> has not been the result in those societies where modern liberalism has
> prevailed. Western men live in a society the public realm of which is
> dominated by a monolithic certainty about excellence – namely that
> the pursuit of technological efficiency is the chief purpose for which
> the community exists. When modern liberals, positivist or existential-
> ist, have criticised the idea of human excellence, they may have
> thought they were clearing the ground of religious and metaphysical
> superstitions which stood in the way of the liberty of the individual.
> Rather they were serving the social purpose of legitimizing the totally
> technological society by destroying anything from before the age of
> progress which might inhibit its victory.[18]

For most of the modern period, liberal societies have assumed
that human freedom is enhanced by technological progress. More
control over nature will provide us with greater freedom to act in
the world. However, more control over nature through technology
can only be achieved with the expansion of the power of collectivities, namely the state and the corporations who fund and implement the scientific research. To achieve more collective power over
nature, individuals must be induced (or seduced) to subject themselves to the power of the state and the corporations. Liberal capitalist democracies have assumed that the freedom of the individual
could be constitutionally protected through something like a charter of rights. A charter of rights and freedoms, however, has no cosmological, ontological, or ethical foundation. It is conventional
and contractual. Individuals can be included in or excluded from
the social contract that forms the basis of a charter of rights.

Hannah Arendt had already diagnosed this problem in her reflections on the plight of refugees, or those whom she calls "state-
less people," in the twentieth century. The displacement of millions
of people in Europe between 1914 and 1945 had created a crisis
for the Western notion of "universal human rights." Arendt observes that "the conception of human rights, based upon the assumed existence of a human being as such, broke down at the very
moment when those who professed to believe in it were for the first
time confronted with people who had indeed lost all other qualities
and specific relationships – except that they were still human. The
world found nothing sacred in the abstract nakedness of being human."[19] The problem, in her view, is that claims concerning the
universality of human rights within modern political philosophies
are devoid of any real meaning. She points out that those who have
been robbed of their citizenship, consigned to internment camps,
or forced into an underground existence seldom put much stock
in the notion of universal human rights; they know that their fate
depends on the existence (or non-existence, as the case may be)
of a state that can put force behind their claims. It is only as citizens of sovereign nations, that is, as parties to the social contract,
that modern individuals can coherently insist upon a recognition
of their rights.

This situation, in Arendt's view, is a peculiarly modern predicament, for it concerns the absence of any transcendent foundation
for political ethics.

A conception of law which identifies what is right with the notion of
what is good for – for the individual, or the family, or the people, or the
largest number – becomes inevitable once the absolute and transcendent measurements of religion or the law of nature have lost their authority. And this predicament is by no means solved if the unit to which
the "good for" applies is as large as mankind itself. For it is quite conceivable, and even within the realm of practical political possibilities,
that one fine day a highly organized and mechanized humanity will conclude quite democratically – namely by majority decision – that for humanity as a whole it would be better to liquidate certain parts thereof.[20]

The regime of human rights, announced in the political philosophies of the eighteenth century and developed into a body of international agreements in the twentieth, derives what little force it

has, according to Arendt, only from agreements between powerful states who recognize a common interest in their enforcement.

To be sure, the great theorists from whom we in the West derive our notions of rights and freedoms (e.g., Locke, Kant, and, more recently, Rawls) often couched these concepts in a language that seems to impart to them a metaphysical, or sacred, character. Immanuel Kant, for example, in one of his formulations of the famous "categorical imperative" insists that reason itself enjoins that we treat all other human beings as ends, never merely as means. This leads him to formulate a vision of the ethical society as a "kingdom of ends." (It is an indication of the enduring influence of this great eighteenty-century theorist that the Health Canada working papers on proposed legislation about genetics technology to which we referred in chapter 7 use precisely this language; they insist that such technology, if it is to be developed or used or both in Canada, must be consistent with the understanding that all human beings are "ends in themselves.")

John Rawls' book *A Theory of Justice* is a more recent example of a liberal theory of rights and freedoms within this tradition.[21] Rawls is strongly influenced by Kant, although he dispenses with some of the latter's metaphysical talk, and offers us a theoretical model by which to calculate rights and obligations in such a way that it does not unfairly privilege the interests of some over others. Without getting into the mechanics of Rawls' proposal, let us say that he, like many of the others in the tradition of liberal theory, grounds his claims regarding the universality of rights in a further claim about the universality of reason.[22] But the understanding of reason implied within this tradition is quite different from the one put forward by the ancient Greeks or by traditional Christianity. To the ancients, reason was, among other things, a capacity to discern the order of the universe and to understand one's place within the whole. Within modernity, reason has come to be understood as the capacity to calculate. In political terms, this means the capacity to calculate with regard to one's own interests and obligations. Although Kant appears to sit somewhere between these two accounts, modern liberal theory faces a fundamental contradiction when it attempts to define political reasoning as calculation, and justice as a matter of convention, while making high-minded claims regarding the universality of rights and freedoms. The substance of the arguments for rights and freedoms makes the metaphysical tone of the rhetoric ring hollow. As George Grant has pointed out, Nietzsche saw clearly through this contradiction, but the English-speaking world, partly as a result of the historical success of its experiments in constitutional liberalism, has not had to face up to the problem.

Grant explains, in his analysis of Rawls, that this theory of justice and the universality of rights fails to take account of the very real fact that the tradition of liberal theorizing has been carried out within the heartlands of the two great English-speaking imperial powers. "[Rawl's] theory of justice is written in abstraction from the facts of war and imperialism."[23] Grant's claim is that the reality of the practice of liberal justice belies the theory. And in this case the failure of the theory to inform the practice is not a matter of weak will or historical contingencies, but rather is a fundamental contradiction in the theory. A conventional, essentially contractual, account of justice gives us no reason why some human beings should not be excluded from the calculations.

In terms of the realities of "war and imperialism" we need only consider the case of the prisoners of the "war on terrorism" held by the United States at Guantanamo Bay. In spite of the fact that the Geneva Convention was presumed to extend *universal* rights to prisoners of war, and in spite of the fact that American judicial procedures and American legal rights ensuring due process for accused criminals were presumed to reflect the American constitution's declared respect for the *universal* rights of all human beings, it would seem that neither of these frameworks apply to the prisoners at Guantanamo. Legal challenges by those who decry the inhumane treatment of these prisoners have failed because, although they are in the custody of US forces, they are not held on American soil, and although they would appear to be prisoners of war (even if it is the dubiously named "war on terror"), they are in fact legally defined as "unlawful combatants." Grant foresaw that, within an account of justice as conventional, "the imprisoned," among others who are, for various reasons, "too weak to enforce contracts," could be excluded from the regime of liberal rights, even in their minimal articulations.

Organizations such as the American Civil Liberties Union and various human rights groups continue the legal and political fight to get the Guantanamo detainees out of legal limbo. As Hannah Arendt observed, "No paradox of contemporary politics is filled with a more poignant irony than the discrepancy between the efforts of well-meaning idealists who stubbornly insist on regarding as 'inalienable' those human rights, which are enjoyed only by citizens of the most prosperous and civilized countries, and the situation of the rightless themselves."[24] The real problem is that no states are prepared to get behind the "rights" of the detainees. British human rights activists have, for example, long decried the complete silence of their government concerning the documented abuse of British citizens in US detention centres. As Arendt writes, "The calamity of the rightless is not that they are deprived of life, liberty, and the pursuit of happiness, or of equality before the law and freedom of opinion – formulas which were designed to solve problems *within* given communities – but that they no longer belong to any community whatsoever. Their plight is not that they are not equal before the law, but that no law exists for them."[25]

· The modern liberal account of reason as calculation, and of universal rights as a principle corresponding to this universality of the faculty of calculation and negotiation with regard to one's own interest, is the predictable political articulation of the modern metaphysical conception of the universe as it is unfolded within the post-Enlightenment physical sciences. Politics itself has become a science among sciences.

George Grant summarized the relation between modern political science and physical science in this way:

Modern theories of justice present it as something human beings make and impose on human convenience. This is done in a physical environment which is understood in terms of necessity and chance. Obviously, the traditional belief, as much as the modern, included cognizance that human beings were responsible for doing things about justice. Human beings built cities, empires, etc. and some regimes were better than others. To use the favorite expression of the Enlightenment, human beings have in modernity taken their fate into their own hand. Their theories of justice teach them that our institutions are what we make in terms of our own convenience. The central cause of this great change has been modern natural science. Brilliant scientists have laid before us an account of how things are, and in that account nothing can be said about justice. It is indeed not surprising therefore that in the coming to be of technological science the dependence of our objective science upon calculus has been matched by the dependence for knowledge of justice upon calculation.[26]

Liberalism has from the outset been plagued by a civilizational contradiction insofar as it has attempted to embrace the new non-teleological natural sciences that issue in the mastery of nature and, at the same time, hold onto a teleological view of humans as in some sense fitted for justice understood as freedom and equality. Current liberal theories of justice do not, because they cannot, eliminate this civilizational contradiction. The history of the twentieth century demonstrated that technological progressivism is an ideology that is capable of transforming and eviscerating liberalism itself. As liberalism has itself become a tradition in which freedom has no end beyond its own expansion, it becomes unable to offer any criteria by which to judge techniques except on their own terms. Efficient they are, but to what end? A society where the good has been privatized and a teleological ethic has been abandoned offers no answer to this question.

George Grant contended that in the history of English-speaking justice, the emptiness at the core of liberalism has been papered over, and social life has been held together by Calvinist Protestantism, which offered a vertical or transcendental basis for human equality in the face of the clear inequality of people.[27] But Calvinist Protestantism has been secularized and replaced with liberalism as a tradition. The liberal good has become, according to Grant, technological progressivism.

At the level of politics this has meant the emergence of a technological regime. This does not mean that technicians have replaced politicians. It does mean that politicians are dependent on technicians at every stage of their careers. They are dependent on technicians to get elected and stay in power. They are dependent on experts to develop and implement policy and law, which in turn are developed in the light of liberal society's commitment to technological progressivism. "Technology becomes our comprehensive destiny as the prevalent modes of thinking our existence either preclude any conception of a human end that could direct or limit technological expansion or declare a human purpose that is contained and actualized in technological development itself."[28] But liberalism itself as a tradition is not compatible with technological innovation, which threatens the rights and freedoms of the individual insofar as they are grounded only in a contract.

Technological progressivism involves a clear commitment to the improvement of the quality of life, that is, to the "free creation of richness and greatness of life and all that is advantageous thereto."[29] As we have seen, we mortals are called upon to create ourselves and to create our world. There is no human nature to realize; there is history to create. Technological progressivism calls into question precisely what liberalism assumes (the equality of all human beings and their "rights"), because the creation of quality of life for some may require the annihilation of certain other human beings who stand in the way of that creation. Grant makes clear what liberals have not wanted to see: at its heart, technological progressivism is Nietzschean. And "in Nietzsche's conception of justice, there are human beings to whom nothing is due – other than extermination."[30]

The nihilism of technological progressivism is obvious to liberals when other political regimes are involved in determining which human beings have no due. These are the "useless eaters" and the mental defectives of the Third Reich for whom euthanasia is prescribed. These are the Kulaks who, for refusing to collectivize their farms, are forced by Stalin to starve. Grant has articulated the nihilism at the heart of technological progressivism in this way:

The human creating of quality of life beyond the little perspectives of good and evil by a building, rejecting, annihilating way of thought is the statement that politics is the technology of making the human race greater than it has yet been. In that artistic accomplishment, those of our fellows who stand in the way of that quality can be exterminated or simply enslaved. There is nothing intrinsic in all others that puts any given limit on what we may do to them in the name of that great enterprise. Human beings are so unequal in quality that to some of them no due is owed.[31]

The pursuit of a superior quality of life by genetic experimentation or reproductive technologies, for example, should not be slowed down by any qualms about the humanity of those upon whom we must experiment.

It is rarely appreciated that this is the beginning of the end of politics as conceived by those modern liberal philosophers who assumed that belief in equality could be sustained in the face of a scientific world view that defines reality in terms of necessity and chance and the human being as "an accidental collocation of matter."[32]

9

Technology and the End of Ethics

Throughout this book we have described the many ways in which technology has both transformed and overridden traditional ethical considerations as it has altered every aspect of our society; agriculture, economics, energy, war, medicine, and reproduction have been radically changed as the Baconian project has taken shape. Many would argue that these changes have been all to the good even if labour, scarcity, disease, and war have not been banished from the face of the earth. They would say that our technical progress has not meant the end of ethics but the emergence of a new ethics that grapples with the techniques that have emerged and the challenges that have accompanied them. Business ethics, biomedical ethics, environmental ethics, feminist ethics, health care ethics, and defence policy are burgeoning areas of study. The development of these branches of ethics, it could be claimed, is a sign that ethics is not at an end but is thriving.

However, our deeper examination of the debates that have dominated these fields reveals that certain fundamental questions have been ignored and that, as in the fields of moral philosophy or political theory, there are no common ethical standards that are applied, and no means (in politics, the academy, the defence establishment, the health care system, or the business world) of determining the superiority of a particular ethical approach. This is arguably a feature of the postmodern condition, but, if so, it would be a prolongation of the implicit nihilism at the heart of the modern project, which is to say that it leads us to the conclusion that it does not matter what we do.

At the practical level this theoretical inadequacy does not seem to make any difference to politicians, managers, doctors, lawyers, hospital administrators, perhaps even to ethicists themselves. Liberal capitalist society seems to function well with a non-ethic that derives from what Alasdair MacIntyre has called "bureaucratic individualism."[1] It accepts and reflects the radical distinction, so popular among liberal social scientists, between facts and values. The contemporary social world is divided into "the realm of the organizational in which ends are taken to be given and are not available for rational scrutiny, and the realm of the personal in which judgement and debate are central factors but … no rational resolution of issues is available."[2] Neither of these two realms is hospitable to the development of an ethics that transcends the pragmatic will to power. "There are only two alternative modes of social life open to us, one in which the free and arbitrary choices of individuals are sovereign and one in which the bureaucracy is sovereign, precisely so that it may limit the free and arbitrary choices of individuals."[3] Bureaucratic individualism entails the acceptance of emotivitist[4] or existentialist (that is to say, irrationalist) theories of moral judgment at the personal level and some brand of utilitarianism (often placed within the context of rights theory or contractualism or both) at the public and institutional level.

Alasdair MacIntyre has, we have seen, argued that in the realm of moral philosophy, the Enlightenment project failed as Western society abandoned a traditional ethical framework. This traditional ethical framework has had many historical manifestations, all of which have been variants on what John Rist has called "transcendental realism."[5] Platonism and neo-Platonism, Aristotelianism, stoicism, and Christian ethics, whether dependent on Augustine or Aquinas, are all forms of transcendental realism. Traditional ethics, as we have argued in chapter 1, committed itself to the doctrine of "natural law": there is an order in the universe, and right action consists in attuning ourselves to that order. That natural order could be altered and improved to enhance legitimate human ends, but it had an integrity of its own that set clear limits to the manipulation of the environment. Although natural law was not a univocal or unambiguous notion, it generally assumed that human desire or human will was to be regulated by and attuned to both the natural order and to the supernatural good. This ordering was achieved through the personal development of virtue, which enables human beings to respect the integrity of the natural order and to seek the unity or integrity of the self in relation to both the natural order and the good. Transcendental moral realism, which implies a virtue ethics, assumes that we can discern a good beyond our desire, passions, or will. It assumes that the self can be unified or be moved toward unification as it aspires toward that good.[6] We can contemplate that good and act (or withhold ourselves from action) with reverence in the face of the mysterious and the incalculable. Life is not a problem to be solved.

Modern ethics, on the other hand, tends to assume that the emancipation of the passions (or the satisfaction of immediate and immanent desires) is the goal of human striving, that the order of nature is completely knowable through scientific research, and that nature (understood as raw material or "standing reserve")[7] is malleable and manipulable in the service of the realization of human desire or will. Human creativity and ingenuity in transforming nature and human nature, rather than obedience or attunement to something beyond the human will (whether natural or supernatural), is the highest aspiration. For the modern ethicist, a supersensuous, supernatural, or metaphysically transcendent good is an illusion to be dispelled as we take upon us the responsibility to create ourselves and the world. Incomplete knowledge about the standards we should use in our creativity should not prevent us from approaching our lives as experimental "works in progress." This creativity demands of us more courage and more calculation. Our challenge is to steadfastly calculate the costs, risks, and benefits of our creative projects within the overall framework of a materialist utilitarianism.

It has not been our purpose in this book (and cannot be our purpose in this final chapter) to argue for the superiority of transcendental moral realism,[8] although we think it is superior. Our purpose has been to demonstrate the inadequacy and inconsistency (and the implicit moral nihilism) of contemporary discussions of many pressing ethical issues on their own terms. Neither utilitarianism nor any of its variants (rights theory, consequentialism, contractualism, pragmatism, etc.) offer any solutions to the moral dilemmas that we face in the technological society.

MacIntyre has described the process by which the traditional view of ethics was abandoned in favour of a moral fiction that combines the notion of utility and the notion of rights. It was naively thought that this moral fiction could provide us with objective and impersonal criteria by which to make ethical judgments in the modern world. It has failed to do so. "When claims invoking rights are matched against claims appealing to utility or when either or both are matched against claims based on some traditional concept of justice, it is not surprising that there is no rational way of deciding which type of claim is to be given priority or how one is to be weighed against another."9

We are arguing that the Enlightenment project in moral theory has failed precisely because it has been unable to offer any coherent ethical framework that might enable us to deal with the crises that have emerged as technological progressivism has reached greater and greater speeds. In other words, the Enlightenment has transformed our view of ourselves and our relation to nature in such a way as to facilitate our domination of that nature, and that very transformation, which had the effect of casting the moral self adrift from its moorings in the natural order, has, not surprisingly, failed to offer any compelling restraints on our collective will to domination. "As moderns we have no standards by which to judge particular techniques, except standards welling up with our faith in technological expansion."10 Regardless, the dynamo must boom on. Decisions must be implemented. And so,

rights theorists, utilitarians, universalizability theorists, contractarians and multifarious protagonists of various blends of these each advance their mutually incompatible solutions to the problems of each particular profession, yet of course with a notably different outcome from that within moral philosophy itself. For in the realm of professional practice matters which affect problems of immediate action cannot be allowed to go unsettled. One way or another codes must be formulated, choices made, dilemmas resolved, with or without rational justification. Hence in this realm what is in fact inconclusive intellectual debate nonetheless issues in the practical resolution of problems, a resolution the arbitrariness of which it is the function of both philosophical and professional rhetoric to conceal.11

We are nothing if not practical, and so practical problems do get resolved. But, as we have shown, professional rhetoric has concealed the failure of moral philosophy to ask, much less answer, fundamental ethical questions. Technological progressivism has made it impossible to do so. In chapter 2, we demonstrated that global economic development has been confined largely to the transfer of technology from the so-called first world to the so-called "developing" world. This has been legitimated in the name of distributive justice. Thanks to global economic development, it has been argued, fewer people will live below the poverty line. But even if it could be shown that the poor are materially better off as their societies have been modernized (and we have argued that it has *not* been so shown), can our calculations factor in the spiritual effects of the cultural uprooting that has taken place as a result of two centuries of colonialism and half a century of technology transfer?[12] As Wolfgang Sachs and Ivan Illich have proposed, economic development, even when it is putatively "sustainable," does not generally "sustain" cultures.

Likewise, we have demonstrated the inadequacy of environmental ethics committed to utilitarianism and sustainable sufficiency where no thought has been given as to what is to be sustained. (For example, is forestry being sustained when old-growth forests are clear-cut and replaced with tracts of newly planted trees?) What can sustainable sufficiency mean if we have no idea how much energy consumption is enough and no commitment to limiting it? And how could we limit it if economic growth is understood as an unqualified good and the advertising industry (dedicated to the emancipation of the passions) is considered essential to guarantee economic growth?[13] Similarly, utilitarianism gives us no wisdom as to what a clean or green source of energy is. (Petro-Canada would have us believe that its gasoline is "clean," in spite of the emission of carbon dioxide. Nuclear power is sold as a "green" energy source, in spite of the radioactivity and the longevity of its carcinogenic waste.) Have the cost-risk-benefit analyses of nuclear power plants dealt with the questions of sustainable sufficiency in light of the as yet unsolved (and, as we have argued, ethically insoluble) problems associated with waste disposal?

Even in the nineteenth century utilitarianism was a blunt (and ideological)[14] tool of analysis when it sought to compare costs (in dollars) and benefits (often in energy that might be used for any purposes, whether good or evil). Now, however, utilitarian calculation is required to include the risks (calculated in terms of probable deaths over time) of the power plant operation and of the waste disposal.

We are dealing with incommensurables here. How do we calculate the value of one life in dollars, and how would its value be discounted over time? And how would we factor in the risk that a certain number of human beings will die of cancer if we use nuclear energy? At what point might we conclude that we should not use nuclear energy to "maintain our standard of living"?

The questions we have posed are hypothetical and unanswerable. Our point in asking them is to highlight the inadequacy of utilitarianism (cost-risk-benefit analyses) to determine what we ought do in the real world. The notion of sustainable sufficiency has been introduced by some ethicists as a principle for the guidance of ethical reflection on our technology and our economics. But sustainable sufficiency cannot (any more than the utilitarianism that it qualifies) provide any clear guidelines for the limitation of technological innovations; it, in fact, offers no clear principle that could guide ethical reflection. Cost-risk-benefit calculations ultimately obscure the question of what we owe to future generations. And, perhaps more to the point, they give us no indication as to what are appropriate human ends or lifestyles for future generations if we cannot discern what these ends are for us now. Again, the notion of sustainable sufficiency leaves open the question of exactly what is to be sustained. If we have no means by which to determine how much intervention into, and manipulation of, nature is commensurate with some clear notion of the human good, then the notion of sustainable sufficiency proves to be a meaningless concept. Do we, for example, "sustain" a kind of social order in which a nature preserve in Alaska would be demolished in order to secure a supply of energy "sufficient" to maintain our increasing dependence on the automobile?

The development of hydrogen fuel is a case in point. It will gobble up billions of dollars in research money before the ethical implications of its development are clarified.[15] Utilitarianism cannot clarify them. The ideal of sustainable sufficiency cannot provide us with any clear idea as to how many automobiles we should operate on this planet (given their average annual energy consumption) if we wish to avoid the worst effects of air pollution and global warming. Sustainable sufficiency cannot tell us whether the risks associated with the disposal of radioactive waste require the abandonment of nuclear power as a primary source of energy. It cannot tell us whether nuclear weapons can be used to meet our "security" needs, in part because those needs themselves are undefined and the methods used to enhance our security as we wage an interminable war on terror entail immense risks themselves. Any conceivable answers to these kinds of questions presuppose answers to deeper questions about appropriate human ends: to what extent is it appropriate for human beings to subordinate the integrity of nature to their own wills? Do we continue to be recognizably ourselves when we seek to emancipate our passions by reducing all being, including, ultimately, our own being, to the status of raw material for that great endeavour? Whether or not we find it adequate today, a natural law ethic at least offered human beings some principles by which to deal with such questions, but these are precisely the questions that modern ethical theories have ruled out of court.

Lacking any answers to these truly ethical questions (in fact, in public terms, lacking the questions themselves), and having moved into a full-blown technological system, we have, without any public debate, accepted all of the implications of what has been called the "risk society."[16] The notion of risk analysis, as we saw in our study of nuclear power generation, was initially applied to specific technologies like spacecraft or reactors. Risk was initially merely a problem *of* technology. Over the past thirty years it has become a problem *for* technology. "In the concept of 'risk society,' risks enter the stage already appropriated and managed by science and technology – as their appropriate domain."[17] In a risk society, we experience "a fundamental insecurity about activities that people have successfully engaged in for tens of thousands of years. One is not to rely on one's own experience but on expert knowers, to a degree detrimental to the human individual."[18] One is, of course, not *able* to rely on his or her own experience because modern technology has expanded the range of human activity and its possible effects well beyond the horizon of any individual's capacity to discern and understand. The reliance on expert knowers is simply a logical consequence of this situation. However, in a technological society, expert knowers do not develop ethical norms but deal in statistical probabilities regarding the consequences of our actions. These statistical probabilities are calculated by a range of individual tests that may not reveal the cumulative risk that is accruing. Such a piecemeal approach to risk assessment leads, at best, to piecemeal regulation. But, as Willem Vanderburg has pointed out, "a piecemeal regulation tends not to be very effective. Consider, for example, the area of chemical technology. There are some 65,000 chemicals in current use [Vanderburg is writing in 1988]. Estimates of the number of new chemicals that are added each year range from about 500 to 1000. Some of these are tested by exposing animals to large doses of these chemicals. No testing occurs for low-dosage, long-term exposure, nor are there any methods for assessing the overall impact on our health of the many chemicals in our environment to which we are exposed every day. Yet their overall effect cannot be deduced from the specific effects taken one at a time."[19]

The risk society is, as Zygmunt Bauman argues, technology's last stand. However, since technology is likely with us for better or for worse, we might modify the formula and say that the risk society is also modern ethics' last stand, a last-ditch attempt to subordinate the technological imperative to some modest form of critical scrutiny. Risk analysis, which began as an adjunct to the insurance industry, has become a technique to evaluate risks and develop the consumer products and public policies to defend us against them. Scientific analysis is essential to the process. The dioxin we generate as a carcinogenic byproduct of industry ends up in our lakes, and so it becomes necessary to conduct sophisticated scientific tests that will reveal its concentration in parts per billion. The acceptable concentration level will be determined over time in light of cancer rates among the populations that drink or bathe in the water. What impairs health or destroys nature is no longer evident to the naked eye. "The focus is more and more on hazards which are neither visible nor perceptible to the victims; hazards that may not even take effect within the life spans of those effected but instead during those of their children."[20] Only science can enable us to deal with the problems that science has produced, and only technology can enable us, we hope, to limit the hazards produced. But Bauman points out that, as consumers, we all participate in the production of the risks and would protest strongly if forced to give up our cars or vacation travel or lifestyles predicated on urban sprawl and economic growth.[21] As taxpayers, however, having been raised on neoconservative rhetoric, we are inclined to deal with the risks individually and privately until it becomes clear that this is impossible.[22]

The deeper ethical problem is, however, that the risk society makes the globe the laboratory for its technological experiments and the object of the experimentation. The crisis that emerged when Oppenheimer's team decided to go ahead with the splitting of the atom in the New Mexico desert (when some said there were three chances in a million that it would give rise to a runaway explosion in the atmosphere) has now become paradigmatic. In a wide range of experimentation, we still lack an understanding of the criteria by which to judge whether to proceed. We have incredibly sophisticated computer programs that enable us to model the changes introduced by new techniques to the environment, to human society, or to the human body. We have to decide which techniques we will apply to deal with the effects of techniques already implemented, but the question of limit has still not surfaced. And models are only models. The real experiment, as Ulrich Beck explains, takes place in (and with) the real world.

Theories of nuclear reactor safety are testable only after they are built, not beforehand. The expedient of testing partial systems [what, in our discussion of nuclear energy, we have called risk or fault-tree analysis] amplifies the contingencies of their interaction, and thus contains the sources of error which cannot themselves be controlled experimentally. If one compares this with the logic of research that was originally agreed upon, this amounts to its sheer reversal. We no longer find the progression, first laboratory, then application. Instead, testing comes after application and production precedes research. The dilemma into which the mega-hazards have plunged scientific logic applies across the board; that is for nuclear, chemical and genetic experiments science hovers blindly above the boundary of threats. Test-tube babies must first be produced, genetically engineered artificial creatures released and reactors built, in order that their properties and safety can be studied.[23]

Hans Jonas has attempted to respond to the emergence of the risk society, the transformation of ethics, and the failure of both classical political theory and modern liberalism to deal with what is happening as technology provides us with unprecedented powers to (collectively) transform nature and human nature. Our ability to "act into nature" with serious consequences for those who live at great spatial distance from us on the planet now and great temporal distance from us in the future has changed the very nature of human action and the reality of ethics.[24]

Paradoxically, the quest for utopia inherent in what we have called technological progressivism has introduced the real possibility of extinction or oblivion. It has brought us, as we have argued, closer and closer to the edge of the abyss along which we are forced to tread. "Now we shiver in the nakedness of a nihilism in which near-omnipotence is paired with near-emptiness, greatest capacity with knowing least for what ends to use it."[25] What is required, Jonas argues, is an ethics of futurity that acknowledges the uncertainty of our scientific projects and their apocalyptic potential. Practically speaking, this means that "the prophecy of doom is to be given greater heed than the prophecy of bliss."[26]

It is not our purpose here to describe in detail Jonas's thoughtful attempt to develop a politics and ethics of responsibility. It has been summarized admirably by Ronald Beiner.[27] We do wish to highlight the fact that Jonas's ethical proposal is inconsistent with liberalism (and bureaucratic individualism) in two important ways. It is not neutral about foundations or about a minimalist notion of the good. Unlike Heilbroner, whose *Inquiry into the Human Prospect* we discussed in chapter 1, Jonas believes that his concern for future generations can be grounded in metaphysics and ontology. Though posterity has done nothing for us, there is a *rational* basis for a person to make sacrifices for future generations. "This idea that ethics should proceed from ontology and metaphysics is a deeply unfashionable one, but it is," Jonas says, "unavoidable nonetheless."[28] He asserts that there are teleological phenomena in nature and that human beings "are purposive beings through and through."[29] The methods of modern science may be non-teleological – purpose is not used to explain nature – but this does not mean that we can do without purpose. "It is simply not true that an 'Aristotelian' understanding of being contradicts the modern causal explanation of nature or is inconsistent with it, let alone that it has been refuted by it."[30] Nature has purpose and thus adheres to values. "Nature in adhering to values, also has the authority to sanction them and may demand their acknowledgment by us and by every knowing will dwelling in her midst."[31] Jonas uses this ontological argument to ground his ethical imperatives.

We are not convinced of the adequacy of Jonas's ontological argument, but we are persuaded of the need for ethics to be grounded in more than subjective will or individual choice if our care for future generations is to become socially binding rather than a personal option. And Jonas is right to assert against liberalism that our responsibility to preserve a future for the human race is a *collective*, not merely an individual, one. Such responsibility gives rise to a supreme principle that must be implemented socially: "Never must the existence or the essence of man as a whole be made a stake in the standards of action."[32] An ethics of limitation or restraint with regard to technological innovation can alone defend this principle.

Contra liberalism, Jonas also contends that the "language of rights and duties is inappropriate to the ethic of responsibility." To future generations, we have a responsibility or duty that is clearly not contractual, since "generations that do not exist cannot be the bearers of rights. Rather, their very existence is a crucial part of the responsibility."[33] We have the responsibility to guarantee not only the continued existence of future generations but the continued existence of their ability to engage in politics. The models of such responsibility are the statesman and the parent, but more the latter:

Just as we feel obliged to protect and preserve the infant when we are actually presented with it, as the guardian of an open future, without knowing how the child will turn out, so too we ought to labor on behalf of future generations without any assurance as to what use they will make of their inheritance or what content they will give to their humanity. Parental responsibility thus offers a "primal" paradigm of what political responsibility might become. Indeed, if we are to avert the prospect of self-inflicted global catastrophe, we must come to feel the same weight of responsibility in the relations between whole generations that we naturally do in the concrete immediacy of the parent-child relationship.[34]

The implications of Jonas's ethic of responsibility, based on what he calls a "heuristics of fear," are not spelled out in great detail. They can be summarized briefly. An ethic of responsibility is not prescriptive. It gives no positive advice as to what we should do. Like liberalism, it remains agnostic about the good. But unlike liberalism, it can tell us what not to do. Whenever we cannot know with certainty what the consequences of a technological innovation will be, caution is in order. Ignorance, knowing that we do not know – for example, about the long-range environmental effects of nuclear waste and about whether such effects may be irreversibly destructive – should have led us to reject this type of energy production regardless of its potential to provide a cheap and easy source of power. Similarly, as soon as we learned that there was a chance that climate change was the result of carbon dioxide emissions due to the burning of fossil fuels and that this would likely have destructive consequences for the planet, caution and conservation were in order. Everything should have been done to minimize our individual and collective use of those fuels.

In 1984 Jonas was not so much afraid of an apocalypse as of the slow perversion or poisoning of the basic processes of life by the "unintended dynamics of technical civilization as such, inherent in its structure, whereby it drifts willy-nilly and with exponential acceleration: the apocalypse of the 'too much,' with exhaustion, pollution, desolation of the planet."[35] His ethic of restraint and limitation of technological innovation had the goal of averting disaster. As such, however, he argued that it "asks for a revocation of the whole life style, even of the very principle of the advanced industrial societies, and will hurt an endless number of interests (the habitual interests of all.)"[36] The demand for such radical restraint was not, Jonas concluded, permanent or based on an anti-technological bias. At the end of his sobering and insightful book, Jonas came to this rather naive and toothless conclusion: "There are times when the [technological] drive needs moral encouragement, when hope and daring rather than fear and caution should lead. Ours is not one of them. In the headlong rush, the perils of excess become uppermost. This necessitates an ethical emphasis which we hope is as temporary as the condition it has to counteract."[37]

In our view, this is good but not good enough. We refer to Jonas's conclusion as naive and toothless for two reasons. First, it fails to provide the criteria for rejecting a particular technological innovation, and thus has been totally ineffectual in slowing down the acceleration due to the introduction of computers of technological innovation and growth. Twenty years after he wrote *The Imperative of Responsibility*, his ethical critique has sunk without a trace. Second, Jonas approaches today's problems of technology as accidental and temporary, to be cured by the imposition of a new ethic of restraint on a system that can be brought back under human control and then allowed to follow its own developmental path once the "apocalypse which threatens from a total development" has passed.[38] But this is to fail to understand technology as a system with its own dynamics, dynamics that been described by Jacques Ellul in terms of autonomy and self-augmentation.[39] Those dynamics affect both society and the individuals who make up that society.

The result, as we have suggested, is that we rarely ask ethical questions that have anything to do with the integrity of the human person or the limits to what we may do in the world in the light of human ends or the ends of nature. Following Ulrich Beck, we ask, rather, "How can the risks and hazards systematically produced as part of modernization be prevented, minimized, dramatized or challenged?"[40] Zygmunt Bauman agrees with Ulrich Beck that "the gravest of problems mankind confronts today and technology has to cope with are those 'resulting from techno-economic development itself.'"[41] But Bauman is surely more perceptive than Beck when he suggests that reflexivity about these problems and their attendant risks "may well increase, rather than diminish, the suicidal tendency of technological rule."[42] Like Vanderburg, Bauman sees contemporary scientific research as adding to the cumulative risks we must meet. "Science is busy producing or encouraging the production of the objects of its future indignation. It reproduces its own indispensability through piling up blunders and threats of disasters according to the principle, 'We have made this mess; we will clean it up'; and more pointedly yet, 'This is a kind of mess only we know how to clean up.'"[43]

Bauman points out that the language of risk is associated with gambling rather than ethics. The gambler enjoys the play even if he loses his bet. What is at stake in a technological society, however, is not merely the loss of a wager. We have shown that what is at stake is the loss of the planet. But, equally importantly, what is at stake is the loss of the moral self. Human beings are transformed by the system. They too become "technological objects. Like anything else they have been analyzed (split into fragments) and then synthesized in novel ways (as arrangements or just collections of fragments)."[44] However, the fragmented self, as Zygmunt Bauman explains (in agreement with Rist, although for postmodern rather than classical Augustinian reasons)[45] is not a moral subject. "The subject never acts as a 'total person,' only as a momentary carrier of one of the many 'problems' that punctuate her life; neither does she act upon the other as a person, or upon the world as a totality."[46]

The absence of a coherent account of moral subjectivity is perhaps one inevitable outcome of the Enlightenment project. We lack a language by which to discern, in ethical terms, the right relationship of human beings to themselves, to one another, and to the natural order precisely because we are only able to conceive of the human subject in terms of an indeterminate range of possibilities. Which possibilities will be realized can only be determined by the creative exercise of the will. The reality of the human being, and thus of nature, is fluid and dynamic. Being is subordinated to becoming. And the Delphic injunction "Know thyself!", which inaugurated the history of Western reason, has been answered within modernity by precisely this account of the self: as a set of possibilities to be realized, or not, through the exercise of creative willing. It goes without saying that this kind of answer is at an infinite remove from the spirit in which the meaning of the injunction was first pondered by the ancient Greeks.

What our ancient predecessors understood was that the ability to discern the appropriate range of action with respect to ourselves, each other, and nature depended on an answer to that question. Nothing in our history has disproved that assumption. In fact, we might say that the civilization of the Enlightenment has proved the rule by ignoring it and, as a consequence, bringing humanity to the possibility of self-destruction, either by catastrophe or by perversion. If the attempt to discern a proper relationship to the natural order (including the order of human nature) is at least in part constitutive of who we are, then it is not surprising that in ignoring the crucial question of who we are, we have put nature itself in the balance.

It has not been our intention in this book simply to be prophets of doom, although we have been convinced by Simone Weil that modern science, in spite of all its undeniable and impressive accomplishments, has lost its way,[47] and that the technological society harbours within its own inflexible algebraic logic the capacity to destroy itself and the planet. (Who among us can deny the fear of collapse that we suppress through our restless activity?)[48] We are convinced that any attempt to avert such a disaster simply by mobilizing in novel ways the instrumental rationality that characterizes that system is bound to fail. We have also argued that the adoption of the Enlightenment worldview has involved the progressive silencing of meaningful discussion of who we are as moral subjects in relation to a natural (and supernatural) order that transcends us. According to traditional ethics, the appropriate modalities for the discovery of such essential relationships were contemplation and reverence. And, according to this older world view, the occasions of our running up against the limits of calculative reason disclosed a horizon beyond which the only appropriate human comportment was that of wonder or awe. Practically, this horizon confronted us with a limit to our creative willing. Of course that horizon could not always be absolutely fixed and always had to be rediscovered in the course of something like a dialogue between human agents and that transcendent reality (taking into consideration human needs and the capacity of nature to meet those needs while being preserved in its own integrity). It was indeed a novel step that was taken, however, when the civilization of the Enlightenment sought to efface that horizon altogether by denying the notion of the human subject as the site of an essential relation between active willing (or obedience) and an order that gave that willing its very purposiveness and limits.[49]

George Grant has spoken of the need for human beings "whose liberal horizons fade in the winter of nihilism" to attune themselves to what he has called "intimations of deprival."[50] If indeed we have silenced the language of meaningful discourse about proper human ends, then we must now turn to those other modalities that, at least according to tradition, could alone disclose those ends: awe and gratitude. On the practical level, the level of ethics and politics, this would mean reinterpreting and re-evaluating the meaning of ignorance in a way more profound than that of a "heuristics of fear." When we cannot know the consequences of our actions, we should seek the humility to draw back from action; when the weighing of costs and benefits seems to involve the comparison of incommensurables, we should resist the temptation to measure.

By honestly coming to terms with "the end of ethics" (understood as the failure of ethics as conceived within the modern account), we are forced to reconsider the ends by which ethical reasoning is itself to be guided. This is the other meaning of the "end of ethics," and it is in terms of both of these meanings (the one negative, the other positive) that we have engaged in the reflections contained in this book. We will not be aided by an analysis that fails to discern the true magnitude and depth of the crisis we are in. Nor will we be served by a naiveté or religious optimism that fails to acknowledge that there is a crisis and pretends that there is a safety net to save us from the results of our actions. But finally, we will not be served by those who say that our fate is rigidly determined and is not open to thought, or that we are the kinds of beings who must inevitably destroy ourselves in the pursuit of our narrow desires and in the exercise of our implacable wills. Should we succumb to the temptation to think of ourselves as fated, it will be because we have failed to know ourselves as truly capable of thought or love. But if the ancient Greeks and Christians were correct in asserting that it is our vocation as human beings to truly know ourselves, then our fate is not determined, and reflection on the nihilism of modern ethics can open up the possibility of meditation on the true end of ethics.

Notes

PREFACE

1 See, for example, Kahn and Simon, *The Resourceful Earth*; Simon, *The Ultimate Resource 2*; Negroponte, *Being Digital*.
2 Candu: the nuclear reactor developed by Atomic Energy of Canada.
3 See, for example, Jungk, *The New Tyranny*; Mander, *Four Arguments for the Elimination of Television*; Stoll, *Silicon Snake Oil*.
4 Postman, *Technopoly*.
5 See Kaczinski, "The Unabomber Manifesto."
6 Gore, *Earth in the Balance* and *An Inconvenient Truth*.
7 Franklin, *The Real World of Technology*, 1.
8 Rosen, *Nihilism*, xiii
9 Kaczinski, "The Unabomber Manifesto," 233.
10 Jonas, *The Imperative of Responsibility*.
11 See Ellul, *The Technological System*, 125–55.
12 Davis, *Technology – Humanism or Nihilism*.
13 See Weil, "Draft for a Statement of Human Obligations," and *The Need for Roots*.
14 See Voegelin, *The New Science of Politics*, 130: "The death of the spirit is the price of progress … The more fervently all human energies are thrown into the great enterprise of salvation through world immanent action, the farther the human beings who engage in this enterprise move away from the life of the spirit."

INTRODUCTION

1 See Mumford, *The Myth of the Machine* and *The Pentagon of Power*; Winner, *Autonomous Technology* and *The Whale and the Reactor*;

Schumacher, *Small Is Beautiful* and *Good Work*; and Ellul, *The Techno-logical Society*, *The Technological System*, and *The Technological Bluff*.

2 Ellul, *The Technological System*, 77.
3 See Kroker, *Technology and the Canadian Mind*. Kroker moved on to a hy-per-modern approach to the discussion of communication and media. The moral sensitivity of his mentors has been abandoned in the service of the sullenness and hyperactivity of postmodern trendiness. For an excellent discussion of sullenness and hyperactivity as traits of the post-modern, see Borgmann, *Crossing the Postmodern Divide*, chapter 1.
4 Bauman, *The Individualized Society*, 18.
5 See Innis, *The Bias of Communication* and *Empire and Communications*.
6 McLuhan, *Understanding Media*.
7 Franklin, *The Real World of Technology*, 1. See Heidegger, *The Question Concerning Technology*.
8 Franklin, *The Real World of Technology*, 10.
9 Ibid., 12.
10 Ibid., 10.
11 Ibid., 15. See also Innis, *Empire and Communications*, 36.
12 Franklin, *The Real World of Technology*, 30.
13 Ibid.
14 Ibid., 17.
15 Havelock, *Preface to Plato*; see Ong, chapter 2, "Transformations of the Word," in *The Presence of the Word*.
16 See Voegelin, *Order and History, Vol. IV*.
17 McLuhan, *The Gutenburg Galaxy*.
18 Franklin, *The Real World of Technology*, 34.
19 Ibid., 31.
20 See Ellul, *The Technological System*, chapter 9. 209–31.
21 See Franklin, *Canada as a Conserver Society*.
22 Franklin, *The Real World of Technology*, 120.
23 Vanderburg, *The Labyrinth of Technology*, 427.
24 Ibid., 430.
25 For an insightful but ethically superficial discussion of the problems that technology itself creates, see Thomas Homer-Dixon, *The Ingenuity Gap*.
26 See Voegelin, *The New Science of Politics*.
27 Vanderburg, *Living in the Labyrinth of Technology*, 72.
28 Ibid., 78.
29 Ibid., 82–3.
30 See Voegelin, "The Origins of Scientism."

31 See, for example, Logan, *The Fifth Language.*

32 Grant, *Technology and Justice*, 12. Grant acknowledged that he had learned this from reading Heidegger. See Arthur Davis, "Justice and Freedom."

33 Grant, *Technology and Empire*, 129.

CHAPTER ONE

1 See, for example, Cox, *The Secular City.*

2 See Grant's comments in "Conversation: Theology and History" in Schmidt, *George Grant in Process*, 103: "Both western accounts of Christianity – Protestant and Catholic – have emphasized the arbitrary power of God in a way that seems fundamentally wrong and which has produced a picture of God whom one should not worship. I think those emphases on the power of God are related to the exclusivity and dynamism that have led to the worst sides of western civilization. We in the West are called to rethink all of this, which started somewhere close to Augustine."

3 See Noble, *The Religion of Technology*, chapter 1, "The Divine Likeness."

4 Max Weber describes the link between the Protestant notion of the calling, the spirit of capitalism, and the practical approach to technical invention as manifest in the life of Benjamin Franklin in *The Protestant Ethic and the Spirit of Capitalism.* See also Merton, *Science, Technology and Society in Seventeenth-Century England*, particularly chapter 4, "Puritanism and Cultural Values."

5 See Berman, *The Reenchantment of the Earth.*

6 See Cullmann, *Christ and Time.* See also Voegelin, *From Enlightenment to Revolution*, 6: "For Bossuet in the seventeenth, as for St Augustine in the fifth century, the universality of history lies in the providential guidance of mankind toward the true religion. The history of Israel, the appearance of Christ, and the history of the Church are the meaningful history of mankind, while the profane history with its revolutions of empire has only the function of providing the educative tribulations for Israel and the Church preparatory to the ultimate triumph."

7 See Voegelin, *From Enlightenment to Revolution*, 19–23, "The Dynamics of Secularization."

8 For a discussion of this term, see Braaten, *History and Hermeneutics.*

9 For a description of this process and a discussion of its significance for the development of "religion" as a topic, see Voegelin, *Order and History, Vol. IV*, 43–9. See also Schmidt, "Simone Weil on Religion."

10 See Fortin, "St. Augustine."

11 See MacIntyre, *Three Rival Versions of Morality*, chapter 6.

12 Grant, *Technology and Empire*, 20.

13 Ibid., 21. For a discussion of the complexity of the process by which the alchemist vision of the world was defeated and the mechanistic vision triumphed, see Berman, *The Reenchantment of the Earth*, chapter 3.

14 This attack, led by Voltaire, is described by Voegelin, *From Enlightenment to Revolution*, 27–8. It is significant for the transformation of ethics, and so we quote it at length:

The spiritual obscurantism of Voltaire makes it impossible for him to center a philosophy of morals in the idea of the spiritually integrated personality. The problems of ethics are dealt with under the title of "natural religion": "I understand by natural religion the principles of morals which are common to the human species." (Voltaire, *Elemens de Philosophie de Newton* [1738] *Oeuvres* pt. 1, ch. 6.) Such common rules are supposed to exist because they have their source in the biological structure of man and serve the purpose of making possible life in society. The fundamental rule is, therefore, a collectivized version of the Golden Rule; that you should act towards others as you would wish them to act toward you. The rule is not founded on the assumption of a spiritual person or of the recognition of the spiritual person in fellowman; rather it is founded on the utility for society of a conduct in accordance with the rule ... The transcendental constitution of mankind through the pneuma of Christ is replaced by faith in the intraworldly constitution of mankind through "compassion." On this point Voltaire follows Newton closely. "Newton thought that the disposition that we have to live in society is the foundation of natural law." The disposition of compassion in man is as general as his other instincts. "Newton has cultivated this sentiment of humanity and he extended it even to the animals." This compassion which he had for animals turned into true charity with regard to man. Indeed, without humanity, the virtue which comprises all virtues, a man hardly merits the name of philosopher. (*Elemens*, pt. 1, ch. 6.) Elements of Stoicism and Averroism obviously have entered the belief in humanity as rarefied biological instinct which serves the existence of the animal tribe. The chattering discourse of Voltaire, furthermore, betrays more openly than the more carefully considered formulations of later thinkers the relations between humanitarian tribalism and certain other phenomena. The attack on the saint as the prudent person who takes care of himself and forgets the neighbor is on principle already the

Communist and National Socialist attack on the freedom and the achievements of the spirit, as well as on the spiritual formation of personality, as socially useless and perhaps even dangerous private concerns. The sphere of the socially valuable is restricted to the procurement of animal comforts and to scientific discoveries which may serve this purpose. Behind the phrase that a man who is not socially useful in the restricted sense does not count looms the virtuous *terreur* of Robespierre and the massacres by the later humanitarians whose hearts are filled with compassion to the point that they are willing to slaughter one half of mankind to make the other half happy. The complacent assumption that charitable compassion is a general disposition of man abandons the healthy Christian cynicism which is aware of the precarious ascendancy of the spirit over the passions and takes its precautions. The identification of the good with the socially useful foreshadows the compulsory goodness of the social planner as well as the idea of revolutionary justice, with the assumption that right is what serves the proletariat, the nation or the chosen race.

15 It has been argued that Kant is as much an Enlightenment figure as is Voltaire and that Kant affirms an otherworldly God. The Enlightenment is therefore not simply antitheistic or anti-Christian. Without wishing to argue the point in detail, we would say that the mainstream of Enlightenment thought is clearly deist or atheist and that Nietzsche is correct when he says that Kant is the great delayer who legitimated the Enlightenment to pious Protestants.

16 Grant, *Philosophy in the Mass Age*, 1966, 51.

17 See Becker, *The Heavenly City of the Eighteenth Century Philosophers*, 102; Goudzwaard, *Capitalism and Progress*, 45–50; Lasch, *The True and Only Heaven*, 52.

18 See Grant, *Philosophy in the Mass Age*, 1966, chapter 3.

19 See Sartre, *Existentialism and Human Emotions*.

20 Rist, *Real Ethics*, 191:

[P]hilosophers who, like Sartre, want to insist that man has no essence but only a history, no ongoing nature but only a set of experiences, or who, more recently, talk about human life "before the institution of sexuality," can only end by deifying lying and self-deception, and one notes the recurrence of deception as an outcome; we have already considered it in connection with the hypothesized need for social *belief* in objective values even if there are none. As we can pretend that objective values exist, so we can pretend to create ourselves while actually failing to do so. It is easy to see how someone who goes down the road of self-creation will come to entertain delusions of grandeur if not of divinity; he would be so much better off, as he imagines, if he possessed greater or absolute power; he could make others (or "the other") do his will; above all he could make him refuse to challenge the lying claim that we can create ourselves and achieve what are then styled "free" choices and autonomous acts.

21 Elliot, *Twentieth Century Book of the Dead.*

22 See Bauman, *Modernity and the Holocaust.* George Grant earlier described our philosophical dilemma in *Philosophy in the Mass Age,* 1966, 78:

On the one hand, does not the idea of a divine order encourage (humanity) to accept the conditions of the world rather than to improve them. Religious societies have surely accepted the fact of scarcity, have accepted that starvation is one of the vicissitudes men may be called upon to bear, have accepted that human beings must earn their living by the sweat of their brow. The contemplative meditating on the wonders of the divine order, isolated and protected from the floods and famines, illustrates this acceptance. It is rebellion against this which has moved (humanity) in the age of progress ... But as soon as this is said, the necessity for limits to (our) making of history must be stated with equal force. It is undeniable that the worst crimes of the twentieth century have been perpetrated in the name of progress and our right to make history.

23 Grant, *Philosophy in the Mass Age,* 1966, 78.

24 Ibid., viii.

25 Grant's views also went contrary to the assumption (articulated by Leo Strauss) that the United States with its origins in the first (Lockean) wave of modernity was a conservative force in modern global politics. For him, the United States spearheaded the technological transformation of the globe and led the way toward the creation of the universal and homogeneous state that Hegel and Kojève presaged. It could not be a force for the maintenance of even Lockean traditions. See H.D. Forbes, "George Grant and Leo Strauss," 170–1.

26 See Heilbroner, *An Inquiry into the Human Prospect.* 11. This book was originally published in 1974.

27 Ibid., 20.

28 Ibid., 32, 62.

29 Ibid., 68–74.

30 Ibid., 52.

31 Ibid., 72.

32 Ibid., 39–46.

33 Ibid., 56.

34 Ibid., 57. See also Saul, *Voltaire's Bastards*, chapters 6, 7, 8.

35 Heilbroner, *An Inquiry into the Human Prospect*, 93:

> There is the value of the self-evident importance of efficiency, with its tendency to subordinate the optimum human scale of things to the optimum technical scale. There is the value of the need to "tame" the environment with its consequence of an unthinking pillage of nature. There is the value of the priority of production itself, visible in the care that both systems lavish on technical virtuosity and the indifference with which both look upon the aesthetic dimensions of life. All these values manifest themselves throughout bourgeois and "socialist" styles of life, both lived by the clock, organized by the factory or office, obsessed with material achievements, attuned to highly quantitative modes of thought – in a word by styles of life that, in contrast with non-industrial civilizations, seem dazzlingly rich in every dimension except that of the cultivation of the human person.

36 Ibid., 93.

37 Ibid., 160.

38 Ibid.

39 Ibid., 161.

40 Ibid.

41 This enigmatic quotation is found in *Der Spiegel's* 23 September 1966 interview with Heidegger, which was published posthumously on 31 May 1976 and reprinted as a translation by Maria P. Alter and John D. Caputo in *The Heidegger Controversy* (Richard Wolin, ed.): "Philosophy will not be able to effect an immediate transformation of the present condition of the world. This is not only true of philosophy, but of all merely human thought and endeavor. Only a god can save us. The sole possibility that is left for us is to prepare a sort of readiness, through thinking and poeticizing, for the appearance of the god or for the absence of the god in the time of foundering *Untergang* for in the face of the god who is absent, we founder."

42 Heilbroner, *An Inquiry into the Human Prospect*, 185.

43 Ibid., 166.

CHAPTER TWO

1 Statistics from "Rich Planet Poor Planet," in *State of the World 2001*, Worldwatch Institute, 4–8. See also Earth Trends: How many people live on less than $1 a day? December 22, 2005 at http://earthtrends. wriupdates nodes/6 (accessed January 2007)

2 Homer-Dixon, "The Rich Get Richer, and the Poor Get Squat." Review of Branko Milanovic, *Worlds Apart.*

3 Ibid.

4 Ibid. See also Milanovic, *Worlds Apart,* chapter 10, "A World without a Middle Man."

5 Bauman pointed out that "all the tigers together embrace no more than 1 per cent of the population of Asia alone." Bauman, *Globalization: The Human Consequences,* 73.

6 See Bauman, *The Individualized Society,* 18–19:

> Most economic historians agree ... that so far as levels of income are concerned, there was little to distinguish between diverse civilizations at the peak of their powers: the riches of Rome in the first century, of China in the eleventh and India in the seventeenth were not much different from those of Europe at the threshold of the industrial revolution. By some estimates, the income per head in Western Europe in the eighteenth century was no more than 30 per cent higher than that of India, Africa or China at that time. Little more than one century was enough to transform the ratio beyond recognition. By 1870, income per head was eleven times higher than in the poorest countries of the world. In the course of the next century or so, the factor grew fivefold – and reached 50 by 1995. As the Sorbonne economist, Daniel Cohen points out: "I dare to say that the phenomenon of inequality between nations is of recent origin; it is a product of the last two centuries." (Daniel Cohen, *Richessse, du monde, pauvretés des nations,* [Paris: Flammarion, 1998], 31.)

7 See Stivers, *Hunger, Technology and Limits to Growth.*

8 See Jackson, *The Rich Nations and the Poor Nations, Towards a World of Plenty,* and *Progress for a Small Planet.*

9 See also Gheddo, *Why Is the Third World Poor?*

10 Genesis, 1:28.

11 See Berger, *The Sacred Canopy,* 117.

12 See Voegelin, *Order and History: Volume I.*

13 See Polanyi, *The Great Transformation*; Heilbroner, *The Great Ascent*; and Boulding, *The Meaning of the Twentieth Century.*

14 See Ortega y Gasset, *The Revolt of the Masses,* 50.

15 See Ashton, *The Industrial Revolution,* chapter 1.

16 See Lukacs, *The Passing of the Modern Age,* chapter 18, "The Bourgeois Interior," 191–207.

17 I accept Lukacs' distinction between bourgeoisie and middle class. The former is a historical phenomenon related to the rise of the city in Europe in the modern period; it entails the co-existence of aristocratic

standards and democratic ideals. The latter is a sociological category that implies nothing more than the group in the middle of society with standard aspirations for comfort, convenience, security, leisure, and standard possessions of food, clothing, and shelter. See Lukacs, *The Passing of the Modern Age,* 192–6.

18 See Lukacs, *Outgrowing Democracy.*

19 See Ehrlich, *The Population Bomb.* Ehrlich argued in his later book, *The Population Explosion,* that the bomb was already exploding. We find the metaphor "population bomb" offensive because it views human beings rather than technological expansion as the problem. It is clear that modern population growth has been the result of technological expansion, rather than vice versa. Without denying the importance of population limitation – which is clearly not a problem in the "developed" world – it seems to me that those interested in "saving the planet" should be more concerned to limit the growth of the automobile population rather than the human population. As yet no one has written a book entitled *The Automobile Bomb.* What is good for General Motors or Toyota, it is assumed, is good for the planet.

20 The classic description of this process is found in Galeano, *Open Veins of Latin America.*

21 See Myrdal, *Against the Stream,* 71–3.

22 Ibid., 73–88.

23 Rostow, *The Stages of Economic Growth.*

24 Sachs, *Planet Dialectics,* 5.

25 Ibid.

26 Cited in Sachs, *Planet Dialectics,* 12.

27 Hardin, "Lifeboat Ethics."

28 In 1976 John Crispo, who was dean of the Faculty of Management Studies at the University of Toronto from 1970 to 1975, published an article in the *Globe and Mail* entitled "All Foreign Aid Should Be for Birth Control."

29 Bello, "Structural Adjustment Programs," 285–93.

30 Ibid., 287.

31 Ibid., 289–92.

32 Daly, "Free Trade," 230. See also Daly, *Beyond Growth.*

33 See Joseph Kahn, "A Fork in the Road to Riches," *New York Times,* 25 June 2000.

34 *State of the World 2001,* 113.

35 Schumacher, *Small Is Beautiful,* 19–25.

36 Ibid., 12–17.

37 Sachs, *Planet Dialectics*, 11.
38 Schumacher. *Small Is Beautiful.*, 136–42.
39 Myrdal, *Against the Stream*, 107.
40 Ibid., 102.
41 Ibid., 112–16.
42 Ibid., 122–4.
43 See Collins and Lappé, *World Hunger.*
44 Ibid.; See George, *How the Other Half Dies*; McGinnis, *Bread and Justice.*
45 See Commoner, *The Closing Circle.*
46 Commoner, *Making Peace with the Planet*, 153.
47 Ibid., 166.
48 Mander, *In the Absence of the Sacred*, 120.
49 For a thoughtful Canadian perspective on the function of transna-
    tional corporations see the last chapter of Kierans, *Remembering*, 250–
    69. Kierans argues that American corporations, are not quite as value
    neutral as they claim and that they do not rise above nationalism, at
    least not above American nationalism. Rather, they have been deliber-
    ately turned into battering rams for the national policies of the United
    States. Witness the changes demanded by Congress as the price of U.S.
    support for the International Monetary Fund, as recorded by Robert
    Gilpin, Eisenhower Professor of Public and International Affairs at
    Princeton. Gilpin's most recent book notes among the conditions laid
    down by Congress, the following: "The U.S. Treasury must certify that
    IMF loans do not subsidize industries that compete against American
    industry." (Robert Gilpin, *The Challenge of Global Capitalism* [Princeton:
    Princeton University Press, 2000], 334).
50 Sachs, *Planet Dialectics*, 29.
51 Crocker, "Towards Development Ethics," 457–83.
52 Ellul, "The Ethics of Nonpower," 208.
53 Ibid., 210.
54 Sachs, *Planet Dialectics*, 33.

CHAPTER THREE

1 Daniel Howden, "Deforestation: The Hidden Cause of Global Warming," *The Independent*, 3 May 2007.
2 Gore, *An Inconvenient Truth*, 66–7, 72–3.
3 Monbiot, *Heat*, 6.
4 Brown, Flavien, French, et al., *State of the World 2000*, 3–21, and Gore,
   An Inconvenient Truth, 182–3.

5 Pearce, *The Last Generation*, 3.

6 Brown, Flavin, French, et al., *State of the World 2000*, 3–21.

7 Monbiot, *Heat*, 10.

8 Gore, *An Inconvenient Truth*, 10.

9 Stivers, *Hunger, Technology and Limits to Growth*, 13.

10 See Kahn and Simon, *The Resourceful Earth*, and Simon, *The Ultimate Resource* and *The Ultimate Resource 2*.

11 Lovins, *Soft Energy Paths* and *Energy/War: Breaking the Connection*; Commoner, *Making Peace with the Planet*.

12 Daly and Cobb, *For the Common Good*.

13 World Commission on Environment and Development, *Our Common Future*.

14 Thiele, *Environmentalism for a New Millennium*, 51.

15 Ibid., 53.

16 Kurien, "Economics of the Just and Sustainable Society," 222.

17 Sachs, *Planet Dialectics*, 82.

18 Daly, *Steady-State Economics*.

19 See Daly, "The Ecological and Moral Necessity."

20 A slogan used by Ontario Hydro to encourage electricity consumption in the sixties and seventies.

21 See "Growthmania" in Daly, *Towards a Steady-State Economy*.

22 For an excellent theoretical critique, see MacIntyre, "Utilitarianism and Cost-Benefit Analysis."

23 Simon, *The Ultimate Resource*, 49–50.

24 See Ellul, *The Technological Bluff*, 20, and Corten, *When Corporations Rule the World*.

25 See Barnett, *Global Reach*, and Barnett and Cavanagh, *Global Dreams*. Michael Jordan is said to have received more for his involvement in Nike's commercials for basketball shoes than did the entire production staff in Indonesia where they are made. See Crawford, "Historian Walter LaFeber Goes One-on-One."

26 See Lovins' optimistic views in *Soft-Energy Paths*, 23.

27 See CNN, "Bush Has Plan to End Oil 'Addiction,'" 1 February 2006. http://www.cnn.com/2006/POLITICS/01/31/bush.sotu/ (accessed 6 February 2007)

28 Daly and Cobb, *For the Common Good*, 198.

29 Ibid., 13.

30 Ibid., 141–4.

31 Ibid., 155.

32 Commoner, *Making Peace with the Planet*, 3–10.

33 Ibid., 193.

34 Brown, Flavin, French, et al., *State of the World 2000*, 96–9.

35 Commoner, *Making Peace With the Planet*, 193–4.

36 Ibid., 194–5.

37 Ibid., 193.

38 Ibid., 240.

39 Ibid., 242.

40 Daly and Cobb, *For the Common Good*, 145–6.

41 Thiele, *Environmentalism for a New Millennium*, 17–28.

42 Ibid., 57.

43 Rasmussen, *Earth Community, Earth Ethics*, 349.

44 Daly and Cobb, *For the Common Good*, 369.

45 Ibid., 377.

46 Ibid., 388.

47 White, "The Historical Roots of Our Ecological Crisis."

48 See Hall, *The Steward*.

49 Daly and Cobb, *For the Common Good*, 388.

50 Ibid., 398.

51 Ibid., 399.

52 Oelschlager, *Caring for Creation*, 236.

53 Ibid., 233. See also Shell Renewable's information page "About Shell Renewables" at www.shell.com/home/content/rw-br (accessed 18 June 2007).

54 Brown, Flavin, French, et al., *State of the World 2000*, 94–5.

55 Information for the following discussion of hydrogen fuel technology is largely taken from Brown, Flavin, French, et al., *State of the World 2000*, 96–8.

56 In a letter to the *Globe and Mail* (17 March 2003), David H. Martin of the Sierra Club of Canada responded to Geoffrey Ballard's proposal to use nuclear power:

Hydrogen as portable transportation fuel is no panacea, because it is itself an energy product, similar to electricity. So it depends on how it is made. If it is made with electricity through electrolysis, then the question is how the electricity is generated. Electricity generated by fossil fuels is not desirable because of the acid and climate-change gases produced. Nuclear-generated electricity is not desirable because of its high cost, unreliability, risk and the radioactive pollution produced.

Building 20 prototype reactors to generate hydrogen for cars is a wacky idea. Ontario Power Generation's four Darlington reactors cost

more than $14 billion when they were completed 10 years ago
and Ontario ratepayers have been paying for the disaster ever since.
A saliva test should be mandatory for anybody proposing a project five
times the size of Darlington, with an untested reactor design.

57 See Energy Bulletin, http://www.energybulletin.net/primer.php
(accessed 30 May 2007).

58 See Colin Campbell, "The Coming Global Oil Crisis," http://
www.oilcrisis.com/summary.htm (accessed 23 February 2007)

59 See "THE END OF SUBURBIA: Oil Depletion and the Collapse
of The American Dream," directed by Gregory Crane. http://
www.endofsuburbia.com/index.htm (accessed 30 May 2007).

60 Heinberg, *Powerdown*, 160

61 Sachs, *Planet Dialectics*, 88.

62 Ibid., 48.

63 Ibid., 46.

64 Ibid., 49.

65 Ibid., 122.

66 Ibid., 61.

CHAPTER FOUR

1 This epigraph is from a letter published in the *University of Toronto Bulletin*, Monday, 8 February 1982. It was written by Dr D.G. Andrews, Canada's first professor of nuclear engineering and a founder of the Canadian Nuclear Association, in response to a letter of mine. I (Schmidt) was critical of the then president of the University of Toronto for supporting the establishment of a Hydrogen Institute, which, if successful, would have required massive amounts of (mostly nuclear-generated) electricity for its functioning. (The institute cost over $5 million to set up and was dismantled by 1985.) This chapter is an attempt to spread our ethics evenly.

2 As quoted in Davis, *Technology – Humanism or Nihilism*, 1.

3 Sufficiency is concerned with the present demands of justice, specifically distributive justice. It is "the timely supply to all persons of basic material necessities defined as the resources needed for food, clothing, shelter, transportation, health care and some margin above subsistence … This emphasis on basics implies a reduction in consumption by those consuming in excess of basics and an increase in consumption by those who find themselves short of basics" (Stivers, *Hunger, Technology and Limits to Growth*, 128–9). Sustainability, "the

long-range capacity of the earth to supply resources for basic needs at
a reasonable cost to society and the environment" (129), is concerned
with the future and is based on our "duties to future generations" or
our concern for the environment. Liberal capitalist societies, as Heilbroner has pointed out, have great difficulty grounding these duties or
this concern. What has posterity ever done for those living in the
present? Why should you or I be concerned about the survival of our
species? No "is" implies an "ought." And future citizens are in no position to participate in the contract that binds the members of the
present polity.

4 For a good introductory summary of the debate as it took place in the
World Council of Churches in the 1970s, long before concerns about
nuclear power were of major concern to the general public, see
Francis and Abrecht, *Facing up to Nuclear Power.* Most of this text was
photographed directly from *Anticipation* nos 20 and 21 (May and
October 1975). The general tenor of the book is encapsulated in the
recommendations of the report to the churches of the ecumenical
hearing on nuclear energy, Sigtuna, Sweden, 24–29 June 1975: "Our
group cannot put forward categorical recommendations. It would not
feel justified either in entirely rejecting, nor in wholeheartedly recom-
mending large scale use of nuclear energy" (Francis and Abrecht,
Facing up to Nuclear Power, 200).

5 The assumption that more energy is always better than less, and that
therefore a society can never have enough, has been questioned by
many like E.F. Schumacher, Amory Lovins, and others in the environmental movement. But few have argued that less energy would be better even if there were no environmental consequences. Ivan Illich was
one of the earliest to try to move the debate to an ethical level by arguing that the use of more energy per capita (a common measure of
"quality of life") is bad. In *The Right to Useful Unemployment,* 71–3, Illich
summarized his argument in this way:

Atomic energy reactors have been widely criticized because their radiation is a threat, or because they foster technocratic controls. So far
only very few have dared to criticize them because they add to the energy glut. The paralysis of human action by socially destructive energy
quanta has not yet been accepted as an argument for reducing the call
for energy. Similarly, the inexorable limits to growth that are built into
any service agency are still widely ignored ... At some point in every domain, the amount of goods delivered so degrades the environment for
personal action that the possible synergy for use-values turns negative.

On this basis, Illich contrasted industrial versus "convivial" tools, and argued for social reform of technology to encourage the development of the latter (see Illich's *Tools for Conviviality*). The vagueness of the term "convivial," its dissociation from any consideration of the scientific basis of technological development, and the impossibility of its social and cultural, as opposed to personal, realization in a scientific society will become evident later.

6 Patterson, *Nuclear Power*, 216.

7 Mazur, "Three Mile Island and the Scientific Community," 216, quoting the declaration presented to Congress and the President of the United States on the thirtieth anniversary of the atomic bombing of Hiroshima. It was signed by more than 2000 biologists, chemists, engineers, and other scientists and published by the Union of Concerned Scientists, Cambridge, Mass.

8 Commoner, *The Poverty of Power*, 86–7.

9 Canadian Nuclear Association, *Nuclear Power in Canada*, 40.

10 US Regulatory Commission, Reactor Safety Study, WASH-1400 (Washington, D.C.: US Government Printing Office, 1975) as cited in Morone and Woodhouse, *Averting Catastrophe*, 62–3. The authors state:
"For nuclear power, the most vivid example of such conflict among experts was the dispute over the Rasmussen report. This major study of reactor safety, sponsored in 1975 by the Atomic Energy Commission and directed by MIT professor Norman Rasmussen, estimated that the worst plausible reactor accident would lead to thirty-three hundred early fatalities, forty-five thousand early illnesses, and fifteen hundred latent cancer fatalities. However, it gave the probability of such a severe accident at one in a billion (per reactor per year).

Nuclear power advocates seized on this report as support for their cause. The exceedingly low probability of an accident, they argued, demonstrated the safety of nuclear power. But others, including the American Physics Society, countered that, because of substantial uncertainties, … the likelihood and effects of a serious accident could be considerably greater than estimated. The effects of low-level radiation would add several thousand to the estimated latent cancer fatalities."

By 1985 the debate over the Rasmussen report had not been resolved.

11 Canadian Nuclear Association, *Nuclear Power in Canada*, 40.

12 One of the common arguments for taking these risks is that the human community is subject to such risks at the hands of nature. For example, the population of the Los Angeles area is subject to

low-probability, high-consequence (LOPHIC) risks due to earthquakes
caused by the shifting of the San Andreas fault. But we do not force
these populations to leave the area. The counter argument is that in
Los Angeles no human agency is responsible for the creation of the
LOPHIC risk and no human being is forced to live in the area. Where
there is no human agency, it seems to me, there can be no ethical responsibility. The construction of the Pickering station or the burying
of its waste in northern Ontario imposes a human risk that, it is argued, could be eliminated if we used less energy and produced it in
other ways.

13 Canadian Nuclear Association, *Nuclear Power in Canada*, 41.
14 Commoner, *The Poverty of Power*, 88.
15 Jungk, *The New Tyranny*, 65. Jungk goes on to say that "the Nuclear
    Regulatory Commission in January 1979 officially repudiated the find-
    ings of the Rasmussen report, specifically the report's claim that the
    risk of a serious nuclear accident was minimal."
16 Commoner, *The Poverty of Power*, 89.
17 Ibid., 90.
18 Knelman, *Nuclear Energy*, 112–13. Note that Knelman assumes that we
    can distinguish our genuine energy requirements from false or spuri-
    ous demands, yet he offers no way to do this. In an affluent society, the
    "need" to use energy to play video games or watch television is very
    difficult to distinguish from the need to cook dinner.
19 Mazur, "Three Mile Island and the Scientific Community."
20 See Morone and Woodhouse, *The Demise of Nuclear Energy*, 19. The au-
    thors make no judgment about the safety of reactors or the tractability
    of the problems of waste disposal or terrorism. They are modern polit-
    ical scientists who make no *ethical* judgments at all. They begin, how-
    ever, with the assumption that nuclear energy is a *"politically* [my
    emphasis] unsafe technology" (3).
21 Weinberg, *Nuclear Reactions*, 245. The problem with this approach was
    explained by the dean of the German reactor industry, Wolf Häfele,
    who wrote in 1974:

    It is precisely the interplay between theory and experiment or trial
    and error which is no longer possible for reactor technology ... Reac-
    tor engineers take account of this dilemma by dividing the problem of
    technical safety into subproblems. But even the splitting of the prob-
    lem can only serve to approximate ultimate safety ... The remaining
    residual risk opens the door to the hypothetical ... The interchange
    between theory and experiment which leads to truth in the traditional

sense is no longer possible ... I believe it is this ultimate indecisive-
ness hidden in our plans which explains the particular sensitivities
of public debates on the safety of nuclear reactors. Wolf Häfele,
"Hypotheticality and the New Challenges: The Pathfinder Role of
Nuclear Energy," *Minerva*, 12, 1 (1974): 313–21, as quoted in Beck,
World Risk Society, 60.

22 See Canada, Nuclear Fuel Waste Act (2002).

23 See Sims, *The Anti-Nuclear Game*, 136: "Most of the radioisotopes in the
used fuel have short half-lives, with about a dozen classified as medium, and another classified as long. These radioisotopes are all decay-
ing and giving off energy. As a result, the fuel is generating both heat
and radio-activity and must be managed with great care."

24 Commoner, *The Poverty of Power*, 94.

25 Canadian Nuclear Association, *Nuclear Power in Canada*, 26. Plutonium
has a half-life of approximately 24,000 years, and it would take about
ten half-lives for it to become harmless.

26 Ibid.

27 Weinberg, "Salvaging the Atomic Age" reprinted in *Nuclear Reactions*,
243.

28 Sims, *The Anti-Nuclear Game*, 143.

29 Ibid., 140.

30 Ibid. It is true that scientists can know the rate of decay of the radioactive material, but it is not true that they can know for certain how long
the material can be isolated from the environment.

31 Ibid., 142.

32 Even as Bill C-27 (the Nuclear Fuel Waste Act) was being debated in
the Canadian Parliament in 2002, Dr Derek Lister, a nuclear engineer
and advisory committee member, contended that "the toxicity of spent
fuel becomes less than that of natural uranium ore after 600 to 1000
years." This calculation was disputed later by AECL, who said that it was
"underestimated by a fact[or] of 16." See "Nuclear Notes," November
2002, page 2.

33 Sims, *The Anti-Nuclear Game*, 136.

34 Ibid. The transition is either to solar technologies or to breeder reactors. Breeder reactors use plutonium as fuel. Although this would dispose of the waste (and lower the risks associated with its permanent
storage), it would also add to the risks associated with transportation
and sabotage in a "plutonium economy." If the transition is to solar energies, why not make the transition now and shut the nuclear facilities
down as soon as possible?

35 Canadian Nuclear Association, *Nuclear Power in Canada*, 26.
36 Schumacher, *Small Is Beautiful*, 121. One can contrast this dire judgment with the cavalier attitude expressed by some officials in the
   nuclear industry. In the letter referred to in the epigraph of this
   chapter (*University of Toronto Bulletin*, 8 February 1982), Professor D.G.
   Andrews stated:
      "Regarding nuclear wastes, Professor Schmidt should know that they
   can be divided into two main groups. Fission products present no
   problems as they fall below natural toxic backgrounds in 400 to
   500 years. (The other toxics are of course 'forever.') The other major
   group comprises the heavy elements, most of which are present in the
   ground anyway and in much larger quantities. Why go into a syndrome
   about a 250,000 year 'heavy' when we are surrounded by a four and
   a half billion year 'heavy' (U-238) which spawns (or is it spews?)
   13 other pests, including radium and radon? We plan to burn these
   things out anyway, soon."
      Some twenty-five years later, we are still waiting.
37 Ferré, *Philosophy of Technology*, 80.
38 The distinction has its origin in the writings of Hume, was developed
   by Nietzsche, and became part of social science largely through the
   work of Max Weber. The inadequacy of Weber's approach (which
   would have denied the social scientists any basis for a condemnation of
   National Socialism or Stalinism) is demonstrated (conclusively, in our
   view) by Voegelin in chapter 1 of *The New Science of Politics*, 11–12:
      The terms "value-judgment" and "value-free" science were not part
   of the philosophical vocabulary before the second half of the nineteenth century. The notion of a value-judgment (*Werturteil*) is meaningless in itself; it gains its meaning from a situation in which it is
   opposed to judgments concerning facts (*Tatsachenurteile*). And this situation was created by the positivistic conceit that only propositions
   concerning facts of the phenomenal world were "objective" while
   judgments concerning the right order of the soul and society were
   "subjective." Only propositions of the first type could be considered
   "scientific," while propositions of the second type expressed personal
   preferences and decisions, incapable of critical verification and therefore devoid of objective validity. This classification made sense only if
   the positivistic dogma was accepted on principle; and it could be accepted only by thinkers who did not master the classic and Christian
   science of man. For neither classic nor Christian ethics and politics
   contain "value judgments" but elaborate, empirically and critically, the

problems of order which derive from philosophical anthropology as part of a general ontology. Only when ontology as a science was lost and consequently when ethics and politics could no longer be understood as the sciences of the order in which human nature reaches its maximum actualization, was it possible for this realm of knowledge to become suspect as a field of subjective critical opinion.

39 See Lowrance, *Of Acceptable Risk.*

40 See Canadian Environmental Assessment Agency, "Report of the Nuclear Fuel Waste Management and Disposal Concept Environmental Assessment Panel."

41 Ibid.

42 Sierra Club of Canada,"Backgrounder."

43 Nuclear Waste Management Organization, "Mandate."

44 Sierra Club of Canada,"Backgrounder."

45 "Nuclear Notes," 2.

46 Nuclear Waste Management Organization, "NWMO Recommends Adaptive Phased Management."

47 Dowdeswell, "Speech to the National Press Club of Canada, Final Study Report Release," 3 November 2005.

48 Ibid.

49 Nuclear Waste Management Organization, "Choosing a Way Forward," 4.

50 Ibid., 5.

51 Dowdeswell, "Speech to the National Press Club of Canada, Final Study Report Release," 3 November 2005.

52 See Angela Jameson, "Uranium Shortage Poses Threat," *Times Online*, 15 August 2005. Available at http://www.relocalize.net/node/514. In "Salvaging the Atomic Age," Weinberg pointed out that "if there are eventually throughout the world 10,000 reactors – as could happen, were nuclear energy to become the world's primary energy source – then, unless the probability of an accident for each reactor is reduced, one could expect one such accident every two years" (*Nuclear Reactions*, 244).

53 Canadian Nuclear Association, *Nuclear Power in Canada*, 34.

54 Commoner, *The Poverty of Power*, 96.

55 Knelman, *Nuclear Energy*, 115.

56 Commoner, *The Poverty of Power*, 96.

57 Knelman, *Nuclear Energy*, 116.

58 In 1972, Weinberg wrote in "Social Institutions and Nuclear Energy":
    We nuclear people have made a Faustian bargain with society. On the one hand we offer – in the catalytic nuclear burner – an inexhaustible

source of energy. Even in the short range, when we use ordinary reactors, we offer energy that is cheaper than energy from fossil fuels. Moreover, this source of energy, when properly handled, is almost non-polluting. Whereas fossil fuel burners must emit oxides of carbon and nitrogen, and probably will always emit some sulfur dioxide, there is no intrinsic reason why nuclear systems must emit any pollutant – except heat and traces of radioactivity.

But the price we demand of society for this magical energy source is both a vigilance and a longevity of our social institutions that we are quite unaccustomed to (*Nuclear Reactions*, 234).

After the accident at Three Mile Island in 1979 Weinberg restated with qualifications the legitimacy of the Faustian bargain in "The First and Second Fifty Years of Nuclear Fission":

I have since been corrected both by nuclear advocates (who prefer Prometheus to Faust) and by scholars (who say that Faust didn't really make a bargain at all). Nevertheless, what I meant was clear: nuclear energy, that miraculous and quite unsuspected source of energy, demands an unprecedented degree of expertise, attention to detail, and social stability. In return, mankind has, in the breeder reactor, an inexhaustible energy source.

Three Mile Island has undoubtedly turned many away from nuclear energy, has reinforced their belief that nuclear energy is simply too hazardous. Three Mile island for me has a rather different significance. I have often said that Goethe's Faust was redeemed – "Who e'er aspiring, struggles on,/For him there is salvation" – and that mankind in its striving, will finally master this complex and unforgiving technology (*Nuclear Reactions*, 329–30).

59 Weinberg, *Nuclear Reactions*, 250.
60 The experience of Ontario Hydro with its Pickering reactors is a case in point. Originally, it was assumed that these reactors would function efficiently for over thirty years and the cost of construction could be amortized over that length of time. It now looks like the lifespan is closer to twenty years, after which the cost of required repairs becomes prohibitive. (In the summer of 1997 Ontario Hydro announced that it would be shutting down seven of its nuclear reactors, including two at Pickering. In some cases this decision seems to have been based on the extensive cost of repairs; in others, on safety concerns that in turn were the result of poor management practices.) This means that the projected costs of the energy produced (and, one assumes, the rates charged for it) have been seriously underestimated. It is interesting to

note that schemes to privatize Ontario Hydro always assume that the nuclear component will remain publicly owned. The public will thus bear the risk and deal with the debt associated with nuclear power production, while the profitable segments of the corporation may be sold off to private companies. See: April Lindgren, "Pickering and Bruce Restart," Southam News, 13 January 2002. Available at http://www.energyprobe.org/energyprobe/index.cfm?DSP=content&ContentID=3125 (accessed 30 May 2007).

61 See Patterson, *Nuclear Power*, 158

62 Canadian Nuclear Association, *Nuclear Power in Canada*, 3.

63 Commoner, *The Poverty of Power*, 104.

64 See Eric Reguly, "Ontario Needs Market Electricity Prices," *Globe and Mail*, 6 December 2003: "The larger Darlington nuclear plant opened in 1992 – a decade late and $12-billion over its original budget. Darlington alone cost as much as Quebec's massive James Bay hydroelectric project."

65 Commoner, *The Poverty of Power*, 108.

66 See Paul Guinnessy, "Stronger Future for Nuclear Power," *Physics Today* 59, 2 (2006): 19–20. Available at http://www.physicstoday.org/vol-59/iss-2/p19.html (accessed 23 February 2007).

67 Commoner, *The Poverty of Power*, 91.

68 Weinberg, "Social Institutions and Nuclear Energy," *Science* 177 (1972): 27, as quoted by Commoner, *The Poverty of Power*, 84.

69 This is the basis of Alvin Weinberg's 1990 defence of nuclear power in "Nuclear Energy and the Greenhouse Effect" in *Nuclear Reactions*, 307–19.

70 Knelman, *Nuclear Energy*, 234.

71 Weinberg, "Social Institutions and Nuclear Energy," *Science* 177 (1972): 27, as quoted by Commoner, *The Poverty of Power*, 84.

72 Knelman, *Nuclear Energy*, 235.

73 Morone and Woodhouse claimed that "nuclear power has been drastically slowed or stopped in most nations that have ready channels for translating citizens' demands into policy, and even in some nations that do not. Large scale, expanding nuclear power programs remain in full swing only in political systems that make it very difficult for citizens to influence policy: France, Japan and some of the authoritarian political systems" (*The Demise of Nuclear Energy*, 19). Policy regarding these nuclear power programs may begin to reverse as climate change becomes more threatening.

74 Knelman, *Nuclear Energy*, 236.

75 Commoner, *The Poverty of Power*, 243.

76 Ibid., 246.

77 Bauman, *Postmodern Ethics*, 217. Bauman goes on to say: "Moral responsibility prompts us to care that our children are fed, clad and shod; it cannot offer us much practical advice, however, when faced with numbing images of a depleted, desiccated and overheated planet which our children and the children of our children will have to inhabit in the direct or oblique result of our collective unconcern" (218).

78 See Vanderburg, "Collective Prerequisites for Preventive Approaches," chapter 3 in *The Labyrinth of Technology*.

79 Beck, *Risk Society*. Note that Jacques Ellul on page 97 of *The Technological Bluff* had earlier cited P. Lagadec, "La Civilisation du risque" (Paris: Seuil, 1981), as providing the first discussion of this topic: "Lagadec's theory of 'major technological risk' seems to me irrefutable, even though understandably it has been poorly received."

80 Beck, *World Risk Society*, 60.

81 Ibid., 130.

82 Ibid., 147.

83 Bauman, *Postmodern Ethics*, 199.

84 Ibid., 204

85 Ibid., 200

CHAPTER FIVE

1 Quoted from a speech by Robert Oppenheimer to the Association of Los Alamos Scientists, 2 November 1945, Los Alamos Scientific Laboratory as quoted in Kunetka, *Oppenheimer*, 84.

2 Quoted in Gray, *Postmodern War*, 212.

3 We are grateful to Brian McGowan for his research into the historical development of Christian attitudes to war and peace.

4 See Bainton, *Christian Attitudes towards War and Peace*.

5 Ibid., 73.

6 Luke 6:27–35.

7 See Augustine, *The City of God against the Pagans*, 19.7.

8 See Aquinas, *Summa Theologica*, Part II, 2, Question 40.

9 See, for example, Coll, "Kosovo and the Moral Burden of Power." In this essay, Coll who was an assistant to the secretary of defense in the first Bush administration and currently serves as dean of the Centre for Naval Warfare Studies, analyzes the war in Kosovo in light of each of the principles of the just war tradition.

10 See Sebold, *On the Natural History of Destruction.*

11 Barbour, *Ethics in an Age of Technology,* 202.

12 See chapter 8, "Military Expenditure," by Petter Stalenheim, Damien Fruchart, Wuyi Omitoogun, and Catalina Perdomo, in Stockholm International Peace Research Institute, *SIPRI Yearbook 2006.* Available at http://yearbook2006.sipri.org/chap8 (accessed 5 February 2007).

13 Jungk, *Brighter than a Thousand Suns,* 8–9.

14 Clark, *The Scientific Breakthrough,* as quoted in Szasz, *The Day the Sun Rose Twice,* 56.

15 Szasz, *The Day the Sun Rose Twice,* 56.

16 Ibid. The Nazi nuclear program also feared a runaway explosion. See Cornwell, *Hitler's Scientists,* 26: "Speer meanwhile [in 1939] reported that the head of the official nuclear programme, Werner Heisenberg, had been unable to confirm that a chain reaction could be controlled 'with absolute certainty.' There had been suspicions among the scientists that a chain reaction, a release of massive energy in fissile material by the instantaneous splitting of its atomic structure, once started, would continue on through the material of the entire planet."

17 Szasz, *The Day the Sun Rose Twice,* 56–7.

18 Ibid., 58.

19 See Cornwell, *Hitler's Scientists,* 307–8: "The Allies had no certain knowledge of the German project until December 1944 when the intelligence team know as Alsos arrived in Strasbourg."

20 Szasz, *The Day the Sun Rose Twice,* 60.

21 Ibid.

22 Quoted in Kunetka, *Oppenheimer,* 84.

23 Michelmore, *The Swift Years,* 121.

24 Ibid., 124.

25 *In the Matter of J. Robert Oppenheimer: Transcript of Hearing Before Personnel Security Board,* US Atomic Energy Commission (Washington, D.C.: Government Printing Office, 1954), 251, as quoted in Kunetka, *Oppenheimer,* 180.

26 Becker, *The Heavenly City of the Eighteenth Century Philosophers,* 50–1.

27 Rouzé, *Robert Oppenheimer,* 142.

28 Ibid., 148–9.

29 Ibid., 149.

30 See Rhodes, *The Making of the Atomic Bomb,* 627.

31 Rouzé, *Robert Oppenheimer,* 83.

32 Novak, *Moral Clarity in the Nuclear Age*. More recently some of Novak's ideas were recycled by George Weigel, who echoed his title in a defence of the recent war on Iraq. See Weigel, "Moral Clarity in a Time of War."

33 Novak, *Moral Clarity in the Nuclear Age*, 56–7.

34 Ibid., 59.

35 Cameron, "Nuclear Catholicism."

36 Novak, *Moral Clarity in the Nuclear Age*, 59.

37 Ibid., 63.

38 Ibid.

39 Cameron, *Nuclear Catholics and Other Essays*, 40–1.

40 Finnis, Boyle, and Grisez, *Nuclear Deterrence, Morality and Realism*.

41 The American Catholic Bishops, *The Challenge of Peace*.

42 Ibid., sections 162–99.

43 We are grateful to Elana Summers of the University of Toronto for her research into, and advice about, the relation between the just war theory and weapons systems developed since the end of the Cold War.

44 Elshtain, *Just War against Terror*.

45 George and Meredith Friedman, *The Future of War*, xi.

46 Gray, *Postmodern War*, 46.

47 Ibid.

48 The figure of 100,000 Iraqi military casualties is an estimate of the US Defence Intelligence Agency. "Toting the Casualties of War," *Business Week*, 6 February 2003. Available at http://www.businessweek.com/bwdaily/dnflash/feb2003/nf2003026_0167_db052.htm (accessed 19 February 2007).

49 For more detailed figures, see Sidel and Levy, *War and Public Health*.

50 See http://www.iraqbodycount.org (accessed 19 February 2007). This widely publicized remark is printed at the top of the homepage on the website of the British-based organization Iraq Body Count, which keeps a running tally of casualties on the basis of confirmed media reports.

51 The Human Rights Watch report, "Needless Deaths in the Gulf War," can be found at http://www.hrw.org/reports/1991/gulfwar/INTRO.htm (accessed 19 February 2007).

52 This revealing episode was reported in "Toting the Casualties of War," *Business Week*, 6 February 2003.

53 Cited in Gray, *Postmodern War*, 45.

54 Ignatieff, *Virtual War*, 161.

55 Ignatieff's more recent work, *Empire Lite*, for example, makes it clear that he is perhaps more worried about an American isolationism

that would prevent it from functioning as an intervener in the name of human rights and constructive nation-building.

56 Cohen, "Kosovo and the New American Way of War," 54.

57 Ibid., 44.

58 Coll, "Kosovo and the Moral Burden of Power," 144.

59 Ibid., 145.

60 Cordesman, *The Lessons and Non-Lessons of the Air and Missile Campaign in Kosovo*, 122.

61 Ignatieff, *Virtual War*, 162.

62 Bacevich and Cohen, *War over Kosovo*, xi.

63 Coll, "Kosovo and the Moral Burden of Power," 149.

64 Kurth, "First War of the Global Era," 69.

65 Ibid., 78–9.

66 Weigel, "Moral Clarity in a Time of War," 20–7.

67 Elshtain, *Just War against Terror*, 23.

68 See also O'Donovan, *The Just War Revisited*, and Ignatieff, *The Lesser Evil*. O'Donovan argues that the just war theory's principle of discrimination was largely ignored in the early twentieth century because of the emergence of air power as a crucial feature in modern warfare. It began to return to prominence during the cold war as critiques of the policy of nuclear deterrence began to rely on just war principles. The emergence of more precise guided munitions actually began in the 1960s, as nuclear strategists began to realize the strategic limitations of their reliance on a policy of mass nuclear counter-attack. The technology originally developed for the guidance of nuclear weapons has more recently been applied to the kind of conventional weaponry that was used in the first Gulf war. But here again we see that the acceptance of just war ethics by those in a position to make decisions on its basis has largely been determined by the historical unfolding of the potentialities of our technology.

Ignatieff's book does not rely so much on the language of the just war tradition, and his ethics of the "lesser evil" is addressed to wider range of issues – including torture and "necessary" abridgements of civil liberties in an "age of terror" – but it certainly includes a revival of, and an insistence upon, certain features of the just war tradition.

69 For example, see Elshtain, *Just War against Terror*, 213n14.

70 See "Iraq Surveys Shows 'Humanitarian Emergency,'" 12 August 1999, UNICEF Information Newsline. http://www.unicef.org/newsline/ 99pr29.htm (accessed 19 February 2007).

71 Elshtain, *Just War against Terror*, 88.

72 Howard Kurtz, "CNN Chief Orders 'Balance' in War News," *Washington Post*, 31 October 2001.

73 See Seumas Milne, "The Innocent Dead in a Coward's War," *The Guardian*, 20 December 2001. Available at http://www.guardian.co.uk/afghanistan/story /0,1284,622000,00.html (accessed 19 February 2007).

74 Elshtain, *Just War against Terror*, 69.

75 See Amnesty International, "Iraq: Civilians under Fire."

76 Michael R. Gordon, "U.S. Air Raids in '02 Prepared for War in Iraq." *New York Times*, 20 July 2003.

77 For regularly updated figures and an account of their methodology, see: http://www.iraqbodycount.org.

78 Les Roberts, Riyadh Lafta, Richard Garfield, Jamal Khudhairi, and Gilbert Burnham, "Mortality Before and After the 2003 Invasion of Iraq: Cluster Sample Survey," *The Lancet* 364, 9448 (20 November 2004): 1857–64.

79 Elshtain, *Just War against Terror*, 70.

80 Ibid., 23. Italics in the original.

81 Fisk, *The Great War for Civilization*, 1036–7. Fisk's book of over 1300 pages is a chilling account of the recent history of Western folly in the Middle East.

CHAPTER SIX

1 See Noonan, *Contraception*, chapter 1.

2 See Lifton and Markusen, *The Genocidal Mentality*, 54:

Nazi racial thought and policy were wildly visionary and romanticized on the one hand, and narrowly technocratic and scientistic on the other. These two seemingly contradictory patterns were, in fact, inseparable. Consider two comments by Nazi doctors. A leading medical administrator for the regime reported that he had joined the Nazi party the day after hearing a speech by Rudolph Hess in which the deputy party leader had declared, *"National Socialism is nothing but applied biology"* [my emphasis]. And a still more malignant comment was made by a Nazi doctor in Auschwitz when he was asked by a prisoner physician how he could reconcile the smoking crematoria in the distance with the Hippocratic oath: "Of course I am a doctor and I want to preserve life. And out of respect for life, I would remove a gangrenous appendix from a diseased body."

3 Mander, *In the Absence of the Sacred*, 170.

4 Kerby Anderson, Probe Ministries, "Genetic Engineering," 1998 at http://www.leaderu.com/orgs/probe/docs/gen-engr.html (accessed 20 February 2007).

5 See Kass, *Toward a More Natural Science*, 122, where he comments on the persistence of this term in spite of its inaccuracy:

There has been much objection, largely from the scientific community, to the phrase "test-tube baby." More than one commentator has deplored the exploitation of its "flesh-creeping" connotations. They point out that a flat petri-dish is used, not a test-tube – as if that mattered – and that the embryo spends only a few days in the dish. But they don't ask why the term "test-tube baby" remains the popular designation, and whether it does not embody more of the deeper truth than a more accurate laboratory appellation. If the decisive difference is between "in the womb" or "in the lab," the popular designation conveys it.

6 McCormick, *How Brave a New World?*, 321.

7 Ramsey, *Fabricated Man*, 122–3.

8 See Vaux, *Biomedical Ethics*, 29. The first principle of the Nuremberg code is: "The voluntary consent of the human subject is absolutely essential. This means that the person involved should have the legal capacity to give consent; should be so situated as to be able to exercise free power of choice, without the intervention of any element of force, fraud, deceit, duress, overreaching or other ulterior form of constraint or coercion; and should have sufficient knowledge and comprehension of the elements of the subject matter involved as to enable him to make an understanding and enlightened decision. The latter element requires that before the acceptance of an affirmative decision by the experimental subject, there should be made known to him the nature, duration and purpose of the experiment; the method and means by which it is to be conducted; all inconveniences and hazards reasonably to be expected; and the effects upon his health or person which may possibly come from his participation in the experiments. The duty and the responsibility for ascertaining the quality of the consent rests upon each individual who initiates, directs or engages in the experiment. It is a personal duty and responsibility which may not be delegated to another with impunity."

9 Ramsey, *Fabricated Man*, 134–5.

10 See The President's Council on Bioethics at http://www.bioethics.gov/about/kass.html (accessed 28 May 2007)

11 Kass, *Toward a More Natural Science*, 51.

12 Ibid.

13 This was certainly the case before Edwards and Steptoe undertook to produce a child for Mr and Mrs Brown. See Kass, *Toward a More Natural Science*, 52–3, where he elaborates the unknown risks in this way:

The truth is that the risks were very much unknown. Although there had been no reports of gross deformities at birth following successful transfer in mice and in rabbits, the number of animals produced in this way was much too small to exclude even a moderate risk of such deformities. In none of the research had the question of abnormalities been systematically investigated. No prospective studies had been made to detect defects that might appear at later times or lesser abnormalities apparent even at birth. In species more closely related to human (e.g., in primates) successful in vitro fertilization had yet to be accomplished. Many respected researchers in the field believed – even after the birth of Louise Brown – that the ability regularly to produce normal monkeys by this method was a minimum prerequisite for using the procedure in humans.

But it must in fairness be added that even after normal young were produced in monkeys, one would not yet be fully certain that normal young would be produced in humans. There might be species differences in sensitivity to the physical manipulations or to possible teratogenic agents in a culture medium …

In sum there is still no way of finding *in advance* whether or not the viable progeny of the procedures of *in vitro* fertilization, culture and transfer of human embryos will be deformed, sterile or retarded. Only the made babies, after their birth and growth, can show whether it was safe to have made them in the first place.

14 Ramsey, *Fabricated Man*, 34.

15 I am grateful to Judy Vivacqua of Erindale College, the University of Toronto at Mississauga, for her research assistance and ethical insight. We have relied heavily on her 1996 Individual Studies undergraduate paper "In Vitro Fertilization: An Ethical Analysis" for some of the analysis of the feminist approaches in the following section.

16 Warnock, *A Question of Life*, 99.

17 Ibid., 34.

18 Ibid., 32.

19 Ibid., 15. This provision of donor anonymity was reversed in Great Britain in 2005. See The Foundation, Dr Susan Wallace, www.pheu.org.uk/ecard?Link_10=798 (accessed 20 February 2007).

20 Warnock, *A Question of Life*, 23.

21 Ibid., 16.
22 Ibid., 26.
23 Ibid., 25–8.
24 Ibid., 56.
25 Ibid., 57.
26 Ibid., 63.
27 Ibid., 64.
28 Ibid., 79.
29 Ibid., 66.
30 Ibid., 67.
31 Ibid., 12.
32 Ibid., 46.
33 Warnock, *Nature and Mortality*, 116.
34 Ibid., 121.
35 Overall, *Ethics and Human Reproduction*, 1.
36 Ibid., 49.
37 Ibid., 50.
38 Ibid., 52.
39 Ibid., 156.
40 Ibid., 157.
41 Ibid., 158.
42 Ibid., 144.
43 Ibid., 57.
44 Ibid., 58.
45 Ibid., 59.
46 Ibid., 60.
47 Ibid., 59.
48 Ibid., 177
49 Raymond, *Women as Wombs*, viii. See also Raymond, "Reproduction, Population, Technology and Rights," and Corea, *The Mother Machine*.
50 Raymond, *Women as Wombs*, 2.
51 Ibid., 6.
52 Ibid., 3.
53 Ibid., 137.
54 Ibid., 27.
55 Ibid., 209.
56 Ibid., 40.
57 Ibid., 40.
58 See Kass, *Toward a More Natural Science* and *Life, Liberty, and the Defense of Dignity*.

59 See, for example, Bailey, "Petri Dish Politics."

60 Lewis, *The Abolition of Man*, 69–71, as quoted in Kass, *Toward a More Natural Science*, 28.

61 Kass, *Toward a More Natural Science*, 31.

62 Ibid., 35. A similar judgment forms the basis of Ronald K.L. Collins and David Skover's argument that the greatest threat to free speech (and to the first amendment of the American Constitution) is not governmental constraint but the Huxleyan crossing. See particularly Book I, Part 1, of *The Death of Discourse*, 3–8.

63 Kass, *Toward a More Natural Science*, 45.

64 Ibid., 30. "The New Biology: What Price Relieving Man's Estate?" was originally published, largely in its present form, in *Science* 174 (18 November 1971): 779–88.

65 Kass, *Toward a More Natural Science*, 52.

66 Ibid., 55.

67 Ibid., 103.

68 Ibid., 104.

69 Ibid., 105.

70 Ibid., 106. Italics in the original.

71 Ibid.

72 Ibid., 107.

73 Ibid.

74 Ibid., 107–8.

75 This was the later position of Richard McCormick, the Roman Catholic bioethicist. See his *How Brave a New World?*

76 Kass, *Toward a More Natural Science*, 57–8.

77 Ibid., 108.

78 Ibid., 110–11.

79 Ibid., 111–12.

80 Ibid., 112.

81 Ibid., 113.

82 Ibid.

83 See Kass, *The Ethics of Human Cloning*; *Life, Liberty, and the Defense of Dignity;* and "Preventing a Brave New World."

84 See President's Council on Bioethics, *Human Cloning and Human Dignity.*

85 Kass, "Preventing a Brave New World," Section V.

86 Ibid.

87 Ibid.

88 Ibid.

89 See the "New Reproductive Technologies, Royal Commission on," in *The Canadian Encyclopedia,* available at http://www.canadianencyclope-dia.ca/index.cfm?PgNm=TCE&Params=M1ARTA0011545 (accessed 24 February 2007).

90 Ibid.

91 Baird, "Regulation of Reproductive Technologies is Long Overdue."

92 Canada, Assisted Human Reproduction Act," at http://laws.justice.gc.ca/en/A-13.4/, and "Regulating 'Assisted Human re-production,'" CBC News in Depth, at www.cbc.ca/news/back-ground/genetics_reproduction/rgtech.html (accessed 18 June 2007).

93 Ronan Mullen, "Designer Babies Made to Order," *Irish Times,* 5 February 2003.

94 Stock, *Redesigning Humans,* as cited in Warnock, *Nature and Mortality,* 129

95 Warnock, *Nature and Mortality,* 129.

96 Ibid., 130

97 Grant, *English Speaking Justice,* 70.

98 See Grant, "The Triumph of the Will," in *The George Grant Reader,* Christian and Grant, eds., 149: "Alone among Western countries, West Germany has a law which gives the fetus a legal right to life with some conditions. The Constitutional Court says that this is to make plain the German historical experience and 'the present spiritual moral confrontation with the previous system of National Socialism.' In 1988, West Germany has forbidden surrogate motherhood and the production of human embryos for research."

99 George Grant, *English Speaking Justice,* 71.

100 The Assisted Human Reproduction Act prohibits the creating of embryos for research. See Section 5(1)(b): "(1) No person shall knowingly (b) create an in vitro embryo for any purpose other than creating a human being or improving or providing instruction in assisted reproduction procedures." Embryos must be created to enable a woman to have a child. The question is, when more than one embryo is created, can those not used for procreation be used for research?

101 "Lords Back Cloning Research," BBC News, 27 February 2002. Available at http://news.bbc.co.uk/1/hi/sci/tech/1843368.stm (accessed 24 February 2007). In the US, see Denise Grady, "February Debate over Cloning in U.S. Remains Intense," *The New York Times,* 12 February 2004.

102 We have not entered into the thorny debate about embryonic stem-cell research, which, until recently, required the destruction of embryos (either surplus embryos or those specifically produced for therapeutic purposes).

CHAPTER SEVEN

1 See Sophia Koliopoulos, "Prenatal Genetic Testing: Do You Really Want to Know Your Baby's Future?":

Prenatal diagnosis is used to diagnose a genetic disease or condition in a developing fetus. The techniques currently in use or under investigation for prenatal diagnosis include (1) fetal tissue sampling through amniocentesis, chorionic villus sampling (CVS), percutaneous umbilical blood sampling, percutaneous skin biopsy, and other organ biopsies, including muscle and liver biopsy; (2) fetal visualization through ultrasound, fetal echocardiography, embryoscopy, fetoscopy, magnetic resonance imaging, and radiography; (3) screening for neural tube defects by measuring maternal serum alpha-fetoprotein (MSAFP); (4) screening for fetal Down syndrome by measuring MSAFP, unconjugated estriol, and human chorionic gonadotropin; (5) separation of fetal cells from the mother's blood; and (6) preimplantation biopsy of blastocysts obtained by in vitro fertilization. The more common techniques are amniocentesis, performed at the 14th to 20th week of gestation, and CVS, performed between the 9th and 13th week of gestation. If the fetus is found to be affected with a disorder, the couple can plan for the birth of an affected child or opt for elective abortion.

2 See Centre for Genetics and Society, "Preimplantation Genetic Diagnosis (PGD) and Screening": "Preimplantation genetic diagnosis (PGD) tests early-stage embryos produced through in vitro fertilization (IVF) for the presence of a variety of conditions. One cell is extracted from the embryo in its eight-cell stage and analyzed. Embryos free of conditions that would cause serious disease can be implanted in a woman's uterus and allowed to develop into a child."

3 Lippman, "Prenatal Genetic Testing and Screening," 19.
4 Ibid., 24.
5 Wolbring, "Renewal of Canadian Biotechnology Strategy 1998."
6 Lippman, "Genetic Testing and Screening," 20–1
7 Rifkin, *The Biotech Century*, 128.
8 Lippman, "Genetic Testing and Screening," 25.
9 Condorcet as quoted in Rifkin, *The Biotech Century*, 170–1.

10 Kevles, "Out of Eugenics," 5–6.
11 Ibid., 10.
12 Pernick, *The Black Stork,* 32.
13 Ibid., 36.
14 Ibid., 35.
15 McLaren, *Our Own Master Race,* 7–9.
16 Ibid., 100–25.
17 Proctor, *Racial Hygiene,* 22.
18 Ibid., 49.
19 Ibid., 58.
20 Ibid., 297.
21 Gallagher, *By Trust Betrayed,* 7.
22 Kevles, "Out of Eugenics," 18.
23 Ibid., 19.
24 Ibid., 32.
25 Asch and Geller, "Feminism, Bioethics, and Genetics in Feminist Perspective," 323.
26 Health Canada, "New Reproductive and Genetic Technologies," 15–17.
27 Health Canada, "Reproductive and Genetic Technologies," Health Canada, 1999, 9.
28 See *Genetic Crossroads no. 38.*
29 See Wolbring, "Renewal of Canadian Biotechnology Strategy 1998," 9. See also *Genome(s) and Justice.*
30 Ibid.
31 Singer, *Practical Ethics,* 186.
32 Carolyn Abraham, "Gene Pioneer Urges Wakening to Dream of Human Perfection." *Globe and Mail,* 26 October 2002, A1, A8.
33 Asch and Geller, "Feminism, Bioethics, and Genetics in Feminist Perspective," 331. See also Asch, "Why I Haven't Changed My Mind."
34 Cowan, "Genetic Technology and Reproductive Choice," 262.
35 Ibid.
36 See Natalie Angier, "Baby in a Box," *New York Times Magazine,* 16 May 1999.
37 Bryan Appleyard, "The Most Extraordinary Person I Have Ever Known," *Toronto Star,* 10 January 1999.

CHAPTER EIGHT

1 See Weil, "Classical Science and After," 6–7. In an essay written toward the end of her brief life, Simone Weil explained that "the science

which was revived by the Renaissance and perished around 1900, tried to represent all the phenomena occurring in the universe by imagining, between two successive states confirmed in a system by observation, intermediate stages analogous to those traversed by a man executing a simple manual labor ... It conceived the universe on the model of the relation between any human action and the necessities which obstruct it by imposing conditions." Modern science was able to subsume the study of every natural phenomenon under the simple notion of energy, and thereby exclude or deny the relevance of those types of knowledge that can only be achieved by participation in, or attention to, the good. It ignored the ethical structure of human life.

2 See Lasch, *The True and Only Heaven*; see also Beiner, "Left-Wing Conservatism."

3 Grant, *Lament for a Nation*, 59.

4 Miller, "Leo Strauss," 76.

5 Strauss, "What Is Political Philosophy?" 47.

6 See MacIntyre, *After Virtue*, 93: "Wherein does Machiavelli differ from the Enlightenment tradition? Above all in his concept of *Fortuna*. Machiavelli certainly believed as passionately as any thinker of the Enlightenment that our investigations should issue in generalizations which may furnish maxims for enlightened practice. But he also believed that no matter how good a stock of generalizations one amassed and no matter how well one reformulated them, the factor of *Fortuna* was ineliminable from human life."

7 Thucydides, *Peloponnesian War*, Book 5, 105, as quoted in MacIntyre, *A Short History of Ethics*, 12. For commentary, see Bolotin, "Thucydides." See also Weil, *Notebooks I*, 190, quoting Thucydides: "'We believe by tradition in the case of the gods, and we see by experience in the case of men, that always through a necessity of nature, every being exercises all the power at his disposal.' This is not true of the God of the Christians."

8 Strauss, "What Is Political Philosophy?" 78.

9 Strauss, "Three Waves of Modernity," 87.

10 MacIntyre, *After Virtue*, 52.

11 Ibid., 53.

12 See Lewis, *The Abolition of Man*, 16, where he explains that the alternative to emotivism is "the doctrine of objective value, the belief that certain attitudes are really true, and others really false to the kind of thing the universe is and the kind of things we are."

13 See 198–99n38.

14 MacIntyre, *Whose Justice? Which Rationality?*, 335.

15 Ibid., 336

16 See MacIntyre, "The Privatization of Good," 346.

17 See MacIntyre, "Liberalism Transformed into a Tradition." See also Beiner, "Liberalism in the Cross-Hairs of Theory."

18 Grant, *Technology and Empire*, 129.

19 Arendt, *The Origins of Totalitarianism*, 299.

20 Ibid.

21 Rawls, *A Theory of Justice*.

22 Rawls defines a "right" in the following terms: "a conception of right is a set of principles, general in form and universal in application, that is to be publicly recognized as a final court of appeal for ordering the conflicting claims of moral persons" (*A Theory of Justice*, 135). While Rawls gives us a procedure for determining rights and obligations that would, at the end of the day, include the idea of universal application, thereby managing to build some of Kant's metaphysical claims about the kingdom of ends into a simple practical tool for calculation (or moral reasoning), he still implicitly relies on metaphysical principles when stipulating whose interests should be considered in the procedure. After Darwin, Nietzsche, and Freud, we can no longer take for granted what eighteenth and nineteenth century theorists could, namely that there is widespread consensus with regard to the metaphysical category – "moral persons."

23 Grant, *English Speaking Justice*, 41.

24 Arendt, *The Origins of Totalitarianism*, 279.

25 Ibid., 295–6.

26 Grant, *Technology and Justice*, 60–1.

27 See Grant, *English Speaking Justice*, 58–68.

28 Mathie, "The Technological Regime," 160.

29 Grant, *Technology and Justice*, 30.

30 Ibid., 94.

31 Ibid., 94.

32 Bertrand Russell, as quoted in Herrick, "Bertrand Russell: A Passionate Rationalist."

CHAPTER NINE

1 See MacIntyre, *After Virtue*, 71: "The culture of bureaucratic individualism results in their [the politics of modern societies] characteristic overt public debates being between an individualism which makes its

claims in terms of rights and forms of bureaucratic organization which make their claims in terms of utility."

2 MacIntyre, *After Virtue*, 34.

3 Ibid., 35.

4 See *The Abolition of Man*, 17, where C.S. Lewis described this moral universe: "The world of facts, without one trace of value, and the world of feeling without one trace of truth or falsehood, of justice or injustice, confront one another and no *rapprochement* is possible."

5 Rist, *Real Ethics*, 2.

6 See Rist, "The Soul and the Self," in *Real Ethics*, 61–94.

7 The term is of course Heidegger's. See Heidegger, *The Question Concerning Technology*, 19: "Thus when man, investigating, observing, ensnares nature as an area of his own conceiving, he has already been claimed by a way of revealing that challenges him to approach nature as an object of research, until even the object disappears into the objectlessness of standing reserve."

8 The arguments are well put by Rist in *Real Ethics*.

9 MacIntyre, *After Virtue*, 70.

10 Grant, *Technology and Empire*, 34.

11 MacIntyre, *Three Rival Versions of Moral Inquiry*, 226.

12 See Weil, *The Need for Roots*, particularly "Part One: The Needs of the Soul," 3–42.

13 It has been interesting to note that, as the concerns about climate change have finally become front page news, the chief concern among economists has been to assure the public that growth of the GDP will continue upward as carbon emissions are reduced. See Mittelstaedt, "A Climate Change Message Dressed in Green Pin Stripes," *Globe and Mail*, 20 February 2007.

14 See MacIntyre, *After Virtue*, 64: "To have understood the polymorphous character of pleasure and happiness is of course to have rendered those concepts useless for utilitarian purposes; if the prospect of his or her own future pleasure cannot for the reasons I have suggested provide criteria for solving the problems of action in the case of each individual, it follows that the notion of greatest happiness of the greatest number is a notion without any clear content at all. It is indeed a pseudo-concept available for a variety of ideological uses."

15 See Heinberg, *Powerdown*, 124–9.

16 Beck, *Risk Society*. Ellul in *The Technological Bluff* had earlier cited P. Lagadec, "La Civilisation du risque" (Paris: Seuil, 1981), 97, as

providing the first discussion of this topic: "Lagadec's theory of 'major technological risk' seems to me irrefutable, even though understandably it has been poorly received."

17 Bauman, *Postmodern Ethics*, 199–200.
18 Vanderburg, "Political Imagination in a Technical Age," 10.
19 Ibid., 9.
20 Beck, *Risk Society*, 27.
21 See Bauman, *Postmodern Ethics*, 205–6.
22 The Walkerton water crisis and the SARS crisis in Toronto recently brought this home to citizens of Ontario.
23 Beck, *World Risk Society*, 60.
24 Jonas, *The Imperative of Responsibility*, 9. See also Cooper, "The Political Significance of Technological Action" for an explanation of "action into nature," 36.
25 Ibid., 24
26 Ibid., 34.
27 See Beiner, "Ethics and Technology."
28 Ibid., 343.
29 Ibid.
30 Jonas, *The Imperative of Responsibility*, 71.
31 Ibid., 78.
32 Ibid., 37.
33 Beiner, "Ethics and Technology," 342.
34 Ibid., 347.
35 Jonas, *The Imperative of Responsibility*, 202.
36 Ibid.
37 Ibid., 203.
38 Ibid., 202.
39 See Ellul, *The Technological System*.
40 Beck, *Risk Society*, 19–20, as quoted in Bauman, *Postmodern Ethics*, 199.
41 Bauman, *Postmodern Ethics*, 199.
42 Ibid., 204
43 Ibid., 200.
44 Ibid., 194.
45 See Rist, *Augustine*, chapter 4, "Soul, Body and Personal Identity."
46 Bauman, *Postmodern Ethics*, 198.
47 See Weil, "Classical Science and After."
48 A spate of books have recently appeared that express the fear of civilizational collapse: Jacobs, *Dark Age Ahead*; Wright, *A Short History of Progress*; Diamond, *Collapse*.

49 See Schmidt and Marratto, "The Measure of Justice."
50 Grant, *Technology and Empire*, 40, and 137–43. See Robertson, "George Grant: Intimations of Deprival, Intimations of Beauty."

Bibliography

American Catholic Bishops. *The Challenge of Peace: God's Promise and Our Response.* Washington: United States Catholic Conference, 1983.

Amnesty International. "Iraq: Civilians under Fire." April 2003. Available at http://web.amnesty.org/library/index/ENGMDE140712003?open&of=eng-irq) (accessed 25 February 2007).

Aquinas. *Summa Theologica,* Part II, 2, Question 40 (of War). Available at http://ethics.sandiego.edu/Books/Texts/aquinas/justwar.html (accessed 24 February 2007).

Arendt, Hannah. *The Origins of Totalitarianism.* New York: Meridian Books, 1958.

Asch, Adrienne. "Why I Haven't Changed My Mind: Reflections and Refinements." In *Prenatal Testing and Disability Rights,* ed. Erik Parens and Adrienne Asch. Washington, D.C.: Georgetown University Press, 2000.

Asch, Adrienne, and Geller, Gale. "Feminism, Bioethics, and Genetics in Feminist Perspective." In *Specific Problems in Bioethics,* ed. Susan Wolf. Oxford: Oxford University Press, 1996.

Ashton, T.S. *The Industrial Revolution: 1760–1830.* London: Oxford University Press, 1962.

Augustine. *The City of God against the Pagans.* Ed. and trans. R.W. Dyson. Cambridge: Cambridge University Press, 1998.

Bacevich, Andrew J., and Eliot A. Cohen, ed. *War over Kosovo: Politics and Strategy in a Global Age.* New York: Columbia University Press, 2001.

Bailey, Ronald. "Petri Dish Politics." *Reason,* December 1999. http://www.reason.com/news/show/31207.html (accessed 28 April 2007).

Bainton, Roland. *Christian Attitudes towards War and Peace: A Historical Survey and Critical Re-evaluation.* New York: Abingdon, 1960.

Baird, Patricia. "Regulation of Reproductive Technologies is Long Overdue." *Paediatrics and Child Care* 9, 2 (February 2004): 91-2. Available at
http://www.pulsus.com/paeds/09_02/bair_ed.htm (accessed 24 February 2007).

Barbour, Ian. *Ethics in an Age of Technology.* New York: HarperCollins, 1993.

Barnett, Richard. *Global Reach: The Power of the Multinational Corporations.*
New York: Simon and Shuster, 1974.

Barnett, Richard, and John Cavanagh. *Global Dreams: Imperial Corporations
and the New World Order.* New York: Simon and Shuster, 1994.

Bauman, Zygmunt. *Globalization: The Human Consequences.* New York:
Columbia University Press, 1998.

– *The Individualized Society.* Cambridge: Polity Press, 2000.

– *In Search of Politics.* Stanford: Stanford University Press, 1999.

– *Liquid Fear.* Cambridge: Polity Press, 2006.

– *Liquid Love: On the Frailty of Human Bonds.* Cambridge: Polity Press, 2003.

– *Modernity and the Holocaust.* Cambridge: Polity Press, 1989.

– *Postmodern Ethics.* Cambridge, Mass.: Blackwell, 1993.

– *Postmodernity and Its Discontents.* Washington Square: New York University
Press, 1997.

Beck, Ulrich. *Risk Society: Towards a New Modernity.* London: Sage, 1992.

– *What is Globalization?* Cambridge: Polity Press, 2000.

– *World Risk Society.* Cambridge: Polity Press, 1999.

Becker, Carl. *The Heavenly City of the Eighteenth Century Philosophers.* New
Haven: Yale University Press, 1932.

Beiner, Ronald. "Ethics and Technology: Hans Jonas' Theory of Responsibility." In *Democratic Theory and Technological Society,* ed. Richard B. Day,
Ronald Beiner, and Joseph Masciulli. Armonk, N.Y.: M.E. Sharpe, 1988.

– "Left-Wing Conservatism: The Legacy of Christopher Lasch." In *Philosophy in a Time of Lost Spirit: Essays on Contemporary Theory,* ed. Ronald
Beiner, 139–50. Toronto: University of Toronto Press, 1997.

– "Liberalism in the Cross-Hairs of Theory." In *Philosophy in a Time of Lost
Spirit: Essays on Contemporary Theory,* ed. Ronald Beiner, 3–17. Toronto:
University of Toronto Press, 1997.

Beiner, Ronald, ed. *Philosophy in a Time of Lost Spirit: Essays on Contemporary
Theory.* Toronto: University of Toronto Press, 1997.

Bello, Walden. "Structural Adjustment Programs: 'Success' For Whom."
In *The Case against the Global Economy,* ed. Jerry Mander and Edward
Goldsmith. San Francisco: Sierra Club Books, 1997.

Berger, Peter L. *The Sacred Canopy: Elements of a Sociological Theory of Religion.* New York: Doubleday, 1969.

Berman, Morris. *The Reenchantment of the Earth*. New York: Bantam Books, 1984.

Boffy, P. "Nuclear Power Debate: Signing up the Pros and Cons." *Science* 192 (1976): 120–2.

Bolotin, David. "Thucydides." In *History of Political Philosophy: Third Edition*, ed. Leo Strauss and Joseph Cropsey. Chicago: University of Chicago Press, 1987.

Borgmann, Albert. *Crossing the Postmodern Divide*. Chicago: University of Chicago Press, 1992.

– *Power Failure: Christianity in the Culture of Technology*. Grand Rapids, Mich.: Brazos Press, 2003.

Boulding, Kenneth. *The Meaning of the Twentieth Century: The Great Transition*. New York: Harper and Row, 1963.

Braaten, Carl E. *History and Hermeneutics*. Philadelphia: Westminster Press, 1966.

Brown, Lester R., Christopher Flavin, Hilary French, et al. *State of the World 2000: A Worldwatch Institute Report on Progress Toward a Sustainable Society*. New York and London: W.W. Norton, 2000.

Cameron, James M. "Nuclear Catholicism." In *Nuclear Catholics and Other Essays*, ed. James M. Cameron. Grand Rapids, Mich.: W.B. Eerdmans, 1990.

– *Nuclear Catholics and Other Essays*. Grand Rapids, Mich.: W.B. Eerdmans, 1990.

Canada. Assisted Human Reproduction Act (2004, c. 2).

– Nuclear Fuel Waste Act (2002, c. 23).

Canadian Environmental Assessment Agency. "Report of the Nuclear Fuel Waste Management and Disposal Concept Environmental Assessment Panel." February 1998. Available at http://www. ceaa.gc.ca/010/0001/0001/0012/0001/report_e.htm (accessed 27 May 2007).

Canadian Nuclear Association. *Nuclear Power in Canada: Questions and Answers*. Toronto: Canadian Nuclear Association, 1975.

Carson, Rachel. *Silent Spring*. New York: Fawcett Publications, 1962.

Cayley, David. *The Rivers North of the Future: The Testament of Ivan Illich*. Toronto: House of Anansi Press, 2005.

Centre for Genetics and Society. "Preimplantation Genetic Diagnosis (PGD) and Screening." http://www.genetics-and-society.org/technologies/other/pgd.html (accessed 19 February 2007).

Christian, William. *George Grant: A Biography*. Toronto: University of Toronto Press, 1993.

Christian, William, and Sheila Grant, ed. *The George Grant Reader*. Toronto: University of Toronto Press, 1998.

Cohen, Eliot. "Kosovo and the New American Way of War." In *War over Kosovo: Politics and Strategy in a Global Age*, ed. Andrew J. Bacevich and Eliot A. Cohen. New York: Columbia University Press, 2001.

Coll, Albert R. "Kosovo and the Moral Burden of Power." In *War over Kosovo: Politics and Strategy in a Global Age*, ed. Andrew J. Bacevich and Eliot A. Cohen. New York: Columbia University Press, 2001.

Collins, Joseph, and Lappé, Frances Moore. *World Hunger: Twelve Myths.* New York: Grove Press, 1986.

Collins, Ronald K.L., and David M. Skover. *The Death of Discourse.* Boulder, Colo.: Westview Press, 1996.

Commoner, Barry. *The Closing Circle: Nature, Man, and Technology.* New York: Knopf, 1971.

– *Making Peace with the Planet.* New York: Pantheon Books, 1990.

– *The Poverty of Power: Energy and the Economic Crisis.* New York: Bantam Books, 1976.

Cooper, Barry. *Action into Nature: An Essay on the Meaning of Technology.* Notre Dame: University of Notre Dame Press, 1991.

– "The Political Significance of Technological Action." *National Forum* 74, 2 (Spring 1994): 32–6.

Cordesman, Anthony H. *The Lessons and Non-Lessons of the Air and Missile Campaign in Kosovo.* Westport, Conn.: Prager, 2001.

Corea, Gina. *The Mother Machine: Reproductive Technologies from Artificial Insemination to Artificial Wombs.* New York: Harper and Row, 1985.

Cornwell, John. *Hitler's Scientists: Science, War and the Devil's Pact.* New York: Viking, 2003.

Corten, David C. *When Corporations Rule the World.* West Hartford, Conn.: Kumarian Press, 1995.

Cowan, Ruth Schwartz. "Genetic Technology and Reproductive Choice: An Ethics for Autonomy." In *The Code of Codes: Scientific and Social Issues in the Human Genome Project*, ed. Daniel J. Kevles and Leroy Hood, 244–63. Cambridge: Harvard University Press, 1992.

Crawford, Franklin. "Historian Walter LaFeber Goes One-on-One with Michael Jordan and Nike." *Cornell Chronicle* 31, 1 (19 August 1999). Available at http://www.news.cornell.edu/Chronicle /99/8.19.99/ LaFeber_book.html (accessed 23 February 2007).

Cox, Harvey. *The Secular City.* New York: Macmillan, 1965.

Crocker, D. "Towards Development Ethics." *World Development* 19, 5 (1991): 457–83.

Cullmann, Oscar. *Christ and Time: The Primitive Christian Conception of Time and History.* London: SCM Press, 1965.

Daly, Herman E. *Beyond Growth: The Economics of Sustainable Development.* Boston: Beacon Press, 1996.

– "The Ecological and Moral Necessity for Limiting Economic Growth." In *Faith and Science in an Unjust World,* ed. Roger Shinn. Geneva: World Council of Churches, 1980.

– "Free Trade: The Perils of Deregulation." In *The Case against the Global Economy,* ed. Jerry Mander and Edward Goldsmith. San Francisco: Sierra Club Books, 1997.

– *Steady-State Economics.* San Francisco: W.H. Freeman, 1977.

Daly, Herman E., ed. *Toward a Steady State Economy.* San Francisco: W.H. Freeman, 1973.

Daly, Herman E., and John B. Cobb Jr. *For the Common Good: Redirecting the Economy toward the Community, the Environment and a Sustainable Future.* Boston: Beacon Press, 1989.

Davis, Arthur. "Justice and Freedom: George Grant's Encounter with Martin Heidegger." In *George Grant and the Subversion of Modernity: Art, Philosophy, Politics, Religion and Education,* ed. Arthur Davis. Toronto: University of Toronto Press, 1996.

Davis, Arthur, ed. *George Grant and the Subversion of Modernity: Art, Philosophy, Politics, Religion and Education.* Toronto: University of Toronto Press, 1996.

Davis, Gregory H. *Technology - Humanism or Nihilism: A Critical Analysis of the Philosophical Basis and Practice of Modern Technology.* Washington: University Press of America, 1981.

Day, Richard B., Ronald Beiner, and Joseph Masciulli, ed. *Democratic Theory and Technological Society.* London: M.E. Sharpe, 1988.

De Crespigny, H. and Minogue, K. *Contemporary Political Philosophers.* London: Methuen, 1976.

Diamond, Jared. *Collapse: How Societies Choose to Fail or Succeed.* New York: Viking, 2005.

Dowdeswell, Elizabeth (president, Nuclear Waste Management Organization). "Speech to the National Press Club of Canada, Final Study Report Release." Ottawa, Ontario, 3 November 2005. Available at http://www.nwmo.ca/default.aspx?DN=1507,60,19,1,Documents (accessed 12 June 2007).

Ehrlich, Paul. *The Population Bomb.* New York: Ballantine, 1968.

– *The Population Explosion.* London: Hutchinson, 1990.

Elliot, Gil. *Twentieth Century Book of the Dead.* London: Penguin Press, 1972.

Ellul, Jacques. "The Ethics of Nonpower." In *Ethics in an Age of Pervasive Technology,* ed. Melvin Kranzberg. Boulder, Colo.: Westview Press, 1980.

– *The Technological Bluff.* Grand Rapids, Mich.: W.B. Eerdmans, 1990.

– *The Technological Society.* New York: Knopf, 1964.

– *The Technological System.* New York: Continuum Publishing, 1980.

Elshtain, Jean Bethke. *Just War against Terror: The Burden of American Power in a Violent World.* New York: Basic Books, 2003.

Ferré, Frederick. *Philosophy of Technology.* Athens: University of Georgia Press, 1995.

Finnis, John, Joseph Boyle, and Germain Grisez. *Nuclear Deterrence, Morality and Realism.* Oxford: Clarendon Press, 1987.

Fisk, Robert. *The Great War for Civilization: The Conquest of the Middle East.* London: Fourth Estate, 2005.

Forbes, H.D. "George Grant and Leo Strauss." In *George Grant and the Subversion of Modernity: Art, Philosophy, Politics, Religion and Education,* ed. Arthur Davis. Toronto: University of Toronto Press, 1996.

Fortin, Eugene. "St. Augustine." In *History of Political Philosophy, Third Edition,* ed. Leo Strauss and Joseph Cropsey. Chicago: University of Chicago Press, 1987.

Francis, John, and Paul Abrecht. *Facing up to Nuclear Power.* Philadelphia: Westminster Press, 1976.

Franklin, Ursula. *Canada as a Conserver Society.* Ottawa: Science Council of Canada, Report no. 27, 1977.

– *The Real World of Technology.* Revised edition. Toronto: CBC Enterprises, 1999.

Friedman, George and Meredith. *The Future of War.* New York: Crown Publishers, 1996.

Fukuyama, Francis. *The End of History and the Last Man.* Toronto: Maxwell Macmillan Canada, 1992.

Galeano, Eduardo. *Open Veins of Latin America: Five Centuries of the Pillage of a Continent.* New York: Monthly Review Press, 1973.

Gallagher, Hugh. *By Trust Betrayed: Patients, Physicians, and the Licence to Kill in the Third Reich.* New York: Henry Holt, 1990.

Genetic Crossroads no. 38. The Newsletter of the Center for Genetics and Society. 9 April 2004. Available at http://genetics-and-society.org/newsletter/archive/38.html (accessed 19 February 2007).

Genome(s) and Justice: Reflections on a Holistic Approach to Genetic Research, Technology and Disability. The Roer Institute in Co-operation with Inclusion International. Draft, August 1998.

George, Susan. *How the Other Half Dies: The Real Reasons for World Hunger.* New York: Penguin Books, 1979.

Gheddo, Piero. *Why Is the Third World Poor?* Maryknoll, N.Y.: Orbis Books, 1973.

Gildin, H. *Political Philosophy.* New York: Bobbs-Merrill, 1975.

Gore, Al. *Earth in the Balance: Ecology and the Human Spirit.* New York: Penguin Books, 1992.

– *An Inconvenient Truth: The Planetary Emergency of Global Warming and What We Can Do About It.* New York: Rodale Press, 2006.

Goudzwaard, Bob. *Capitalism and Progress.* Toronto: Wedge Pub. Foundation, 1979.

Grant, George. *English Speaking Justice.* Toronto: House of Anansi Press, 1974.

– *Lament for a Nation: The Defeat of Canadian Nationalism.* Toronto: McClelland and Stewart, 1965.

– *Philosophy in the Mass Age.* With a new introduction by the author. Toronto: Copp Clark Publishing, 1966.

– *Philosophy in the Mass Age.* Toronto: Copp Clark Publishing, 1959.

– *Philosophy in the Mass Age.* Toronto: University of Toronto Press, 1995.

– *Technology and Empire: Perspectives on North America.* Toronto: House of Anansi Press, 1969.

– *Technology and Justice.* Toronto: House of Anansi Press, 1986.

– *Time as History.* Toronto: University of Toronto Press, 1995.

Gray, Chris Hables. *Postmodern War: The New Politics of Conflict.* New York: Guilford Press, 1997.

Hall, Douglas J. *The Steward: A Biblical Symbol Come of Age.* Toronto: United Church Publishing House, 1989.

Hardin, Garrett. "Lifeboat Ethics: The Case against Helping the Poor." *Psychology Today* 8 (September 1974): 38–43. Available at http://www.garretthardinsociety.org/articles/art_lifeboat_ethics_case_against_helping_poor.html (accessed 23 February 2007).

Havelock, Eric. *Preface to Plato.* Cambridge: Harvard University Press, 1963.

Health Canada. "New Reproductive and Genetic Technologies: Setting Boundaries, Enhancing Health." Minister of Supply and Services Canada, June 1996. Available at http://www.hc-sc.gc.ca/dhp-mps/alt_formats/cmcd-dcmc/pdf/tech_reprod_e.pdf (accessed 23 February 2007).

– "Reproductive and Genetic Technologies: An Overview Paper." 1999.

Heidegger, Martin. *The Question concerning Technology.* New York: Harper Torchbooks, 1977.

Heilbroner, Robert L. *The Great Ascent: The Struggle for Economic Development in Our Time.* New York: Harper and Row, 1963.

– *An Inquiry into the Human Prospect: Updated and Reconsidered for the 1980s.* New York: W.W. Norton, 1980.

– *The Worldly Philosophers.* New York: Simon and Shuster, 1953.

Heinberg, Richard. *The Party's Over: Oil, War and the Fate of Industrial Societ-ies*. Gabriola Island, B.C.: New Society Publishers, 2003.

– *Powerdown: Options and Actions for a Post-Carbon World*. Gabriola Island, B.C.: New Society Publishers, 2004.

Herrick, Jim. "Bertrand Russell: A Passionate Rationalist." In *Against the Faith: Essays on Deists, Skeptics and Atheists*. Amherst, N.Y.: Prometheus Books, 1985. Available at http://www.positiveatheism.org/hist/russell6. htm (accessed February 24, 2007)

Homer-Dixon, Thomas. *The Ingenuity Gap: Can We Solve the Problems of the Future?* Toronto: Vintage Canada, 2001.

– "The Rich Get Richer, and the Poor Get Squat." *Globe and Mail*, 30 July 2005. Review of *Worlds Apart: Measuring International and Global Inequality* by Branko Milanovic (Princeton: Princeton University Press). Available at http://www.homerdixon.com/download/worlds_apart.pdf (accessed 25 February 2007).

Ignatieff, Michael. *Empire Lite*. Toronto: Penguin Books, 2003.

– *The Lesser Evil: Political Ethics in an Age of Terror*. Princeton: Princeton University Press, 2004.

– *Virtual War: Kosovo and Beyond*. Harmondsworth, Middlesex: Viking, 2000.

Illich, Ivan. *The Right to Useful Unemployment*. London: Marion Boyars, 1978.

– *Tools for Conviviality*. New York: Harper and Row, 1973.

Innis, Harold A. *The Bias of Communication*. Toronto: University of Toronto Press, 1951.

– *Empire and Communications*. Revised by Mary Q. Innis with a preface by Marshall McLuhan. Toronto: University of Toronto Press, 1972.

Jackson, Barbara Ward. *Progress for a Small Planet*. New York: Norton, 1979.

– *The Rich Nations and the Poor Nations*. Toronto: Canadian Broadcasting Corporation, 1961.

– *Towards a World of Plenty?* Toronto: University of Toronto Press, 1964.

Jacobs, Jane. *Dark Age Ahead*. Toronto: Random House, 2004.

Jonas, Hans. *The Imperative of Responsibility: In Search of Ethics for the Technological Age*. Chicago: University of Chicago Press, 1984.

Jungk, Robert. *Brighter than a Thousand Suns*. New York: Harcourt Brace, 1958.

– *The New Tyranny: How Nuclear Power Enslaves Us*. New York: Warner Books, 1979.

Kaczinski, Ted. "The Unabomber Manifesto." In *Unabomber: On the Trails of America's Most Wanted Serial Killer*, John Douglas and Mark Olshaker, 191–286. New York: Pocket Books, 1996.

Kahn, Herman, and Julian Simon, ed. *The Resourceful Earth: A Response to Global 2000*. New York: Blackwell, 1984.

Kass, Leon. *The Ethics of Human Cloning*. New York: AEI Press, 1998.

– *Life, Liberty, and the Defense of Dignity: The Challenge for Bioethics*. San Francisco: Encounter Books, 2002.

– "Preventing a Brave New World." *The New Republic*, 21 May 2001. http://www.findarticles.com/p/articles/mi_qa3798/is_200107/ai_n8989747/print (accessed 7 February 2007).

– *Toward a More Natural Science: Biology and Human Affairs*. New York: The Free Press, 1985.

Kevles, Daniel J. "Out of Eugenics: The Historical Politics of the Human Genome." In *The Code of Codes: Scientific and Social Issues in the Human Genome Project*, ed. Daniel J. Kevles and Leroy Hood. Cambridge: Harvard University Press, 1992.

Kevles, Daniel J. and Leroy Hood, ed. *The Code of Codes: Scientific and Social Issues in the Human Genome Project*. Cambridge: Harvard University Press, 1992.

Kierans, Eric. *Remembering*. Toronto: Stoddart Publishing, 2001.

Knelman, F.H. *Nuclear Energy*. Edmonton: Hurtig Publishers, 1976.

Koliopoulos, Sophia. "Prenatal Genetic Testing: Do You Really Want to Know Your Baby's Future?" *DNA Files*, October 2001. http://www.dnafiles.org/about/pgm3/topic.html (accessed 24 February 2007).

Kroker, Arthur. *Technology and the Canadian Mind: Innis/McLuhan/Grant*. Montréal: New World Perspectives, 1984.

Kunetka, J.W. *Oppenheimer: The Years of Risk*. Englewood Cliffs, N.J.: Prentice Hall, 1982.

Kurien, C.T. "Economics of the Just and Sustainable Society." In *Faith and Science in an Unjust World*, ed. Roger Shinn. World Council of Churches, 1980.

Kurth, James. "First War of the Global Era." In *War over Kosovo: Politics and Strategy in a Global Age*, ed. Andrew J. Bacevich and Eliot A. Cohen. New York: Columbia University Press, 2001.

Lasch, Christopher. *The True and Only Heaven: Progress and Its Critics*. New York: W.W. Norton, 1991.

Leslie, John. *The End of the World: The Science and Ethics of Human Extinction*. London: Routledge, 1996.

Lewis, C.S. *The Abolition of Man*. London: Collins, 1978.

Lifton, Robert Jay, and Eric Markusen. *The Genocidal Mentality: Nazi Holocaust and Nuclear Threat*. New York: Basic Books, 1990.

Lippman, Abby. "Prenatal Genetic Testing and Screening: Constructing Needs and Reinforcing Inequities." *American Journal of Law and Medicine* 17, 1 and 2 (1991): 15–50.

Logan, Robert K. *The Fifth Language: Learning a Living in the Computer Age.*
  Toronto: Stoddart, 1995.

Lovins, Amory. *Energy/War: Breaking the Connection.* New York: Harper and
  Row, 1980.

– *Soft Energy Paths.* Cambridge, Mass.: Ballinger Publishing Company,
  1977.

Lowrance, W.W. *Of Acceptable Risk.* Los Altos, Calif.: Kaufmann, 1976.

Lukacs, John. *At the End of an Age.* New Haven: Yale University Press, 2002.

– *Historical Consciousness.* New York: Harper and Row, 1968.

– *Outgrowing Democracy: A History of the United States in the Twentieth Century.*
  Garden City, N.Y.: Doubleday, 1984.

– *The Passing of the Modern Age.* New York: Harper Torchbooks, 1970.

McCormick, Richard. *How Brave a New World? Dilemmas in Bioethics.* Washington: Georgetown University Press, 1981.

McGinnis, Jim. *Bread and Justice: Toward a New International Economic Order.*
  Mahwah, N.J.: Paulist Press, 1979.

MacIntyre, Alasdair. *After Virtue.* Notre Dame, Ind.: Notre Dame Press,
  1984.

– "Liberalism Transformed into a Tradition." In *Whose Justice? Which Rationality?* Notre Dame, Ind.: University of Notre Dame Press, 1988.

– "The Privatization of Good: An Inaugural Lecture." *Review of Politics* 52,
  3 (1990), 344–77.

– *A Short History of Ethics.* New York: Macmillan, 1966.

– *Three Rival Versions of Morality: Encyclopedia, Genealogy and Tradition.* Notre
  Dame, Ind.: University of Notre Dame Press, 1990.

– "Utilitarianism and Cost-Benefit Analysis: An Essay on the Relevance of
  Moral Philosophy to Bureaucratic Theory." In *Values in Electrical Power
  Industry,* ed. K. Sayre. South Bend, Ind.: University of Notre Dame Press,
  1977.

– *Whose Justice? Which Rationality?* Notre Dame, Ind.: University of Notre
  Dame Press, 1988.

McKibben, Bill. *Enough: Staying Human in an Engineered Age.* Henry Holt,
  2003.

McLaren, Angus. *Our Own Master Race: Eugenics in Canada: 1885–1945.*
  Toronto: McClelland and Stewart, 1990.

McLuhan, Marshall. *The Gutenberg Galaxy: The Making of Typographic Man.*
  Toronto: Signet Books, 1969.

– *Understanding Media: The Extensions of Man.* Toronto: McGraw Hill, 1964.

Mander, Jerry. *Four Arguments for the Elimination of Television.* New York:
  Morrow, 1978.

– *In the Absence of the Sacred: The Failure of Technology and the Survival of the Indian Nations.* San Francisco: Sierra Club Books, 1992.

Mander, Jerry, and Edward Goldsmith, ed. *The Case against the Global Economy.* San Francisco: Sierra Club Books, 1997.

Mathie, William. "The Technological Regime: George Grant's Analysis of Modernity." In *George Grant in Process: Essays and Conversations,* ed. Larry Schmidt. Toronto: House of Anansi Press, 1978.

Mazur, Allan. "Three Mile Island and the Scientific Community." *Annals of the New York Academy of Sciences,* 365 (1): 216–21.

Merton, Robert K. *Science, Technology and Society in Seventeenth-Century England.* New York: Harper and Row, 1970.

Michelmore, P. *The Swift Years: The Robert Oppenheimer Story.* New York: Dodd, Mead, 1969.

Milanovic, Branko. *Worlds Apart: Measuring International and Global Inequality.* Princeton: Princeton University Press, 2006.

Miller, E.F. "Leo Strauss: The Recovery of Political Philosophy." In *Contemporary Political Philosophers,* ed. H. De Crespigny and K. Minogue. London: Methuen, 1976.

Mitcham, Carl and Jim Grote, ed. *Theology and Technology: Essays in Christian Analysis and Exegesis.* Lanham, Md: University Press of America, 1984.

Monbiot, George. *Heat: How to Stop the Planet from Burning.* Toronto: Doubleday Canada, 2006.

Morone, Joseph, and Edward Woodhouse. *Averting Catastrophe: Strategies for Regulating Risky Technologies.* Berkeley: University of California Press, 1986.

– *The Demise of Nuclear Energy: Lessons for the Democratic Control of Technology.* New Haven: Yale University Press, 1989.

Mumford, Lewis. *The Myth of the Machine: Technics and Human Development.* New York: Harcourt, Brace Jovanovich, 1967.

– *The Pentagon of Power.* New York: Harcourt, Brace Jovanovich, 1969.

Myrdal, Gunnar. *Against the Stream: Critical Essays in Economics.* New York: Vintage Books, 1975.

Negroponte, Nicholas. *Being Digital.* New York: Alfred A. Knopf, 1995.

Nietzsche, Friedrich. *Twilight of the Idols/The Anti-Christ.* Trans. R.J. Hollingdale. London: Penguin Books, 1968.

Noble, David F. *The Religion of Technology.* New York: Alfred A. Knopf, 1997.

Noonan Jr, John T. *Contraception: A History of Its Treatment by Catholic Theologians and Canonists.* Cambridge: Harvard University Press, 1965.

Novak, Michael. *Moral Clarity in the Nuclear Age.* Nashville: Thomas Nelson Publishers, 1983.

"Nuclear Notes." November 2002. Campaign for Nuclear Phaseout. Available at http://www.cnp.ca/resources/nuclear-notes-v1.pdf (accessed 27 May 2007).

Nuclear Waste Management Organization. "Choosing a Way Forward: The Future Management of Canada's Used Nuclear Fuel (Final Study – Summary)." November 2005. Available at http://www.nwmo.ca/adx/asp/adxGetMedia.asp?DocID=1487,20,1,Documents&MediaID=2706&Filename=NWMO_Final_Study_Summary_E.pdf (accessed 23 February 2007).

– "Mandate." Available at http://www.nwmo.ca/Default.aspx?DN=41,18,1,Documents (accessed 23 February 2007).

– "NWMO Recommends Adaptive Phased Management." Press release, 3 November 2005. Available at http://www.nwmo.ca/default.aspx?DN=1498,50,19,1,Documents (accessed 25 May 2007).

O'Donovan, Joan E. *George Grant and the Twilight of Justice*. Toronto: University of Toronto Press, 1984.

O'Donovan, Oliver. *The Just War Revisited*. Cambridge: Cambridge University Press, 2003.

Oelschlager, Max. *Caring for Creation: An Ecumenical Approach to the Environmental Crisis*. New Haven and London: Yale University Press, 1994.

Ong, Walter. *The Presence of the Word: Some Prolegomena for Cultural and Religious History*. New York: Simon and Shuster, 1967.

Ortega y Gasset, José. *The Revolt of the Masses*. New York: W.W. Norton, 1932.

Overall, Christine. *Ethics and Human Reproduction: A Feminist Analysis*. Boston: Allen and Unwin, 1987.

Patterson, W.C. *Nuclear Power*. Markham, Ont.: Penguin Books, 1976.

Pearce, Fred. *The Last Generation: How Nature Will Take Her Revenge for Climate Change*. Toronto: Key Porter Books, 2007.

Pernick, Martin S. *The Black Stork: Eugenics and the Death of Defective Babies in American Medicine and Motion Pictures since 1915*. Oxford: Oxford University Press, 1996.

Polanyi, Karl. *The Great Transformation*. Boston: Beacon Press, 1957.

Postman, *Technopoly: The Surrender of Culture to Technology*. New York: Vintage Books, 1993.

President's Council on Bioethics. *Human Cloning and Human Dignity: An Ethical Inquiry*. Washington, D.C., July 2002. Available at http://www.bioethics.gov/reports/cloningreport/index.html (accessed 23 February 2007).

Proctor, Robert. *Racial Hygiene: Medicine under the Nazis*. Cambridge: Harvard University Press, 1988.

Ramsey, Paul. *Fabricated Man*. New Haven: Yale University Press, 1970.

Rasmussen, Larry L. *Earth Community, Earth Ethics.* Maryknoll: Orbis Books, 1996.

Rawls, John. *A Theory of Justice.* Oxford: Oxford University Press, 1971.

Raymond, Janice. "Reproduction, Population, Technology and Rights." "Health Update" in *Women in Action* 1998:2. Available at http://www.isiswomen.org/wia/wia298/rep00001.html (accessed 23 February 2007).

– *Women as Wombs: Reproductive Technologies and the Battle over Women's Freedom.* San Francisco: Harper, 1993.

Rhodes, Richard. *The Making of the Atomic Bomb.* New York: Simon and Shuster, 1986.

Rifkin, Jeremy. *The Biotech Century: Harnessing the Gene and Remaking the World.* New York: Tarcher/Putnam, 1998.

Rist, John M. *Augustine: Ancient Thought Baptised.* Cambridge: Cambridge University Press, 1994.

– *Real Ethics.* Cambridge: Cambridge University Press, 2002.

Robertson, Neil G. "George Grant: Intimations of Deprival, Intimations of Beauty." *Modern Age* 46, 1–2 (Winter/Spring 2004): 74–83.

Rosen, Stanley. *Nihilism: A Philosophical Essay.* New Haven: Yale University Press, 1969.

Rostow, Walt Whitman. *The Stages of Economic Growth: A Non-communist Manifesto.* Cambridge: Cambridge University Press, 1960.

Rouzé, M. *Robert Oppenheimer, the Man and His Theories.* New York: Paul S. Eriksson, 1965.

Sachs, Wolfgang. *Planet Dialectics: Explorations in Environment and Development.* London: Zed Books, 1999.

Sartre, Jean-Paul. *Existentialism and Human Emotions.* New York: Philosophical Library, 1957.

Saul, John Ralston. *Voltaire's Bastards: The Dictatorship of Reason in the West.* Toronto: Penguin Books, 1993.

Schmidt, Larry, ed. *George Grant in Process: Essays and Conversations.* Toronto: House of Anansi Press, 1978.

Schmidt, Lawrence E. "Simone Weil on Religion: A Voegelinian Critique." *Cahiers Simone Weil* 15, 3 (1992): 263–73.

Schmidt, Lawrence E., and Scott Marratto. "The Measure of Justice: The Language of Limit in the Writings of Simone Weil." ARC: *The Journal of the Faculty of Religious Studies, McGill University* 28 (2000): 53–66.

Schumacher, E.F. *Good Work.* New York: Harper and Row, 1979.

– *Small Is Beautiful: A Study of Economics As If People Mattered.* New York: Harper and Row, 1973.

Sebold, W.G. *On the Natural History of Destruction.* London: Penguin Books, 2004.

Sidel, Victor, and Barry Levy. *War and Public Health.* New York: Oxford University Press and the American Public Health Association, 2000.

Sierra Club of Canada. "Backgrounder: Nuclear Fuel Waste Management." November 2001. Available at http://www.sierraclub.ca/national/ programs/atmosphere-energy/nuclear-free/reactors/nuclear-fuel-waste-11-01.html (accessed 12 June 2007).

Simon, Julian. *The Ultimate Resource.* Princeton: Princeton University Press, 1981.

– *The Ultimate Resource 2.* Princeton: Princeton University Press, 1996.

Sims, Gordon. *The Anti-Nuclear Game.* Ottawa: Ottawa University Press, 1990.

Singer, Peter. *Practical Ethics.* 2nd ed. Cambridge: Cambridge University Press, 1993.

State of the World 2001. Worldwatch Institute. New York: W.W. Norton, 2001.

Stivers, Robert. *Hunger, Technology and Limits to Growth.* Minneapolis: Augsburg Publishing House, 1984.

Stock, Gregory. *Redesigning Humans: Our Inevitable Genetic Future.* London: Profile Books, 2002.

Stockholm International Peace Research Institute. *SIPRI Yearbook 2006: Armaments, Disarmament and International Security.* Oxford: Oxford University Press, 2006.

Stoll, Clifford. *Silicon Snake Oil: Second Thoughts on the Information Highway.* New York: Doubleday, 1995.

Strauss, Leo. "Three Waves of Modernity." In *Political Philosophy,* H. Gildin. New York: Bobbs-Merrill, 1975.

– "What Is Political Philosophy?" In *Political Philosophy,* H. Gildin. New York: Bobbs-Merrill, 1975.

Strauss, Leo, and Joseph Cropsey, ed. *History of Political Philosophy: Third Edition.* Chicago: University of Chicago Press, 1987.

Szasz, F.P. *The Day the Sun Rose Twice.* Albuquerque: University of New Mexico Press, 1984.

Thiele, Leslie Paul. *Environmentalism for a New Millennium: The Challenge of Coevolution.* New York and Oxford: Oxford University Press, 1999.

Vanderburg, Willem. *The Labyrinth of Technology.* Toronto: University of Toronto Press, 2000.

– *Living in the Labyrinth of Technology.* Toronto: University of Toronto Press, 2005.

– "Political Imagination in a Technical Age." In *Democratic Theory and Technological Society*, ed. Richard B. Day, Ronald Beiner, and Joseph Masciulli Armonk. New York: M.E. Sharpe, 1988.

Vanderburg, Willem, ed. *Jacques Ellul Speaks on His Life and Work.* Toronto: CBC Enterprises, 1981.

Vaux, Kenneth. *Biomedical Ethics: Morality for the New Medicine.* New York: Harper and Row, 1974.

Vivacqua, Judy. "In Vitro Fertilization: An Ethical Analysis." Unpublished undergraduate paper, Erindale College, University of Toronto, 1996.

Voegelin, Eric. *From Enlightenment to Revolution.* Durham, N.C.: Duke University Press, 1975.

– *The New Science of Politics.* Chicago: University of Chicago Press, 1952.

– "The Origins of Scientism." *Social Research* 15, 4 (1948): 452–94.

– *Order and History: Volume I, Israel and Revelation.* Baton Rouge: Louisiana State University Press, 1956.

– *Order and History, Vol. IV: The Ecumenic Age.* Baton Rouge: Louisiana State University Press, 1974.

Warnock, Mary. *Making Babies: Is There a Right to Have Children?* Oxford: Oxford University Press, 2003.

– *Nature and Mortality.* London: Continuum Books, 2003.

– *A Question of Life: The Warnock Report on Human Fertilization and Embryology.* New York: Basil Blackwell, 1985.

Weber, Max. *The Protestant Ethic and the Spirit of Capitalism.* London: George Allen and Unwin, 1930.

Weigel, George. "Moral Clarity in a Time of War." *First Things* 128 (January 2003): 20–7.

Weil, Simone. "Classical Science and After." In *Science, Necessity and the Love of God.* Oxford: Oxford University Press, 1968.

– "Draft for a Statement of Human Obligations." In *Selected Essays, 1934–43.* Trans. R. Rees. Oxford: Oxford University Press, 1962.

– *The Need for Roots: Prelude to A Declaration of Duties Toward Mankind.* Trans. Arthur Wills. New York: Harper Colophon, 1971.

– *The Notebooks of Simone Weil: Volume One.* Trans. Arthur Wills. London: Routledge and Kegan Paul, 1956.

– *The Notebooks of Simone Weil: Volume Two.* Trans. Arthur Wills. London: Routledge and Kegan Paul, 1956.

– *Oppression and Liberty.* Trans. Arthur Wills and John Petrie. Amherst: University of Massachusetts Press, 1973.

– *Science, Necessity and the Love of God.* London: Oxford University Press, 1968.

Weinberg, Alvin. *Nuclear Reactions: Science and Trans-science.* New York: American Institute of Physics, 1992.

– "Salvaging the Atomic Age." *Wilson Quarterly* 3, 3 (1979): 88–115. Reprinted in *Nuclear Reactions: Science and Trans-science.*

– "Social Institutions and Nuclear Energy." *Science* 177 (July 1972): 27–34. Reprinted in *Nuclear Reactions: Science and Trans-science.*

White, Lynn, Jr. "The Historical Roots of Our Ecological Crisis." *Science* 155 (1967): 1203–7. Available at http://www.uvm.edu/~gflomenh/ENV-NGO-PA395/articles/Lynn-White.pdf (accessed 23 February 2007.)

Winner, Langdon. *Autonomous Technology: Technics-Out-of-Control as a Theme in Political Thought.* Cambridge: MIT Press, 1977.

– *The Whale and the Reactor: A Search for Limits in an Age of High Technology.* Chicago: University of Chicago Press, 1986.

Wolbring, Gregor, on behalf of the Council of Canadians with Disabilities. "Renewal of Canadian Biotechnology Strategy 1998." International Center for Bioethics, Culture and Disability. Presentation to Health Canada by David Martin and Paula Kierstead. Available at http://www.bioethicsanddisability.org/submissi.html (accessed 23 February 2007).

Wolf, Susan, ed. *Specific Problems in Bioethics.* Oxford: Oxford University Press, 1996.

Wolin, Richard, ed. *The Heidegger Controversy: A Critical Reader.* New York: Columbia University Press, 1991.

World Commission on Environment and Development [The Brundtland Commission]. *Our Common Future.* Oxford: Oxford University Press, 1987.

Wright, Ronald. *A Short History of Progress.* Toronto: House of Anansi Press, 2005.

Index

abortion, 16, 156; on basis of disability, 145–6; on basis of gender, 145; ethics of, 117; legalization of therapeutic, 117; selective, 115; transformation of societal attitudes to, 117

Act Respecting Human Reproduction and Related Research (Canada, 2004), 135; its prohibition against cloning, 137

adoption, 133

Afghanistan, 100, 102; casualties after 11 September 2001, 105–6

agriculture, 25; and loss of farmland, 40; and organic farming, 35

al Qaeda, 106, 109, 110

American Catholic Bishops (*The Challenge of Peace*), 95

American Civil Liberties Union, 97, 160

American Statistical Association, 97

Amnesty International, 107

amniocentesis, 139

Andrews, D.G. (Canadian Nuclear Association), 57, 193n1, 198n36

apocalypse, xii, 12, 175

Appleyard, Bryan, 147

Aquinas, Thomas, 12, 202

Arendt, Hannah, 108; on the calamity of the rightless, 160; on the plight of refugees, 158–9

Aristotle, 12, 173

arms race, 86

artificial innovulation, 114

artificial insemination, 115; and the ethics of respect for fetal life, 117; from a donor, 114–15

Asch, Adrienne, 146–7

Assisted Human Reproduction Act (Canada), 211n92

atomic bomb, and the just war doctrine, 84–5

Augustine, St, 11; *The City of God*, 12; on the fallen sate of human nature, 152

automobile, 26; increasing global dependence on, 169; high-compression engines and smog, 48

autonomy: as an ethical criteria, 138; and genetic technology, 147; as the right not to have to make choices, 147; used to legitimate negative eugenics, 138

Bacon, Francis, 11, 12, 13, 79, 147,
    165
Bainton, Roland, 81, 202
Baird, Patricia, 135
Barbour, Ian, 86
Barth, Karl, 13
Bauman, Zygmunt, 4; on the frag-
    mented self, 176; on the risk
    society, 76–7, 171
beatific vision, 14
Beck, Ulrich, 176; on the risk soci-
    ety, 77–8
Becker, Carl, 89–90
Beckett, Samuel, xiii
Beiner, Ronald, 173, 217
Bello, Walden, 30
Berlin Wall, 152
Bethe, Hans, 58, 88
Bible, 13
biological determinism, 122, 142
biopolitics, 144
biospheric thinking, 50
biotech industry, 144
birth control, 30
birth defects, 139
Blackmun, Justice, 136
Blair, Tony, 40
blastocyst, status of *in vitro*, 130
Bosnia, and the NATO campaign
    (1999), 98
breeder reactors, 197n34
Bruce nuclear plant (Ontario),
    201n60
Brundtland, Gro, 41
bureaucratic individualism, 165,
    215n1
Bush, George W., 40, 97, 111, 191

Calvinist Protestantism, 162
Cameron, James, 93

Campbell, Colin (peak oil),
    193n58
Canadian Nuclear Association, 59,
    63, 193n1
Candu nuclear reactor, xi, 70
capitalism: and communism as vari-
    ations on a common theme, 151;
    free market and environmental
    problems, 49; laissez-faire, 43
carbon dioxide emissions, 18, 39,
    53
Carson, Rachel, 49
Charo, R. Alta, 147
Charter of Rights and Freedoms
    (Canada), 157
chemicals in the environment, 171
Cheney, Dick, 96
Chesterton, G.K., 141
chorionic villus sampling (CVS),
    139
Christian Church Fathers, 11
civilian casualties, 95–7; and the
    principle of discrimination, 104
civil liberties of terrorists, 156
Clarke, Arthur C., 1
Clinton, President Bill, 100
cloning, xii, 114, 126; for research,
    134
cluster bombs, 107
Cobb Jr, John B., 41
Cohen, Elliot, 97–8
Cold War, 19, 85, 103
Coll, Albert, 98, 100, 202n9
collateral damage, 96–7, 99; in the
    war against Afghanistan, 106
collectivities, 157
colonialism, 23, 27, 30
colonial theory (Myrdal), 27
commodification of reproduction,
    122–3

Commoner, Barry, 34, 47, 68, 73; on distributive justice, 48; on economic development, 35, 41; on militarism, 48; on nuclear reactors, 58–60, 69–70; on political reforms, 48; on socialism, 74; on the technosphere versus ecosphere, 47
communitarianism, 149
Compton, Arthur, 87
computer modelling, 172
Condorcet, Marqis de, 140, 146, 212n9
consequentialism, 166
conservatism of ancient and Christian philosophers, 152
consumer society, 20, 32
contraception, 113
contractualism, 166
contractual liberalism, 136, 149, 150; and its agnosticism about the good, 154
Cooper, Barry, on acting into nature, 217n24
Cordesman, Anthony, 99
corporations, 35; American, and defence spending, 94; and capitalism, 41; and scientists, 45
cosmological myth, 24
Cowan, Ruth Schwartz, 147
creativity, 166, 177
Crocker, D., 36

Daly, Herman, 31, 41; on using up yesterday's sunshine, 42; and Cobb, John, 45–7, 51
danceband on the *Titanic*, 21
Darlington Nuclear Power plant, cost overruns, 69, 201n64
Davis, Gregory, 181n12, 193n2

debiologizing sex, 126
dehumanization of reproductive technologies, 128
Descartes, René, 11, 13
development: economic, 23, 28, 33, 41; authentic, 36; in Latin America, 28; and justice, 36–8
dioxin and cancer rates, 171
disability rights activists, 145
disenchantment of the earth, 24
divorce and remarriage, and lineage, 133
DNA, 143; research, 113, 136
Douglas, Tommy, and eugenics, 141
Dowdeswell, Elizabeth, 66, 199n51
Down syndrome, 142; and DNA research, 143

economy: dual, 32; spermatic, 125
economic growth, 19, 32, 41, 168, 171
economics, 32; and the abandonment of ethics, 36; and environmental degradation, 50; and externalities, 47; success measured by GNP, 46; trickle-down, 41
economic triumphalism, 150
economy of plenty, 14
ecumenic age, 6
Ehrlich, Paul, 189
electricity, 43
electronic media, 7
Elliot, Gil, 17
Ellul, Jacques, 3, 7, 32, 37, 175, 181n11, 182n20, 202n79, 216n16, 217n39
Elshtain, Jean Bethke, 95, 97, 108; on civilian casualties in the Iraq

war, 104–5, 107; as just war defender of the "war on terror," 107, 109; and political realism, 111; on precision-guided missiles, 103

emancipation of the passions, 150, 170

embryo donation and transfer, 132

embryos: cost of, 123; destruction of, 117; moral or ontological status of, 134; research carried out on spare, 121; rights to own, use, or dispose of, 120

embryonic stem-cell research, 134, 212n102

emotivism, 154

Enlightenment, 14, 17, 177–8; and corporations, 35; faith, 149; philosophers and the goodness of knowledge, 89; progressivism, 52, 140; project, 15, 154–6, 167

environmental degradation, 8, 16, 18, 19, 21; and crisis, 40

equality and human rights, 150

Erigena, John Scotus, 11

eschatology, 13, 25

ethics, 15; of assisted human reproduction, 119; classical and Christian tradition of, 15, 154; classical teleological scheme of, 154–5; and disability rights, 145; and economic development, 36; of embryo use, 119; of experimentation on human subjects, 117; feminist, 147; and limits, 76, 174; and metaphysics, 173; modern, and the emancipation of the passions, 166; of parenthood, 121; and reproductive technologies, 115; and risk management, 78

eugenics, 115, 134, 138–41, 146; contemporary branches of, 164; goals, 144; and Nazi experimentation, 114, 138; negative, 114, 138; of normalcy, 144; and the Nuremberg code, 114; positive or progressive, 114; program in Nazi Germany, 142–3; as a privatized industry, 148; in the Weimar Republic, 141

Eugenics Society of Canada, 141

euthanasia, 141, 156; of "useless eaters" in the Third Reich, 163

experimentation on human subjects, 118

expert knowers, 170

fact-value distinction, 155

fault-tree analysis, 60

feminism, and reproductive technologies, 122–7

Ferré, Frederick, 198

fetal life: destruction of in IVF, 119; the "humanity" of, 117

fetal tissue, harvesting of, 125

Fisk, Robert, 109–10

Ford, Henry, 26

foreign aid, 29, 33

Foucault, Michel, 101

Franklin, Ursula, 4, 7, 8, 18n7

Franks, Tommy, 96

freedom, 16, 21; of choice for women, 127; expansion of collective, 150; reproductive, 134

Friedman, George and Meredith, 95, 102, 204

frozen embryos, 115

Fukuyama, Francis, 150

future generations, what we owe to, 169, 173, 194n3

Gallagher, Hugh, 142
Galton, Francis, 140
gambling, 176
Gamow, George, 87
Geller, Gail, 146–7
Genbank (database for DNA sequence information), 143
gene-line therapy, 114
gene pool, 114, 138
genetically transmitted diseases, 114
genetic counselling: and the disabled, 145
genetic engineering, xiii
genetic manipulation, therapeutic, 114
genetics, 113, 140, 143; and racial hygiene, 142; research, 144
genetic screening, 114; and the medical profession, 115
genetic sequences, 114
genetic surgery, 114
genetic testing, 138
Geneva Convention, 160
George, Susan, 34
Gilbert, Walter, 143
globalization, 23, 34; and the environment, 50
Gorbachev, Mikhail, 94
Gore, Al, 181n6, 190n2; *An Inconvenient Truth*, 41
Grant, George, 9, 12, 13, 137, 183n2, 186n17, 215n18, 218n50; and his analysis of Rawls' theory of justice, 160; on contractual liberalism, 136; on "intimations of deprival," 178; on modern theories of justice, 161; on pluralism in a technological society, 157; on the

progressive nature of capitalism, 151; on rights and freedoms in liberal societies, 160
Gray, Chris Hables, 95, 204n46
green energy, 168
greenhouse effects of nuclear energy, 18, 201n69
Greer, Germaine, 123
Guantanamo, 160
Gulf War, 95–7

Hardin, Garrett, 29
Härlin, Benedikt, report on genome research, 144
Harper, Stephen, 40
Haveloc, Eric, 6
Health Canada, 213n27
Hebrew prophets, 11
Hegel, 17
Heidegger, Martin, 4, 21, 187n41, 216n7
Heilbroner, Robert, 17, 173, 186n26, 187n35, 193n3
Heilsgeschichte (salvation history), 11, 12
Heinberg, Richard, 54, 216n15
Heisenberg, Werner, 203n16
hemophilia, 139
Hess, Rudolph, 206n2
heterosexuality, virtues of, 133
heuristics of fear, 174, 178
Hippocratic injunction *primum non nocere* (first do no harm), 123
Hippocratic oath, 206n2
Hiroshima and Nagasaki, 89, 91; and President Truman, 99
historical societies, 6
history-making spirit (Grant), 13, 16, 17, 21
Hobbes, 154

Homer-Dixon, Thomas, 22, 23, 182n25, 188n2
Human Fertilization and Embryo Act (UK, 1990), 122, 135
Human Genome Project, 143
humanism, xi, 13, 14
human nature, classical Christian view of, 152
human rights, 96, 99; and the state according to Hannah Arendt, 158; sacred character of, 159; universality of, 158
Human Rights Watch, 96, 99, 204n41
human scale, 33, 75
Hume, David, 155, 198n38
Huntington's chorea, 139
Hussein, Saddam, 105; possession of poisonous gases, 111
Huxley, Aldous, 128
hydrogen power, 53, 169; and fuel-cell motors, 53

Ignatieff, Michael, 97, 204n55, 205n68; on human rights, 99
Illich, Ivan, 168, 194n5
imperialism, 28
incommensurables, 169
industrial revolution, 25; achievements of, 151; negative aspects of, 151
infertility, 115, 118; as feminine disease, 124; and individual rights, 129; male-factor, 124–5
ingenuity gap, 9
Innis, Harold A., 4, 6, 182n11
International Monetary Fund, 23, 30, 31, 33
International Panel on Climate Change, 40

in vitro fertilization (IVF), 117; clinics, 122; as experimentation on a human subject, 118; homologous, 131; and the recommendations of Mary Warnock, 120
Iraq, 95–7; and the war on terror, 102
Iraq Body Count, 107, 204n50
Islamism, radical, 109
Israel and the occupied territories, 110

Jackson, Barbara Ward, 24, 188
Jameson, Angela, 199n52
Johnston, General Robert B., 96
Jonas, Hans, 172–5, 181n10; and conclusions regarding technological innovations, 175; and the ontological ground for ethics, 173; and the quest for utopia, 173; and the responsibility to preserve a human future, 174
Jungk, Robert, 59, 181n3, 196n15, 203n13
jus ad bellum criteria, 83–8
jus in bello criteria, 84, 95; Suarez on, 83; Vitoria on, 83
justice, 15, 24; as conventional, 160; procedural, 154
just war doctrine: Ambrose, Bishop of Milan, on, 82; Aquinas on, 83; Augustine of Hippo on, 82; and casuistry, 111; and civilian casualties in Iraq, 95–7; and Christianity, 80–2; and Constantine, 81; and the Council of Arles (314 AD), 81; and discrimination, 84, 95, 205; and non-combatant immunity, 83; and precision-guided munitions, 81, 95, 98, 99; and

terrorism, 103; and the war on terror, 108; and weapons of mass destruction, 80

Kaczinski, Ted, xii, xiii, 181n9; *Unabomber Manifesto*, xii
Kahn, Herman, 41; and the beautiful resource future, 45
Kahn, Herman and Simon, Julian, 181n1, 191n10
Kahn, Joseph, 189n33
Kanbur, Ravi, 31
Kant, Immanuel, 152, 185n15; and the categorical imperative, 159; and enlightened self-interest, 153
Kass, Leon, 118, 207n5, 208n13, 210n83; on cloning, 134; contra Ramsey on the acceptability of IVF experimentation, 129; and the disposal of surplus embryos, 130; on IVF, 118; on family values, 133; on the funding of research into IVF, 133; on IVF in the context of genetic engineering and behaviour control, 127; and the naturalist argument, 131; and reasons for a ban on reproductive cloning, 134; on the risks associated with IVF, 129–30
Kevles, Daniel, 213n22
kingdom of God, 152
Kluge, Eike, 145–6
Knelman, Fred, 60, 68, 74, 196n18
Kosovo, 98, 101, 202n9
Kurth, James, 100–2
Kuwait, 98

labour movement, 26
Lancet, the, 108

Lappé, Francis Moore, 34
Lasch, Christopher, 149, 214n2
Lewis, C.S., 127–8, 210n60, 214n12, 216n4
liberal capitalism, 149; and feminism, 127
liberal ethics, xiv; and the distinction between what is human and what is a person, 119; and sexual relations, 119
liberal globalism, 101
liberalism: and social constraints, 150; as dissolver of tradition, 157; as plagued by a civilizational contradiction, 162; and technology, 157; as a tradition, 156
liberal rights, 128
liberal values, 95
limits to growth, 43
lineage, 133
Lippman, Abby, 139, 212n3
Lovins, Amory, 41, 45, 191n26, 194n5
Lukacs, John, 26, 188n17, 189n18

Machiavelli, Nicolo, 11, 16; on the conquering of chance, 152
MacIntyre, Alasdair, 154, 184n11, 191n22, 214n6, 215n16; critique of contractual liberalism, 155–7; critique of modern ethics, 167; on the failure of the Enlightenment project, 157, 165; on magic, 1, 12
maintaining our standard of living, 169
Mander, Jerry, 36, 37, 206n3
Manhattan Project, 86–9
marriage, and traditional Christian morality, 118

Marxist communism (socialism),
149: as attack on pre-modern
conception of politics, 152; as
less progressive form of liberalism, 151
mastery thesis, 24
maternal instincts, 126
McClung, Nellie, 141
McLuhan, Marshall, 4, 7, 9
Mengele, Dr, 117
metaphysical knowledge, 15
Milanovic, Branko, 23, 188n2
militarism, 82
Milosovic, Slobodan, 98
modernization, 31
Monbiot, George, 190n3, 191n7
monetary policy, 23
moral relativism, xiv
moral subjectivity, 176–7
Morone, Joseph and Woodhouse,
Edward, 195n10, 196n20,
201n73
Moses, 11
Mullen, Ronan, 135
Mumford, Lewis, 3
Murphy, Emily, 141
mutually assured destruction (the
MAD doctrine), 92
Myrdal, Gunnar, 27, 33

NATO: and conduct of war in
Bosnia, 98–9; and human rights
in Kosovo, 100; and negotiations
with Serbia (1999), 101; in a
time of globalization, 102
naturalism, 131
natural law, 12, 15, 16, 21; and critique of essentializing, 126; and
sense of human limitations, 152;
and transcendental realism, 165

natural theology, 13
nature: as purposeful, 173; as raw
material, 170
Nazi eugenics program, 142
neo-colonialism, 27, 33
neo-conservative rhetoric and risks,
171
neo-liberal economics, 24, 33
neo-malthusianism, 141
Nietzsche, xiv; on equality, 163; on
nihilists and last men, 128; on
values, 198n38
Nietzschean critique of all essentializing, 126
nihilism, xii, 23, 113; of technological progressivism, 163
non-maleficence, 123
Northwatch, 66
Novak, Michael, 92, 204n32; justification of nuclear deterrence, 93
Nuclear Fuel Waste Act (Canada),
61, 66
nuclear chain reaction, 87
nuclear deterrence, 85, 205n68;
and the just war doctrine, 92;
Oppenheimer on, 91
nuclear power: and cost-risk-benefit calculations, 63; and economics, 57, 69; and ethics, 72–
3; as a Faustian bargain, 73; as a
green source of energy, 168;
and ignorance, 174–5; and risk,
58; and sabotage, 68; and safety,
59–61; and science, 73; and security, 67; and sustainable sufficiency, 57, 74–5; and terrorism,
67–8
nuclear waste, 198; conceptual environmental assessment of, 65;
disposal of, 61–3

Nuclear Waste Management Organization (Canada), 65–6, 199n49
nuclear weapons, 19; and security, 170
Nuremberg code, 117, 138
Nuremberg trials, 114

obligations, xiv
Oelschlager, Max, 52
Office of Technology Assessment (US Congress), 144
old-growth forests, 168
Ong, Walter, 6, 7
Ontario Hydro, 200n60
Oppenheimer, Robert, 79, 86, 171, 202n1, 203n25; and the development of nuclear weapons, 89; and his Enlightenment belief in the goodness of knowledge, 89; and the just war doctrine, 89–91; and the moral autonomy of science, 91; and President Truman, 89; quotation from the Bhagadhvad Gita, 88
oral-aural cultures, 6, 9
Orwell, George, 128
Overall, Christine, 122; on abortion, 124; on the ethics of human parenthood, 124; on IVF, 123; as liberal feminist, 122, 127

Palestinians, and the occupied territories, 110
Paracelsus, 12
parent-child relationship as paradigmatic (Jonas), 174
parousia, 12
participation as ethical ideal, 24
peak oil, 53–4

perfectibility of man, 140
Pernick, Martin, 140
petrochemical industries, 35
pharmaceutical companies, 136
photovoltaic cells, 35, 36
Pickering nuclear plant, 200n60
Pinochet, Augusto, 30
pluralism in a technological society, 157
plutonium, 61
political ethics, 158
political science, 149
population, 18, 25, 33; control, 34; rate of population growth of cars versus humans, 55; as the ultimate resource (Simon), 44; zero population growth, 35
positivism, 149
post-literate societies, 7
postmodern condition and ethics, 164
poverty, 21, 22; and colonialism, 27, 29, 33, 34
precision-guided munitions, 95, 97
pre-implantation genetic diagnosis, 138–9, 212n2
prenatal diagnosis, 138, 212n1; and government interference, 147
President's Council on Bioethics, 207n10, 210n84
privatization of the good, 156–7
procreation, 113; natural, 131; as a purpose of marriage, 118; and sexual love, 133
Proctor, Robert, 142
progeniture, 121
progress, 14, 25, 29, 76; medical, 118; religion of, 151
propaganda, xii

Protestant ethic, 26
protest ideology (Myrdal), 27
providence, 11, 12
public virtues, 56

racial hygiene, 140, 142; *Rassenhygiene* and National Socialism in Germany, 141
radical Islamism, 109
Rambouillet negotiations (1999), 101
Ramsey, Paul, 116–17, and biological experimentation, 117; and Christian purposes of marriage, 118; on IVF as an experiment on a human subject, 118; on "the sphere of love" and "the act of love," 119
Rasmussen, Larry, 192
Rawls, John, 159
Raymond, Janice, 124; on abortion, 125; on IVF, 125; as radical feminist, 124, 127
Reagan, Ronald, 41
reason as calculation, 160
Reformation, 11, 12; and just war doctrine, 83
regional populism, 149
religion of progress, 152
Renaissance, 12
reproductive freedom, 125
reproductive technologies, xii; and eugenics, 113; Canadian legal policy with regard to, 134–5; and feminist concerns, 122; and infertility, 115
resource depletion, 18, 19
responsibility, 76; ethics of (Jonas), 173
Rifkin, Jeremy, 139, 141, 212n9

rights and freedoms, 159; of those who do not yet exist, 174
rights theory, 166–7
risk, 77; analysis, 60–1, 65, 170; of a runaway atomic explosion, 88
risk society, 77–8, 170–1
Rist, John, 165, 176, 185n20, 216n6, 217n45
Roe *v* Wade (1973), 137
Rorty, Richard, 52
Rosen, Stanley, xiii
Rostow, Walter, 28, 189n23
Royal Commission on New Reproductive Technologies (Canada), 135, 144, 211n89
Rumsfeld, Donald, 107
Rutherford, Ernest, 87
Sachs, Wolfgang, 28, 32, 36, 37, 42; and fuel efficiency, 54; and technocratic rationality, 55
safety, technical meaning of, 60
Said, Edward, on the result of the sanctions again Iraq, 104
sanctions, against Iraq, 105
Sartre, Jean-Paul, 16, 185n20; and existentialism, 156
Schumacher, E.F., 3, 31, 34, 194n5, 198n36;on nuclear waste disposal, 64
Schwarzkopf, General Norman, 95–6
science, modern, 7, 13, 17, 21; and ethics, 79; and gnosticism, 80; the moral autonomy of, 91; non-teleological, 162; and risk, 78, 176; and technology, 25
scientific research, 19; following production, 172; on human embryos, 122
Seaborn, Blair, 65

September 11 attacks, 110
Serbia, 98–9, 101
sexual relations, 113; as symbolic or
    sacramental, 118
Sexual Sterilization Act (Alberta),
    140
Shell Renewables, 192n53
Sierra Club, 67, 199n42; on the
    Seaborn Panel Report, 65
Simon, Julian, 41; and limits to
    growth, 43
Sims, Gordon, 62; on nuclear waste
    disposal, 62, 65
Singer, Peter, and infanticide, 146
Sinsheimer, Robert, 143
SIPRI Yearbook 2006, 203
situation ethics, and access to IVF,
    121
Smith, Adam, 45
social contract, 154
social Darwinism, 141
soft energy path, 41
solar technologies, 35, 197
spina bifida, 139
Stalin, Josef, and the collectiviza-
    tion of Kulak farms, 163
State of the World 2000, 190n4,
    191n6, 192n34
sterilization, voluntary, 114; and
    eugenics, 142
Stivers, Robert, 24, 41, 188n7,
    193n3
Stock, Gregory, 136, 211n94; ap-
    proach to germ-line therapy,
    136
Strauss, Leo, 152, 186n25, 214n4
Structural Adjustment Plans, 30
surrogate mothers, 115
sustainable sufficiency, 24, 39, 51;
    adequacy of the concept, 41, 169

symbolization, 9
Szilard, Leo, 87

Taliban, 106
Tay-Sachs disease, 139
technological asymmetry between
    Western powers and rogue states,
    107
technological fix, 52
technological imperative, 10, 92,
    148
technological progressivism, 162,
    167
technological regime, 162
technological society, 157
technologization of reproduction,
    114
technology: eugenics, 146; holistic,
    5; intermediate, 33; prescriptive,
    5, 7; and risk, 47; self-augmenta-
    tion of, 176; as system, 34, 175;
    as tool, 3; of war, 112
teleology, 13
Teller, Edward, 87, 88; and the
    hydrogen bomb, 89
terrorism, 102
terrorist organizations as "unmiti-
    gated evil" (Weigel), 103
test-tube babies, 115
Thatcher, Margaret, 40
Thiele, Lesley Paul, 41, 191n14,
    192n41; on the waves of environ-
    mentalism, 49
Three Mile Island, 60, 200n58
Thucydides, 214
tolerance margins of nature, 32
Torah, 11
transcendental realism, 165
transfer of technology, 28–9, 31, 168
Truman, Harry, 28

UNICEF study of effects of UN sanctions on Iraq, 105
Union of Concerned Scientists, 59–
   60, 195n7
uprootedness, 168
urban sprawl, 171
utilitarianism, 64, 146; of Bentham
   and Mill, 155; Herman Daly's critique of, 43; inadequacy of, 169;
   materialist, 166; and nuclear
   energy, 168
utopia, 13, 16, 77

value-judgment, 198
values, contextual vs. performance, 8
Vanderburg, Willem, 8, 170, 182,
   202n78
Vaux, Kenneth, 207
virtue ethics, 166
Voegelin, 1, 181n14, 182n30,
   183n7, 184n14; on values language, 198–9
Voltaire, 184n14
voluntary self-degradation, 133

Walkerton water crisis (Ontario),
   217n22
war on terror, 102, 108, 109, 111,
   160; "shock and awe," 95; "virtual," against Iraq, 100
Warnock, Mary, 119, 211n95; on
   the effects of globalization on the
   restriction of reproductive technologies, 136; on parental rights
   of sperm donors, 120; later positions on reproductive technolo-

gies, 135; on regulating storage
   and ownership of and experimentation on embryos, 120; on
   surrogate motherhood, 121
wars of distribution, 18–19
WASH-1400, US Regulatory Commission Reactor Safety Study
   (1975), 195n10
Watson, James D., 143, 146, 148
weapons of mass destruction, 79; in
   World War I and II, 85
Weber, Max, 155, 183n4
Weigel, George, 102–3, 204n32
Weil, Simone, xiv, 1, 183n9, 213n1,
   216n12; and modern science,
   177
Weinberg, Alvin, 61, 196n21,
   199n58, 201n71; and the Faustian bargain with nuclear power,
   68–9; on nuclear waste disposal,
   62
White Jr, Lynn, and the Biblical call
   for dominion, 50
Winner, Langdon, 3
Wolbring, Gregor, 212n5, 213n29
women and reproductive technolo-
   gies, 123
World Bank, 30, 31, 33
World Commission on Environ-
   ment and Development, *Our
   Common Future* (Brundtland
   Report), 191n13
World Council of Churches, 24, 41,
   42, 194n4; and the soft energy
   path, 45
World Trade Organization, 23, 37